Tom Stoppard

Tom Stoppard's other work includes *Rosencrantz and Guildenstern Are Dead, The Real Inspector Hound, Jumpers, Travesties, Night and Day, Every Good Boy Deserves Favour* (with André Previn), *After Magritte, Dirty Linen, The Real Thing, Hapgood, Arcadia, Indian Ink, The Invention of Love* and the trilogy *The Coast of Utopia.* His radio plays include: *If You're Glad I'll Be Frank, Albert's Bridge, Where Are They Now?, Artist Descending a Staircase, The Dog It Was That Died* and *In the Native State.* Work for television includes *Professional Foul* and *Squaring the Circle.* His film credits include *Empire of the Sun, Rosencrantz and Guildenstern Are Dead,* which he also directed, *Shakespeare in Love* (with Marc Norman) and *Enigma.*

by the same author

TOM STOPPARD

Plays Four

Dalliance
Undiscovered Country
Rough Crossing
On the Razzle
The Seagull

faber and faber

This collection first published in 1999
by Faber and Faber Limited
3 Queen Square, London WC1N 3AU

Typeset by Country Setting, Kingsdown, Kent CT14 8ES
Printed in England by Mackays of Chatham plc, Chatham, Kent

This collection © Tom Stoppard, 1999

Dalliance © Tom Stoppard, 1986
Undiscovered Country © Tom Stoppard, 1980
Rough Crossing © David Alter, as Trustee, and Tom Stoppard
On the Razzle © Tom Stoppard, 1981, 1982
The Seagull © Tom Stoppard, 1997

Tom Stoppard is hereby identified as author of this
work in accordance with Section 77 of the Copyright,
Designs and Patents Act 1988

All rights whatsoever in these plays are strictly reserved and
application for permission to perform them must be made in advance,
prior to any such proposed use, to Peters, Fraser & Dunlop Ltd.,
Drury House, 34-43 Russell Street, London WC2B 5HA. The amateur rights for
Rough Crossing, *On the Razzle* & *The Seagull* are held by Samuel French.
Amateur applications for permissions to perform these plays must be made
in advance, before rehearsals begin, to Samuel French Ltd., 52 Fitzroy Street,
London W1P 6JR. No performance may be given unless a licence has first been obtained.

A CIP record for this book
is available from the British Library

ISBN 978-0-571-19750-7
ISBN 0-571-19750-7

4 6 8 10 9 7 5

Contents

DALLIANCE

Liebelei
by Arthur Schnitzler
in an English version
by Tom Stoppard

For Peter Wood

Characters

Fritz
Theodore
Mizi
Christine
A Gentleman
Frau Binder
Herr Weiring
A Tenor
A Soprano
Fritz's Manservant
Stage Manager

In addition, at the operetta

Conductor
Musicians
Stage-hands

The play takes place in Vienna
in the 1890s

Dalliance was first performed at the Lyttelton Theatre, London, on 27 May 1986. The cast was as follows:

Fritz Stephen Moore
Theodore Tim Curry
Mizi Sally Dexter
Christine Brenda Blethyn
A Gentleman Basil Henson
Frau Binder Sara Kestelman
Herr Weiring Michael Bryant
A Tenor Neil Daglish
A Soprano Roz Clifton
Fritz's Manservant Alan Haywood
Stage Manager Saul Reichlin
Orchestra Manager Steven Law

Directed by Peter Wood
Designed by Carl Toms

Act One

The reception room of Fritz's flat.

    There is a table to eat at, and a sideboard, etc. There is a piano. There is a divan. French doors at the back give on to a terrace or garden partly visible to us. There are doors to a kitchen and to a lobby leading to the street.

    Fritz is discovered practising marksmanship with a duelling pistol. The Manservant is on hand to bring the paper target back to Fritz for his inspection, and to reload the pistol while Fritz takes a second shot with the second of the pair of Pistols. Fritz aims and fires for the second time. The Manservant brings the target for the second time. It is clear from the way Fritz inspects the target that he is not much of a shot. There does not appear to be a hole in the target at all. Before Fritz shoots again, he steps forward for a shorter range, then shoots.

    Theodore enters the room from the lobby. He is wearing a coat or cloak. He sees Fritz and calls to him.

Theodore Fritz!

    Fritz turns to him, holding the gun.

Don't shoot!

Fritz I don't.

Theodore What exactly . . .?

Fritz Sport. And what . . .?

Theodore Supper.

Fritz I'm afraid I . . .

Theodore It's all arranged.

Fritz All right. Where are we going? Did you keep the cab?

Theodore No.

Theodore takes off his overcoat and throws it down over a chair.

Fritz Well . . . why don't you take your coat off?

Meanwhile the Manservant has put both pistols into a wooden pistol case. Two or three paper targets remain on the ground outside the French windows. The Manservant leaves through the kitchen doors, closing them behind him after saying, 'Goodnight, sir', and being ignored. Meanwhile Fritz spots two or three letters, newly arrived, which have been placed on his desk. He seizes the letters anxiously and sifts through them rapidly.

Ah – the post!

Theodore Love letters? I say, you are in a state. Is this the post-coital one hears so much about?

Whatever Fritz might have been expecting is not there. He starts to open the letters.

I always say one should never put it in writing.

Fritz Nothing. One from Lensky . . . and my father . . .

Theodore Don't mind me. What has your father got to say?

Fritz Not much . . . wants me to go down to the country for a week at Whitsun.

Theodore Very good idea. Six months would be even better. Fresh air, fresh pastures, milkmaids . . .

Fritz It isn't a dairy farm.

Theodore Even so.

Fritz Do you want to come?

Theodore 'Fraid I can't.

Fritz Why not?

Theodore God, I've got my anatomy viva, again! – I'd only go to make sure you stayed there.

Fritz Oh, come off it, I'm all right.

Theodore What you need is a change of scene. Really. It was quite apparent the other when-was-it – as soon as you got out into the country on a bright spring day you became quite tolerable.

Fritz Thanks very much.

Theodore Now it's wearing off again. We're back in the danger zone. No, really, you've no idea how it improved you, getting away from all this, you were really quite sensible. Like old times. Even since then when we went out with those two popsies you were good fun. But all that's over, now that you can't stop thinking of 'that woman'.

Fritz makes an impatient gesture.

If you think I'll let you ruin my life over a woman you're very much mistaken.

Fritz My God, you do go on.

Theodore Fritz, I'm not asking you to give her up. I just want you to treat it as a normal affair instead of this grand opera which'll be the finish of you. Love is

9

for operettas. Honestly, if you could get out of her spell you'd be amazed how much better the two of you would get on. You'd see that there's nothing *fatale* about the *femme*, she's just another pretty wife put into the world to brighten up your day, just like any other woman who is reasonably young and decent-looking and gets about a bit.

Fritz What do you mean, the finish of me?

Theodore I mean exactly that. I'm terrified you're going to run off with her one day.

Fritz Oh, that.

Theodore Not only that.

Fritz That's right, Theo, not only that.

Theodore Just don't do anything silly.

Fritz It's not up to me.

Theodore What isn't?

Fritz Nothing. She's been wrong before.

Theodore How? What are you talking about?

Fritz She's been on edge lately . . . well, on and off.

Theodore Why?

Fritz No reason at all. Nerves. (*Smiles.*) A guilty conscience if you like.

Theodore You said – she'd been wrong before . . .?

Fritz Yes. Only today . . .

Theodore What happened today?

Fritz She thinks we're being watched.

Theodore Watched?

Fritz She's seeing things, that's all. Literally. Hallucinations. She looks through this gap in the curtains and she sees someone or other standing out there on the street corner and she's convinced – I mean, is it possible to make out a face at this distance?

Theodore Hardly.

Fritz Exactly, that's what I tell her. But then it's awful – she's terrified to set foot outside. She gets quite hysterical and bursts into tears and says she wants to die with me.

Theodore Naturally.

Fritz Today she made me go outside to have a look round, as if I just happened to be stepping out of doors. Needless to say there was no one I knew for miles around. So that disposes of that, wouldn't you say? Wouldn't you say, Theo? People don't just disappear into thin air. Theo?

Theodore What do you want me to say? All right, people don't disappear into thin air, sometimes they hide in doorways.

Fritz I looked in every one.

Theodore You must have been the picture of innocence.

Fritz There was nobody. As I said – hallucinations.

Theodore Absolutely. Only let it be a lesson to you to be more careful.

Fritz He can't suspect anything. I would have noticed. I actually had supper with them after the theatre yesterday. They invited me to their musical evening tomorrow, him and her. It was all so ridiculously hail-fellow-well-m– – maybe that means he knows.

Theodore Listen, Fritz – do me a favour – all right, I *am* asking you to give her up. If only for *my* sake. Think of *my* nerves. Now, I know it's absolutely against your nature and your principles to end an affair before you've begun another one, so I've been smoothing the sheets, way, rather.

Fritz Oh, have you?

Theodore You haven't noticed? After I took you on my date with Mizi, and got her to bring along her best friend? And do you deny you took quite a fancy to the little darling?

Fritz She was rather sweet actually . . . yes, awfully sweet. And you can't imagine how I long for a little simple affection without all the drama . . . for someone soothing to stand by me when life gets fraught.

Theodore That's it exactly. The warrior's rest. That's what they're for. Convalescence. That's why I've always been against these so-called fascinating women. Women have no business to be fascinating, their job is to be pleasant. You must find your happiness in pastures where I look for mine, where there are no dramas and no dangers, no grand opera, easy in and easy out from first kiss to fond parting.

Fritz Yes, that's right.

Theodore After all, women are perfectly happy being women, so why do we keep trying to turn them into angels and demons, it's so unhealthy.

Fritz Yes, she really was an angel, Mizi's friend . . .

Theodore You're doing it again.

Fritz No – no –

Theodore You're hopeless –

Fritz No, I'm with you – convalescence, lie them down in fresh pastures, whatever you say.

Theodore Otherwise I withdraw my support. I've had enough of your romantic tragedies. I'm bored with them. And if you feel compelled to demonstrate your famous conscience, I'll tell you my simple philosophy in these matters: better me than somebody else; and there is *always* somebody else.

The doorbell rings.

Fritz (*startled*) Who can that be?

Theodore Well, go and see. Oh God, he's gone white as a sheet – calm down this minute. It's the popsies.

Fritz (*relieved*) What?

Theodore I took the liberty of inviting them round.

Fritz But why didn't you say so? My man will have gone.

Theodore We will have to do.

Fritz goes out to the front door.

Fritz (*outside*) Good evening, Mizi.

Mizi enters carrying a parcel, followed by Fritz.

Where's Christine?

Mizi She's coming on later. How are you, Dory? I hope you don't mind, Fritz, but Theodore asked us.

Fritz Delighted. The only thing he forgot was –

Theodore He forgot nothing. (*to Mizi*) Did you bring everything I wrote down for you?

Mizi Of course. Where should I put it?

Fritz Let me take it. It can go on the sideboard for the moment.

Mizi I brought something extra which wasn't on your list.

Theodore What is it?

Mizi Chocolate éclairs.

Theodore You shall have your cake.

Fritz Let me have your hat, Mizi – that's right. So, why didn't Christine come with you?

Mizi She was taking her father down to the theatre, then she's catching the tram back here.

Theodore What a good girl.

Mizi Well, her father's been a bit down in the dumps since the old lady died.

Fritz Christine's mother?

Mizi No, her auntie who was living with them. She never knew her mother.

Theodore Christine's father – little man with long, grey hair?

Mizi No, he's got short hair.

Fritz How would you know him?

Theodore I was watching the show at the Josefstadt with Lensky the other day and I had a good look at the chap playing the double-bass –

Mizi It's not a double-bass, it's a violin.

Theodore Well, I said he was small.

Mizi (*to Fritz*) You've got a nice place here, *très élégant, monsieur*, really lovely. What's the view?

Fritz This window, *ma'm'selle*, looks out on the Stroghgasse. Next door –

Theodore What's all this coyness? I want us to be on familiar terms, not to say intimate.

Mizi Eat first.

Theodore A very middle-class idea. Still, I suppose it's reassuring. And how is your mother, if I may be so familiar?

Mizi Would you believe –?

Theodore I would. Toothache. She's always got toothache. You must tell her about dentists.

Mizi The doctor says it's her age.

Theodore It is, it is. Everything is our age. Our age is the toothache age, rotten to the teeth.

Mizi picks up a photograph frame.

Mizi Who's this?

Theodore It doesn't show in the photographs.

Mizi (*to Fritz*) Goodness, it's you, in uniform. Were you in the army?

Fritz Yes.

Mizi A Dragoon! Yellow or black?

Fritz The Yellows.

Mizi A Yellow Dragoon!

Theodore She's gone. Mizi, wake up!

Mizi So now you're in the Reserve?

Fritz That's right.

Mizi I bet you look like something in your breeches.

Theodore You seem to know a lot about it. Listen, Mizi, I'm an officer too.

Mizi A Dragoon?

Theodore Yes.

Mizi Why ever didn't you say?

Theodore I wanted to be loved for myself.

Mizi Well, next time we go out anywhere together you must wear your uniform.

Theodore I only put it on for funerals. But I'll be wearing it for August – I've got manoeuvres.

Mizi Heavens, it won't wait till August.

Theodore No, that's true – our love is eternal, of course, but there is a limit.

Mizi Who thinks about August in May? Isn't that right, Fritz? Why did you stand us up last night?

Fritz Where?

Mizi After the theatre, of course.

Fritz Didn't Theo make my excuses?

Theodore Of course I did.

Mizi Excuses are no use to me. I mean to Christine. A promise is a promise.

Fritz I honestly would have much rather been with you.

Mizi Honestly?

Fritz But I couldn't. I was sharing a box with a couple of friends, and I couldn't tear myself away.

Mizi You couldn't tear yourself away all right – who was the lovely lady? Did you think we couldn't see you through the peephole?

Fritz From behind the curtain?

Mizi You sat right to the back of the box.

Fritz I find it helps if you can't see the actors.

Mizi You were sitting behind her, the one in the black velvet dress, and you kept leaning forward like this.

Fritz I see you *were* keeping an eye on me.

Mizi Well, it's none of my affair. But if I were in Christine's shoes . . . How is it that Theo is always free after the theatre – why doesn't *he* have to have supper with a couple of friends?

Theodore (*meaningfully*) Yes, why don't *I* have to have supper with a couple of friends?

The doorbell rings.

Mizi That'll be Christine.

Fritz goes out.

Theodore Mizi, you can do me a favour. Forget your military career, at least for the moment.

Mizi What can you mean?

Theodore You didn't learn how a Hussar dresses from the army manual.

Fritz and Christine enter, Christine carrying a bunch of roses.

Christine Hello . . . (*to Fritz*) Did you mind us coming? You're not cross?

Fritz My dear girl, Theodore is occasionally the one with a good idea.

Theodore Well, is your father fiddling away?

Christine He certainly is. I took him all the way to the Josefstadt.

Fritz So Mizi said. What have you got there?

Christine I've brought you some flowers.

Fritz You're an angel – Isn't she an absolute – (*catching Theo's eye*) – darling! – Wait, let's put them in the vase there.

Theodore No, no, you have absolutely no sense of style. Flowers should be scattered carelessly over the table. Except that it should be after the table is laid. Ideally they should fall from the ceiling but I suppose we can't manage that.

Fritz Hardly.

Theodore I know! – let's put them in the vase over there! (*He puts them in a vase.*)

Mizi It's getting dark, boys and girls, we'll light the lamp in a moment.

Theodore Lamp? Ridiculous idea! We'll light candles! That'll be much prettier. Come on, Mizi, you can give me a hand.

> *There are two silver candelabra, lacking candles, which Theodore picks up and takes out into the kitchen, ushering Mizi out with him.*

Fritz How are you, my pet?

Christine I'm all right now.

Fritz Only now?

Christine I've missed you so much.

Fritz You saw me yesterday.

Christine Saw you?

Fritz Through the peephole, Mizi said.

Christine Don't be unkind.

Fritz You're such a baby. I couldn't get away. You could see that.

Christine Yes . . . but, Fritz – who were the people in the box?

Fritz Friends – what do their names matter?

Christine And the woman in black?

Fritz Oh, my dear girl, I can never remember clothes.

Christine Oh, really!

Fritz Or rather, only in special cases. For instance that dark grey blouse you wore the first time I saw you . . . oh – and your pendant – I recognize that too!

Christine So when did I wear it?

Fritz It was . . . well, some time ago, that day we went for a walk in the gardens along by the railway and we watched all those children playing . . . wasn't it?

Christine Yes. So you do think of me now and then.

Fritz All the time, my sweet.

Christine I think of you all the time, too, Fritz – every minute – I'm only happy when I can see you.

Fritz We see each other all the time.

Christine All the time?!

Fritz Well, so to speak. Come the summer it will be less. What would you say if I went away for a few weeks?

Christine What . . .? You're going away?

Fritz No, but suppose I want to be on my own for a week.

Christine Whatever for?

Fritz I'm only saying suppose – I know what I'm like and sometimes I'm like that. Besides, you might not want to see *me* for a few days. I'd understand.

Christine I'll never feel like that, Fritz.

Fritz You can't be sure.

Christine I am sure. I love you.

Fritz And I . . . you.

Christine You're everything to me, Fritz – I'd do anything, I can't imagine a time when I wouldn't want to see you, for ever and ever.

Fritz Dear girl, don't say that – ever and ever makes me ever so nervous. Don't let's speak of eternity.

Christine Oh, don't worry, Fritz – I know it's not really for ever.

Fritz I didn't mean that. Perhaps it'll happen that we can't live without each other – but we can't know . . . people can't.

> *Theodore and Mizi now enter from the kitchen holding the blazing candles.*

Theodore Now, will you look at that! Isn't that nicer than some silly lamp?

Fritz You're a born romantic, Theo.

Theodore I know. Well, children, what do you think about supper?

Mizi Yes – come on Christine!

Fritz Hang on, I'll show you where everything is.

Mizi The first thing we need is a tablecloth.

Theodore produces one with a flourish from behind his back or from his sleeve.

Theodore (*with an accent*) First – ze cloth de table – I 'ave ze very thing – in fact I 'ave ze veritable cloth – ze true cloth – accept no substitutes –

Mizi (*laughing*) He should be in the music-halls. Dory, when are you going to take me to the Orpheum? You said you would. But Christine has to come too, and Lieutenant Fritz – and then *we'll* be the friends in his box.

Fritz Yes . . . oh yes.

Mizi And the lady in black can go home alone.

Fritz It's really too silly the way you go on about her.

Mizi Oh she's nothing to us . . . Now – cutlery? – good – and plates . . .?

Fritz Plates! – in the plate cupboard.

Mizi Fine, thank you, we can manage without you now – leave it to us, you'll only be in the way. (*to Christine*) Have you seen the photo of Fritz in uniform?

Christine No.

Mizi You should see it – it's devastating.

Mizi goes into the kitchen. Christine picks up the photograph, looks at it long and lovingly and eventually replaces it. She notices the men looking bemusedly at her. Embarrassed, she hurries into the kitchen after Mizi.

Theodore You don't mind, do you? I love evenings like this.

Fritz Yes, they're very nice.

Theodore I feel so at peace, don't you? This is the life, isn't it?

Fritz Well, it's one of them.

Mizi (*off*) I say, Fritz – is there any coffee in the machine?

Fritz Yes, but you could make coffee on the primus, the machine takes ages.

Theodore I'll give you a dozen so-called fascinating women for one unspoiled little popsie.

Fritz They're not to be spoken of in the same breath.

Theodore Absolutely. The trouble with real women is that we can't stand the ones who want us, and we're mad about the ones we can't have.

Mizi and Christine enter with things for the table. They begin to set out the tableware and the food.

Mizi What's all that? We want to be let in on it.

Theodore Nothing for your ears, little girls. We're philosophizing. (*to Fritz*) If this was our last evening with these two it wouldn't be any different, would it?

Fritz Our last evening together . . . well, I don't know . . . partings are always a bit sad, even the ones we put in our diaries.

Christine Fritz, where's the cruet?

Fritz The cruet?

Christine Condiments?

Fritz Condiments! Salt, pepper, oil and vinegar! – in the condiment cupboard!

Theodore (*to Mizi*) Come here, minx.

> *Fritz helps Christine. Mizi comes to Theodore. Theodore sprawls on the divan and Mizi joins him there.*

Christine You've got life organized, haven't you?

Fritz Yes, haven't I?

Christine Fritz – won't you tell me?

Fritz What?

Christine Who the lady was.

Fritz Who was that lady I saw you with last night? No – don't make me cross. Remember what we said. No questions. That's what's so nice about being with you. Nothing else exists. I don't ask you things.

Christine You can ask me anything.

Fritz (*sharply*) But I don't. I don't want to know anything.

> *There is an awkward silence. Mizi hurries over to Christine.*

Mizi Goodness, what a mess you're making of that . . . (*She takes things out of Fritz's hands and arranges the table accordingly.*) There we are . . .

Theodore I say, Fritz, is there anything to drink?

Fritz Oh, yes, I'm sure there's something.

*Fritz finds a couple of bottles in the sideboard.
Theodore surveys the table.*

Theodore Excellent.

Mizi I think that's everything.

Fritz Here we are.

Theodore What about the roses falling from the ceiling?

Mizi Yes, quite right – we forgot the roses.

*Mizi takes the flowers out of the vase, stands on a
chair and scatters the roses on the table.*

There you are!

Theodore Careful! – not on the plates.

Christine Honestly, she's quite out of hand

Fritz Where would you like to sit, Christine?

Theodore Where's the corkscrew?

Fritz In the corkscrew drawer.

Theodore Let's eat first and afterwards Fritz will play
for us. What do you say?

Mizi Oh yes, that would be devastating!

Fritz (*to Christine*) Shall I?

Christine Oh, please! I've been wanting you to for ages.

Fritz You play a bit, don't you?

Christine Oh, heavens . . .

Mizi She plays beautifully – and she can sing.

Fritz Really? You never told me.

Christine When did you ask?

24

Fritz Wherever did you learn to sing?

Christine I didn't learn exactly. Father taught me a bit but I haven't got much of a voice. And there hasn't been a lot of singing in the house since my auntie died.

Fritz What do you do with yourself all day?

Christine Heavens, I've got lots to do.

Fritz Housework, you mean?

Christine And I copy out scores.

Fritz Music scores?

Christine Yes, of course.

Theodore That must be tremendously well paid.

The others laugh.

Well, I'd pay tremendously well for it. Copying music sounds like a frightful chore.

Mizi And she's silly to punish herself. (*to Christine*) If I had your voice I'd have gone on stage years ago.

Theodore You don't need a voice. And I suppose you do nothing all day, being in the theatre.

Mizi I beg your pardon – a seamstress is the busiest person in the Josefstadt.

Theodore 'Seams, madam? I know not seams.'

Mizi (*puzzled, cross*) Are you making fun of me?

Fritz (*to Christine*) You must sing something for us.

Theodore What will you have, Mizi? And before you say anything the cakes come last. First you have to eat some proper food.

Fritz And drink several glasses of wine, starting with this one. (*He starts to pour out the wine.*)

Theodore Not like that. That's not how it's done nowadays. Don't you keep up with society? (*He takes the bottle and pours the wine with considerable pomp, naming it and proclaiming the vintage in a manner which, however, makes the precise year unintelligible.*) Xeres de la Frontera, mil huit cent cinquante . . . (*He repeats the procedure for each glass and then sits down.*)

Mizi He's such a fool.

Theodore Cheers!

Mizi Your health, Theodore.

Theodore (*standing*) Ladies and gentlemen –

Fritz Not yet!

Theodore (*sitting down*) Right!

   They start to eat.

Mizi I love people who make speeches at the table.

Theodore All of them?

Mizi I've got a cousin who does them in rhyming couplets.

Theodore What regiment is he in?

Mizi Oh, do stop it. He recites poetry – he's devastating, Christine, and not as immature as some people either.

Theodore Well, it's not uncommon for elderly folk to speak in rhyme.

Fritz You're not drinking, Christine.

Theodore Here's to old soldiers, may they live to recite again.

Mizi And to young lieutenants who hardly speak at all, like Fritz. Fritz – we'll drink a friendship cup if you like – and Christine must do the same with Theodore.

Theodore But not in this wine – this is no wine for our cups. (*He takes up the other bottle and goes through the same procedure as before.*) Voslauer Auslese . . . You'll find this an affectionate little cup, with just a hint of promiscuity.

Mizi (*sipping the wine*) Ah!

Theodore Can't you wait till we've all got a glass? All right, my friends, before we pledge let's drink to fortune and that happy chance which – which has brought the four of us and the rest of it.

Mizi That'll do.

> *Fritz links arms with Mizi, Theodore with Christine, all with glasses in their hands, as they drink. Fritz kisses Mizi. Theodore tries to kiss Christine.*

Christine (*smiling*) Oh, are we supposed to?

Theodore Certainly, otherwise it doesn't count. (*He kisses Christine.*)

Mizi It's awfully hot in here.

Fritz That's because of all those candles.

Mizi And the wine.

> *Theodore picks up an éclair for Mizi.*

Theodore Here you are, this is what you get for being a good girl. (*He puts the éclair in her mouth.*) There . . . good?

Mizi Very!

Theodore Well, bad girls get two. Come on, Fritz – now's the moment. Play us something.

Fritz Do you want me to, Christine?

Christine Oh, please!

Mizi Play something devastating.

Theodore fills the glasses.

(*drinking*) No more for me.

Christine The wine's so heavy.

Theodore Fritz!

Mizi Lieutenant Fritz – play 'The False Hussar'.

Fritz 'The False Hussar' – how does it go?

Mizi Dory, can't you play 'The False Hussar'?

Theodore I can't play the piano.

Fritz I know it, I just can't remember it.

Mizi I'll sing it for you.

Theodore Brings back fond memories no doubt.

> *Mizi, beginning to sing, leads Fritz into the tune.**
> *Mizi sings the chorus and then starts the verse with
> the others, particularly Theodore, contributing the
> bits they know. When the song reaches the chorus
> for the second time, Theodore gets up and dances
> with Mizi. Meanwhile Christine joins Fritz at the
> piano.*

* The tune used in the original National Theatre production was
'Don't Be So Naughty' from *Der Obersteiger* by Karl Millöcker.
The words, however, were invented for the occasion; as was the title.

The False Hussar

Sweetheart, please don't send me away.
Sweetheart, there's no war on today.
Sweetheart, won't you dally, do.
Or I'll die
Or I'll die for love of you.

Hail and farewell, my gay Hussar.
Handsome and bold and brave you are.
How many girls did you forsake?
Here is one heart that you won't break!
Even with all your gallantry
Here you will have no victory.
What is it that you're waiting for?
Shouldn't you be at war?

Sweetheart, please don't send me away.
Sweetheart, there's no war on today.
Sweetheart, won't you dally, do.
Or I'll die
Or I'll die for love of you.

At the end of the second chorus the doorbell is heard. Fritz stops playing. The dancers, however, carry on heedlessly. Then they realize that the music has stopped.

Has somebody shot the piano player?

Fritz That was the door. Did you invite anyone else?

Theodore Of course not. You don't have to answer it.

Christine What's the matter?

Fritz Nothing.

Theodore and Mizi pick up the dance to their own accompaniment. The doorbell rings again.

Theodore You're not at home.

Fritz You can hear the piano out in the hall. And anyone can see the lights from the street.

Theodore What nonsense. You're simply not at home.

Fritz But it puts me off.

Theodore So what do you think it is – a letter? A telegram?

Fritz Damn it, I'll have to go and see. (*He goes out to the door.*)

Mizi How boring! (*She thumps the piano keys discordantly.*)

Theodore Oh, do stop! (*to Christine*) What's the matter? Has the doorbell put you off too?

Fritz re-enters, closing the door behind him.

Christine Who was it?

Fritz Would you be good enough to give me a few moments . . . Would you mind going into the next room?

Theodore Oh no!

Christine Who is it?

Fritz Nothing, my love – I just have to have a few words with someone.

The two women allow themselves to be shown into the kitchen by Theodore.

Theodore (*to Fritz*) Get rid of her.

Fritz Go on – get in!

Fritz goes out to the front door. After a few moments the Gentleman enters. He is wearing officer's uniform.

I must apologize for keeping you waiting. Please . . .

Gentleman Not at all. I'm sorry to have disturbed you.

Fritz You haven't at all.

Gentleman Oh, but I can see I have. A little gathering?

Fritz Just a few of the chaps.

Gentleman (*still friendly*) Sounds a bit dubious.

Fritz (*awkwardly*) I beg your pardon?

Gentleman They seem to go in for feather boas and picture hats.

Fritz Oh yes. (*smiles*) One or two of them *are* a bit dubious.

Gentleman Life can be so amusing sometimes.

Fritz May I make so bold as to inquire to what I owe the honour of this . . . Why have you come?

Gentleman (*calmly*) My wife left one of her gloves here . . .

Fritz Your wife? Here? There must be some mistake.

Gentleman My wife left one of her gloves here – a glove like this one.

> *The Gentleman slaps Fritz on the face with the glove. Fritz takes a step back. Pause.*

Well? I said – well? A Yellow Dragoon.

> *Fritz snaps to attention.*

Fritz I am at your disposal.

Gentleman And I shall dispose of you. (*The Gentleman produces a bundle of letters.*) Here are your letters. I must ask you to give me those you have received. I wouldn't want them to be found here . . . afterwards.

Fritz They won't be found. (*Fritz stares at him. Pause.*) Is there anything more I can do for you?

Gentleman Anything more? That you might do for *me*? (*The Gentleman turns to leave, then changes his mind.*) You young know-it-alls . . . take-it-alls . . . My box, my table, my – You grab – brag – strut – rut like dogs in the street – and you'll be shot down like dogs.

Fritz I am at your disposal.

Gentleman (*bows coldly*) Good.

Fritz I am entirely at your disposal. I shall be at home tomorrow until noon.

Gentleman Ah – about tomorrow. My wife's musical evening.

Fritz Please ask her to forgive me.

Gentleman I'm sure she will miss you.

Fritz Perhaps another time.

Gentleman Yes, perhaps. After all I might miss you too.

The Gentleman turns to leave. Fritz moves to see him out but the Gentleman stops him with a gesture. The Gentleman lets himself out. Fritz stands for a moment and then goes to the window and peers through it. He goes to the kitchen door and opens it a little.

Fritz Theo, a moment.

Theodore enters, closing the door behind him.

Theodore All right?

Fritz It was him.

Theodore Ah! I hope you didn't do anything silly.

Fritz He knows.

Theodore He knows nothing. He laid a trap for you, and you fell for it. You're a fool . . .

Fritz shows Theodore the letters.

Ah. I've always said one shouldn't put it in writing.

Fritz That must have been him outside this afternoon.

Theodore Well, tell me what happened.

Fritz Theodore, I have the honour to ask of you a certain favour –

Theodore Oh, do stop talking like that. I'll straighten it out.

Fritz It's got beyond that.

Theodore We'll see.

Fritz Anyway it would be as well if you . . . but we can't keep those poor girls waiting any longer –

Theodore Let them wait. What were you going to say?

Fritz It would be as well if you went and got Lensky before the night's out.

Theodore I'll go now if you like.

Fritz You won't get him now. But he'll be in the café between eleven and twelve – you could both come round then.

Theodore Don't look like that. Nine times out of ten it all comes out all right.

Fritz This time it won't. He'll make sure of that.

Theodore Oh, but think of that business last year between Dr Billinger and Herz – same thing exactly.

Fritz Come on, you know as well as I do he might as

33

well have shot me dead here in this room. It would have come to the same thing.

Theodore Oh, yes – what a wonderful attitude. And Lensky and I count for nothing? Do you think we'll let –

Fritz I don't want any of that. Let him have what he wants.

Theodore Fritz –

Fritz What's the point, Theodore? As if you didn't know yourself.

Theodore Nonsense. Anyway there's a lot of luck in these things – you're just as likely to – almost as likely – there's a fair chance – oh God!

Fritz She felt it coming. We both did. We knew it.

Theodore Enough of that.

Fritz What in God's name is she doing at this moment? I wonder if he . . . Theodore, tomorrow you've got to find out what's going on there.

Theodore I'll do my best.

Fritz And make sure there's no delay.

Theodore It can't be before the day after tomorrow.

Fritz Theodore!

Theodore Don't despair – I'm positive that everything will turn out all right – don't ask me why but intuition counts for something. It just struck me, I felt it in my bones – I mean my heart – (*Apologetically he 'shoots' himself in the head for his* faux pas *and then realizes how much worse he has made matters*) – oh God, sorry!

> *Fritz and Theodore catch the humour of the moment and laugh together.*

Fritz You're a real friend. But what on earth are we going to tell the girls?

Theodore Does it matter? Let's get rid of them.

Fritz Oh no. We must be cheerful as can be. I'll go back to the piano and you call them in. What will you tell them?

Theodore To mind their own business.

Fritz No . . .

Theodore I'll tell them it concerns a pal of yours, we'll think of something. (*He opens the door.*) Ladies . . .

Fritz Theo – what a relief, eh?

Mizi and Christine enter.

Mizi At last!

Christine Who was it, Fritz?

Theodore Curiosity killed the cat –

Fritz begins to play the funeral march.

Christine Tell me, Fritz – please.

Fritz Sweetheart, I can't. It concerns people you don't know at all.

Christine What people?

Theodore She won't leave you in peace. Don't tell her a thing – you gave him your word.

Christine Him? Oh, you mean . . .

Mizi Leave off, Christine – don't be a bore. Let them have their little pleasures, they're only trying to make it sound important.

Theodore Mizi and I have to finish our dance – maestro, music if you please!

Theodore and Mizi dance for a few moments but the mood has gone wrong.

Mizi I can't any more.

Theodore kisses her and sits on the arm of the chair. Fritz stays at the piano. He takes Christine's hands and looks at her.

Christine Why have you stopped?

Fritz Enough for tonight.

Christine That's how I'd like to be able to play.

Fritz Do you play much?

Christine I don't get much chance. There's always so much to do at home. And then we've got such a terrible piano.

Fritz I'd like to play it some time, and to see your room.

Christine It's not as nice as here.

Fritz And there's something else I want. I want you to tell me everything about yourself. I know so little.

Christine Little is all there is. And I don't have any secrets either – unlike some people I know.

Fritz Never been in love?

Christine looks at him. Fritz kisses her hand.

Christine And I'll never love anyone else.

Fritz You mustn't say that . . . ever . . . how can you know? Do you always tell your father everything, Christine?

Christine Not any more.

Fritz Don't feel bad about it, little one. In the end we all have our secrets. That's how we live.

Christine If only I knew that you really cared for me, everything would be all right.

Fritz Don't you know?

Christine When you talk to me like this I think I do.

Fritz Christine . . . you can't be comfortable like that.

Christine Oh, no, please, let me stay. I'm all right.

Fritz strokes her hair.

Oh. Oh – that's nice. (*Silence.*)

Theodore So, Fritz, where's the cigar cupboard? (*He exits, then comes back immediately with coffee on a tray.*) Who's for black coffee?

Fritz Mizi –

Theodore Let her sleep. And you shouldn't be drinking black coffee. You ought to get to bed as soon as possible and make sure of a good night's rest.

Fritz glances at him and laughs bitterly.

Well, that's the way things are. Whether you've behaved well or badly is no longer the point. Behaving sensibly is all that counts.

Fritz You will bring Lensky tonight, won't you?

Theodore There's no need. Tomorrow is soon enough.

Fritz I'm asking you.

Theodore Then I will.

Fritz Will you see the girls home?

Theodore Yes – and right now. Mizi – up you get!

Mizi has fallen asleep. She stirs now.

Mizi Is that black coffee? Can I have some?

Theodore Here we are, my dear.

Fritz (*to Christine*) Tired, little girl?

Christine Oh, I love it when you talk to me like that.

Fritz So tired . . .

Christine It's the wine. And it's given me a bit of a headache.

Fritz Some fresh air will put that right.

Christine Are we going already? Are you coming with us?

Fritz No, darling – I shall stay at home now. I've a few things to do.

Christine Now? What could you have to do at this time?

Fritz (*almost sternly*) Christine, you must stop doing that . . . (*more kindly*) Actually I'm dead beat – Theo and I were tramping round the countryside for hours today.

Theodore Oh, it was glorious. We'll all go out in the country together one day soon.

Mizi Oh, that'll be devastating – and you've both got to put on your uniforms.

Theodore She has a real feeling for nature.

Christine (*to Fritz*) When will I see you?

Fritz I'll write.

Christine (*sadly*) Well, goodbye then.

> She turns to go. Fritz notices her sadness.

Fritz Christine. We'll see each other tomorrow then.

Christine (*eagerly*) Really?

Fritz The railway gardens. Same as before. Let's say six o'clock. Will that be all right?

Mizi Aren't you coming with us, we want to be dragooned!

Theodore The woman's obsessed.

Fritz No, I'm staying here.

Mizi Lucky you – we've got quite a trek.

Fritz Wait, Mizi – you're leaving nearly all the cakes behind – you must take them home with you.

Mizi Is that allowed?

Christine Honestly, she's like a child.

Mizi Wait a minute – for that I'll help you blow out the candles.

Christine Should I open a window? It's so stuffy in here.

Fritz Yes, we can go out that way. There you are, children.

Mizi Are the street lights out already?

Theodore Of course they are.

Fritz I'll light the way out for you.

Christine Oh how wonderful to have some air.

Mizi Go on, out you go, quick march – get along with you.

> *There is a general exit through the French doors. Fritz holds aloft one of the candelabra to light the way. He stands watching as they disappear chattering and laughing together. They pick up the tune of 'The False*

Hussar' as they go. Standing outside on the terrace,
Fritz picks up one of his discarded targets. He walks
back into the room, holding up the target, looking
for the bullet hole. He moves the target behind the
candles for a better look. The target catches fire.
He stands holding the candelabra in one hand, and
the blazing target in the other, the only light now in
the room.

Act Two

The living room of the top-floor flat shared by Christine and her father.

It is simply furnished. There are a few books in a bookcase. There is a window with a view over the rooftops. There is also a roof terrace. There is a large stove on which there is a bust of Schubert.

A silver band can be heard playing distantly in the park. Occasionally from nearer at hand a clanking goods train is heard to pass by below.

The room is empty. Then Christine hurries in from within, in the process of getting dressed, carrying a hat and an artificial flower. She hurries to a sewing box and starts sewing the flower on to the hat.

A knock at the door leading to the stairs is followed by Frau Binder calling 'Herr Weiring!' Frau Binder enters (and perhaps helps Christine to finish dressing during the first part of the dialogue).

Frau Binder Yoo hoo, Herr Weiring!

Christine Oh – Frau Binder!

Frau Binder Good evening, Christine. (*She appraises Christine.*) Oh, you look . . . (*She sniffs Christine's perfume.*) Going out?

Christine How are you? – Is everything well downstairs?

Frau Binder Yes, you're quite a stranger. In fact, my husband was wondering if you'd join us for dinner in the Lehnergarten as it's the night the band plays.

Christine Thank you very much, Frau Binder, but I can't this evening. Another time, perhaps. You don't mind, do you?

Frau Binder Why should I mind? You'll have a much nicer time without us. Your father's left for the theatre?

Christine Oh no, he'll be home soon. It's a piano rehearsal and the orchestra isn't called tonight.

Frau Binder In that case I'll wait for him. I've been meaning to ask him for ages for some tickets. I suppose one can get some now?

Christine Oh yes, but why not come to the dress rehearsal in a couple of days? I'll be there too.

Frau Binder If people like us didn't have friends in the theatre we'd never get to go. But don't let me keep you, Christine. My husband will be disappointed of course – not to mention someone else.

Christine Who's that?

Frau Binder Binder's cousin is joining us. Did you know Franz has a steady job now, Christine?

Christine Oh, really?

Frau Binder Good money, too. Such a nice young man. And he thinks the world of you, you know.

Christine Well, I have to be off, Frau Binder.

Frau Binder He won't listen to a word against you – whatever they say. There *are* men who –

Christine Goodbye, Frau Binder.

Frau Binder Goodbye. Don't keep the young man waiting!

Christine Is something the matter, Frau Binder?

Frau Binder Nothing at all – you're quite right, you're only young once.

Christine Goodbye, then.

Frau Binder Only, you ought to be a bit more discreet.

Christine What do you mean?

Frau Binder Vienna is big enough to hide a multitude of – I mean, why do you have to meet him a hundred yards from your own door?

Christine I don't think that's anyone else's business.

Frau Binder I couldn't believe my ears when Binder told me. He saw you. Get on with you, I said to him, you're imagining things. Christine isn't the sort of girl who romps around in the dark with young men. And if she did get up to something she'd certainly know enough not to do it on her own doorstep. Well, he said, you can ask her yourself. And, he said, who's to wonder – she doesn't come in to see us any more, instead she goes about with that Mizi Schlager . . . hardly fit company for a nice girl. Men have such dirty minds, Christine. And of course he felt it was his duty to tell Franz straight away and Franz turned on him. He'd go through fire for his Christine and anyone who says a word against her gets an earful, about how good you are in the house, how kind you always were to auntie, God rest her soul, how well brought up you are and so on . . . Won't you change your mind and come with us to listen to the music?

Christine No.

Christine's father, Herr Weiring, enters holding a sprig of lilac.

Herr Weiring Good evening – oh, Frau Binder, how are you?

Frau Binder Quite well, thank you.

Herr Weiring And how's little Lina? And your husband?

Frau Binder Both well, thanks be to God.

Herr Weiring That's good. (*to Christine*) Still indoors on such a lovely evening?

Christine I was just on my way.

Herr Weiring That's right, it's lovely out in the fresh air. Don't you think so, Frau Binder? Really marvellous. I've just come by the railway gardens. The lilac is out. A magnificent sight. I've been guilty of a misdemeanour. (*He gives the flower to Christine.*)

Christine Thank you, father.

Frau Binder You're lucky the park-keeper didn't see you.

Herr Weiring You should go too, Frau Binder. The scent of the lilac is so strong you won't miss this little sprig.

Frau Binder If everyone thought like that –

Herr Weiring Yes, that would be too bad –

Christine I'll see you later, father.

Herr Weiring Should I come with you?

Christine Well, I . . . I promised to see Mizi.

Herr Weiring Ah yes, a much better idea. Youth must be served. Goodbye, then.

Christine Goodbye, Frau Binder.

Christine goes. Her father looks after her tenderly.

Frau Binder She's very thick with that Mizi.

Herr Weiring I'm glad she has someone to go about with instead of sitting around the house – it's not much of a life for the poor girl.

Frau Binder Yes, I suppose so.

Herr Weiring I can't tell you, Frau Binder, how sad it makes me when I come home from a rehearsal and find her sitting here like Cinderella . . . and after lunch we are hardly up from the table before she's sat down again with her music scores.

Frau Binder Oh, yes, we'd all rather be millionaires. But what about her singing?

Herr Weiring It won't get her very far. Her voice is good enough for the family piano – music to a father's ears – but she'll never make a living with it.

Frau Binder Such a shame.

Herr Weiring I'm glad she knows it – at least she won't be disappointed.

Frau Binder Oh, girls are such a worry! I came up to invite her to come and hear the band in the Lehnergarten. I thought it might cheer her up a bit. She could do with it.

Herr Weiring Why didn't she want to go?

Frau Binder I don't know. I think perhaps because Binder's cousin is coming with us.

Herr Weiring Oh that'll be it – she can't bear him. She told me.

Frau Binder Why not? Franz is a perfectly decent young man. He's got a steady job now. These days that's not to be sneezed at by a . . .

Herr Weiring By a poor girl, you were going to say?

Frau Binder By any girl.

Herr Weiring Come now, Frau Binder – a girl in the springtime of her life, is that what girls like her are meant for – decent young men with steady jobs?

Frau Binder (*surprised*) Yes. One can't wait for Prince Charming to turn up and if some day he comes along he'll ask for everything but her hand and be off again. That's why I always say one can't be too careful with a young girl, especially in the company she keeps.

Herr Weiring So she's supposed to throw her youth out of the window, is she? And what does the poor thing get out of all this decency if she ends up as the wife of a haberdasher?

Frau Binder Herr Weiring, my husband may be a haberdasher but he's a decent and respectable man who has never given me cause for complaint.

Herr Weiring Oh, but Frau Binder – did I mean you? You didn't throw your youth out of the window.

Frau Binder I really can't remember.

Herr Weiring Oh, don't say that – say what you like but memories are the most precious things we have.

Frau Binder I have none.

Herr Weiring Oh, come now.

Frau Binder And what has one got to show for it if they're the sort of memories you're talking about? Nothing but regrets.

Herr Weiring And what has one got to show for it if one doesn't even have those? If one's whole life has just drifted by, one day after another, one day like another, without joy, without love . . . you think that's any better?

Frau Binder Well, think of your sister.

Herr Weiring Yes. Think of her.

Frau Binder Well, aren't you glad that the poor thing always had you to protect her? You were a brother in a thousand –

He protests.

– no, it's true, you had to be mother and father to her when you were hardly more than a boy.

Herr Weiring Yes, at least I had that excuse. I thought I knew what was best for her. Like God. But as time went on and her hair turned grey and her face got lined, and the days followed one another and her youth passed with them till my pretty sister was suddenly an old maid – only then did I realize what I had done.

Frau Binder Oh, but Herr Weiring –

Herr Weiring I can still see her, the way she sat opposite me in the evenings by that lamp there – smiling at me with a gentle resignation, as if she wanted to thank me for something. And I ought to have gone down on my knees and asked her forgiveness for protecting her so thoroughly from any chance of happiness.

Frau Binder Or unhappiness. How is one supposed to know? My husband – (*She changes her mind.*) My husband will be waiting for me. I say, why don't you come with us?

Herr Weiring Perhaps I might.

Frau Binder But do take your overcoat, it'll get quite chilly later on.

Herr Weiring Do you think so?

Frau Binder Of course it will – How can you take so little care of yourself?

Herr Weiring takes his coat and they leave together.

(*As they leave*) And how is the new show?

Herr Weiring Charming. So pretty. So true to life.

This takes them out. The distant music reasserts itself and the evening fades a little.

Christine returns, disappointed. She has closed the door behind her. There is a knock at the door. She ignores it, and starts to leave the room in the direction of the interior. She is halted by the sound of Mizi's voice calling her name and the door opening.

Mizi I was chasing you up the road. Didn't you hear me?

Christine No.

Mizi What's the matter?

Christine Nothing. Bit of a headache.

Mizi It's all that wine last night – I'm amazed I haven't got one. Still, it was fun wasn't it? They're a terrific couple of swells, aren't they? And that's a devastating place Fritz has got, *très élégant*. Now, Dory's place – whoops! – enough of that!

Christine Oh, Mizi, what do you think – he never turned up.

Mizi He stood you up? Well, serves you right!

Christine What do you mean? What have I done?

Mizi You throw yourself at him and let him walk all over you. It makes them too sure of themselves.

48

Christine What do you know about it?

Mizi It's the only thing I do know about. You make me cross sometimes. He doesn't show up, he doesn't walk you home, shares a box with strangers and goes off with them, and you gaze at him like a lovesick duck.

Christine Don't talk like that – stop acting rottener than you are. You know you like Theodore too.

Mizi Like him – of course I like him. But I'm not going to put myself out for him – not for Dory or anyone else. Not all the men in the world are worth it put together and certainly not one at a time.

Christine Mizi, I don't know you like this.

Mizi I took care you wouldn't. I was a bit in awe of you. But all the same I did think – when it hits her it will knock her sideways. The first time always does. But you can be glad of one thing, you had a friend like me around.

Christine Mizi! Mizi Do you think I'm not? What would you take it into your head to do if you didn't have me to tell you? Men are all the same and the lot of them aren't worth one unhappy hour. Let me tell you, girl – you can't believe a thing men say.

Christine Why do you keep talking about *men*? – I'm not interested in any of the others! For the rest of my life I'll only care about one man!

Mizi You won't. The record stands at eighteen months. All the rest is front.

Christine Oh, please stop!

Mizi Maybe there is a man who would devote himself to you for life but only a fool would look for him in Vienna.

Christine Mizi – don't –

Mizi And only a cretin would look for him in the Medical School, and only you in the Dragoons.

Christine Mizi – I can't bear to listen to this today – it hurts me –

Mizi Oh, come on –

Christine I'd rather you went. I'm sorry. I'd rather be left alone. (*She goes out on to the roof terrace.*)

Mizi I'm off. Come and see me at the theatre when you're better. Perhaps that's my trouble – no man is a hero to a wardrobe mistress. They're all the same when they're waiting for their trousers.

> *She turns to go and finds that Fritz has appeared in the doorway. He looks at her inquiringly. She jerks her head towards the door leading to the roof. Fritz comes further into the room. Mizi offers him her hand. Fritz raises her hand to his lips and bows over it. Mizi kisses him passionately on the mouth. He is taken by surprise, disconcerted, and he pushes her away. She laughs at him and leaves, still laughing. Fritz looks carefully around the room and then approaches the piano. He lifts the lid and plays a tune with one finger. Christine hears this and comes to the door and sees him.*

Fritz Hello!

Christine (*joyously*) Fritz! Oh, Fritz! (*She rushes into his arms.*)

Fritz Steady on – darling!

Christine Everybody says you'll drop me but you won't, will you? Not yet – not yet –

Fritz Who says so? What's all this? (*He calms her, stroking her.*) Well, honestly, my darling – I thought you'd be a bit put out to see me up here.

Christine As long as you're here – nothing else matters.

Fritz There, there – calm down.

Christine Why didn't you come?

Fritz I did. I came late. I waited in the gardens but I couldn't see you and I was about to give up and go home when I suddenly felt such a desperation – such a longing to see this dear little face . . .

Christine Is that true?

Fritz And then I suddenly had to see where you lived – yes, I really did – I just had to see it once, I couldn't wait, so I came straight up – you don't mind?

Christine Oh God!

Fritz No one saw me.

Christine What do I care!

Fritz (*looking round*) So here it is. So this is your room. It's so . . . nice.

Christine But you can't see anything. (*She is about to take the shade off the lamp to light it.*)

Fritz No, let it be. I don't want the light in my eyes. It's better as it is. So this is where you are. This is the table you told me about where you sit and work. And what a view – over so many rooftops – and over there – what's that dark mass . . .?

Christine That's the Kahlenberg.

Fritz Of course! You're much better off than I am!

Christine Oh . . .!

Fritz I'd love to live as high as this and look out over the rooftops. It's marvellous. And how quiet this street must be.

Christine Oh, it's quite noisy enough during the day.

Fritz Do you get much traffic going by?

Christine No, but there's the railway –

Fritz Oh, I shouldn't like that.

Christine You get used to it and after a while you stop hearing it.

Fritz Is it really the first time I've been here? Everything seems so familiar – it's exactly as I'd imagined it –

Christine Oh, don't look too closely –

Fritz What are those pictures?

Christine No – don't!

Fritz But I'd like to see them.

Christine *Hail* and *Farewell*.

Fritz So they are. *Hail* and *Farewell*.

Christine I know very well they aren't great art –

Fritz (*another painting*) And what's this? *Forsaken*! Poor girl!

Christine It's those Dragoons, I expect.

Fritz And who's the old boy up there on the stove?

Christine That's Schubert of course.

Fritz So it is.

Christine Because father's so fond of him. My father used to compose songs himself once, beautiful songs which he would teach me . . .

Fritz Not any more?

Christine Not any more.

Fritz Ah – and here's your collection of books.

Christine Don't look at those.

Fritz Why not? Schiller! . . . and Goethe . . . and an encyclopaedia. Well, well!

Christine It only goes up to G.

Fritz So it does. *Everybody's Encyclopaedia.* You look at the pictures, do you?

Christine What do you mean, Fritz?

Fritz You look at the pictures. In the encyclopaedia. You like to look at the pictures.

Christine Well, yes, I look at the pictures too.

Fritz Oh – I didn't mean – it's only because I love your pretty little head, and I don't want it bothered about . . . I've said the wrong thing.

Christine Oh, no Fritz –! I love you loving my head – if you like I'll never read anything again!

Fritz It's so cosy here.

Christine Do you really like it?

Fritz Very much. And what's this?

Christine Now what's he found!

Fritz Oh no, dear girl, these don't belong here – they're faded . . .

TOM STOPPARD

Fritz has picked up a vase containing artificial flowers.

Christine I'm sure they're not.

Fritz Artificial flowers always look faded. You should have real flowers in your room – fresh and fragrant. I'll make sure that from now on . . . (*He breaks off.*)

Christine What? What were you going to say?

Fritz Nothing.

Christine Tell me.

Fritz I was only going to say that I'll send you some flowers tomorrow.

Christine Well, and do you take it back already? Of course! – by tomorrow you'll have forgotten all about me.

Fritz What are you talking about?

Christine Oh yes – I know – I can feel it.

Fritz How can you think that of me?

Christine It's because of you. You make such a secret of yourself. You don't tell me anything about yourself. How do you spend your days?

Fritz But darling, it's all very ordinary. I go to lectures – well, sometimes – and I go to the coffee house – I read – I play the piano – I pass the time with people . . . it's all quite trivial, too boring to talk about.

Christine But you must have done lots of other things.

Fritz No. Not really. That's all I've ever done. And now my time is up. I have to go, my flower.

Christine Already?

54

Fritz Your father will be home.

Christine Not for hours yet, Fritz – stay a bit longer – only for a minute – do stay!

Fritz The other thing is, I have to . . . Theodore's expecting me. There's something I have to discuss with him.

Christine Does it have to be today?

Fritz I'm afraid it does.

Christine You can see him tomorrow.

Fritz I may not be in Vienna tomorrow.

Christine Not in Vienna!?

Fritz Well, yes. It's been known to happen. I might go away for the day – even two days – you funny little girl –

Christine Where to?

Fritz Where to? Here or there. Heavens, don't look like that. I'm going down to my parents. Is there anything wrong with that?

Christine You see! You're secretive about them, too.

Fritz What a baby you are! I can't tell you how lovely it is being alone here with you. Don't you think it's nice?

Christine No, I don't. It isn't nice being told nothing – don't you see? I want to know everything about you. Every little thing. It isn't enough to have you for an hour on the occasional evening – and then you're off again and I'm no wiser. And the whole night to get through and another day, hour after hour, still knowing nothing. It makes me unhappy.

Fritz But why should it?

Christine Well, it's because I miss you so much and you might as well not be living in the same city – you could be somewhere else entirely! You seem so far away it's as if you're dead!

Fritz Christine –

Christine No, it's true!

Fritz Come here a moment.

Christine comes close to him.

There's only one thing you can really know – that you love me *now*. At this moment. Don't look beyond. Sometimes a moment seems to contain the whole of beyond inside it – but that's as close as we come to knowing eternity. It's the only glimpse we get. (*He kisses her. He gets up. Suddenly he bursts out.*) Oh, how lovely it is being here with you! How lovely. One feels so secret here, tucked away among all these rooftops and chimneys, so protected, so alone. So safe.

Christine If you always spoke to me like that I could almost believe . . .

Fritz What, dear?

Christine That you love me as much as I dreamed you did the first time you kissed me. Do you remember?

Fritz I do love you. (*He kisses her and then breaks away.*) But now let me go –

Christine Are you already sorry you said it? After all, you're free. You're free. You can drop me if you want. You made no promises and I made no conditions. What happens to me doesn't matter – I've been happy once and it's all I ask of life. I only want you to know that

I never loved anyone before you and when you don't want me any more I'll never love anyone else.

Fritz Don't say that – don't – it's too – (*distastefully*) it's like that picture –

Christine (*hurt*) I realize your taste is above such sentiment – these clichés –

Fritz Oh, Christine – everything tastes bitter to me now! I'm so sorry I hurt you – please don't, don't cry, Christine, Christine.

They embrace. There is a bold knock at the door. Christine and Fritz fearfully break apart. Christine lights the lamp while Fritz steps outside on to the roof terrace. There is another knock and Theodore enters.

Theodore Hello – I've got a nerve, haven't I?

Fritz (*emerging*) Have you got something to tell me?

Theodore I have.

Christine It must be something very important.

Theodore It is.

Fritz So . . . you're with me tomorrow?

Theodore That's right.

Fritz Good. Why didn't you wait downstairs?

Christine What's all this whispering?

Theodore Why didn't I wait downstairs? Well, if I'd been sure you were up here . . . I wasn't going to risk walking up and down for two hours. I've been looking for him everywhere. I've been run off my feet so I must beg a glass of water.

Christine I'll get one. (*She leaves the room.*)

Theodore What are you doing here?

Fritz Is there any more news?

Theodore What?

Fritz About her.

Theodore Who? Oh, no. I only came to collect you because you're so irresponsible. What's all this excitement? You ought to be resting, this is no place for you.

Fritz You're right. God, how such moments deceive us.

Theodore What moments?

Fritz I almost believed that my happiness is with that girl. But it's one big lie.

Theodore Sentimental rot.

Fritz Yes. That's right, rot. Sweetness and decay, they go together.

Theodore You'll laugh at it tomorrow.

Fritz I doubt I'll get the chance.

Christine re-enters with the water.

Don't you think this room is lovely?

Theodore Yes, very nice. Are you stuck here all day? I mean, it's very cosy but it's a bit high up for my liking.

Fritz That's just what I love about it.

Theodore drinks some of the water and gives the glass back to Christine.

Theodore But now I have to take Fritz away. We have to be up early tomorrow.

Christine So you really are going away.

Theodore He'll be back, Christine!

Christine Will you write to me?

Theodore He's not going far.

Christine Oh, but I know he is. You are, Fritz. Never mind.

Theodore This is nonsense, Christine. She doesn't know what she's saying. All right then, kiss each other goodbye since it's going to seem like for ever – oh God! – pretend I'm not here. Take as long as you like.

Fritz and Christine kiss.

Right, that's enough! Goodbye, Christine.

Fritz (*to Christine*) I don't want to go.

Christine Oh, get on with you – you're just being silly.

Theodore She's absolutely right.

Fritz (*turning on him angrily*) Theo, it's my life!

Theodore, taken aback, hesitates and then leaves. Fritz takes Christine in his arms.

Act Three

*We are backstage at the Josefstadt theatre, the wings
providing our forestage with a partial view of the Josefstadt stage beyond. The transition between Act Two and
Act Three should be made without an intermission. The
effect should be that the scenery of Act Two should now
be seen to be cleared from the stage of the Josefstadt by
the opera stage-hands. The stage-hands get the space into
a 'rehearsal state' while the orchestra, unseen, is tuning
up. The characters in the rehearsal are to be a Hussar
(Tenor) and a girl (Soprano). They are in resplendent
costume. They will be rehearsing a duet – 'The False
Hussar'. The transition is being supervised by a Stage
Manager. During the transition Christine hurries on
holding sheets of music. She hands these to the Stage
Manager, or possibly to an orchestra manager.*

Stage Manager Are those the corrections?

Christine Yes, can I watch the rehearsal from here?

Stage Manager Yes, all right.

*He takes the pages off stage, towards the orchestra.
'The False Hussar' gets under way. It begins with a
verse which we did not hear in Act One, as follows:*

Tenor (*sings*)
Beautiful lady, hail to thee
Surely an angel you must be
How can a man believe his eyes?
How came you here from paradise?
Angel be mine and I'll be yours

Home have I come from foreign wars
Fighting the Turks on land and sea
Will you not comfort me?

The Tenor is without his tunic. This is brought on by Mizi, who hurries in during this first verse.

Christine Mizi, have you heard anything?

Mizi What? – Oh, them. How should I know? Too busy.

Mizi takes the tunic 'on stage' and as the Soprano starts singing the chorus she fits the Hussar's tunic on to the Tenor, helping him to do it up.

Soprano (*sings*)
Mother told me all about you
Mother told me what I should do
Mother said it's all Liebelei
Daughter mine
Daughter mine, you must reply –

Christine No message? Nothing?

Mizi No.

Christine And you've had no letter?

Mizi Why should I get a letter?

Christine It's been two days.

Mizi Exactly. Two days, what's the fuss? You look awful. Your father's bound to notice you've been crying.

Christine I've told him.

Mizi What?

Christine Everything.

Mizi Well, what's the difference? One only has to look at you anyway. Does he know who it is?

Christine Yes. I told him last night.

Mizi What did he say?

Christine Nothing. He wasn't angry.

Mizi He must think Fritz will marry you.

The Soprano has now sung the chorus and her own verse, which is the same verse Mizi sang in Act One. Beginning 'Hail and farewell, my gay Hussar'. At the end of her verse, the Tenor prepares to take up his own chorus.

Tenor (*sings*)
Sweetheart, please don't send me away
Sweetheart, there's no war on today
Sweetheart, won't you dally, do . . .

But at this point there is a mishap in the rehearsal – for example, the Tenor knocks over some insecurely fastened part of the stage set. The song breaks down in disorder. Stage-hands appear to effect repairs. The Stage Manager hurries on to apologize to the unseen 'Maestro'. Mizi and Christine continue their conversation with hardly a pause.

Mizi You know what I think?

Christine What?

Mizi That this story of theirs about a trip is a fraud.

Christine How?

Mizi They probably haven't gone anywhere.

Christine Yes, they have. I know they have. I went past his house yesterday – the shutters were closed – he's not there.

Mizi All right, so they're away. But they're not coming back, not to us anyway.

Christine You say it so calmly.

Mizi Well, tonight or tomorrow or in six months – it all comes to the same thing.

Christine You don't know what you're talking about. You don't know Fritz. He's not what you think. I saw what he was like when he came to see me. He only pretends – sometimes – not to care, but he loves me. Yes, I know, it's not for ever, I do know that – but it won't stop overnight. He's my Fritz and he'll come back.

Mizi You've convinced me. He's probably gone to the country to ask his aged parents for permission to marry.

The repair has now been made, and the duet reassembles itself and picks up with the orchestra. The duet continues with the beginning of the Tenor chorus – 'Sweetheart, please don't send me away'.

Christine Mizi . . . do me a favour.

Mizi Don't worry so much. What do you want?

Christine Go round to Theodore's after rehearsal. It's not very far – just look in and ask if he's back yet. If he's not there they might know when he's expected.

Mizi I'm not running after any man.

Christine He doesn't need to know anything about it. Perhaps you'll bump into him by accident.

Mizi Why don't you do it yourself? – go round to Fritz's place

Christine I daren't. He hates anything like that. And I'm sure he can't be back. But Theodore might be and he'd know. Please, Mizi.

Mizi You're such a baby sometimes.

Christine Do it for me. Go on. It's not asking a lot.

Mizi Well, if it means so much to you. But it won't do any good. They're not at home.

Christine And you'll come and tell me?

Mizi All right.

Christine Thank you, Mizi, you're a friend.

Mizi Yes, I am. Now go home and I'll see you later.

Christine Thank you.

> *Now the duet goes wrong again, for different reasons. The Tenor, singing the chorus solo, explains the reason, improvising out of his song.*

Tenor (*sings*)
Sweetheart, please don't send me away
Sweetheart, there's no war on today
I can't sing in this bloody thing!
It's too tight – it's far far far too tight!

> *So singing, he has taken off the tunic and tossed it back to Mizi who catches it and hurries away in guilty confusion to, no doubt, make it less tight. The orchestra of course has broken down. The Tenor leaves the stage in a huff. The Soprano follows him. Members of the orchestra start crossing our stage from the direction of the musicians' pit. Among them is Herr Weiring.*

Herr Weiring Christine –

Christine What's the matter? What is it?

Herr Weiring I want you to go home. Don't stop on the way.

Christine Father . . .?

Herr Weiring Just go home.

Christine You're angry.

Herr Weiring Of course not. It's my fault. Please go home. I'll come after rehearsals.

Christine What are you talking about? What's happened? I thought you understood.

Herr Weiring I do understand. I understand everything.

Christine What?

Herr Weiring Go home.

Christine Not till you tell me.

Herr Weiring I will tell you. It needs time.

Christine I'll wait.

The Musicians, Stage-hands, etc., have been progressively moving off stage and now Christine and Herr Weiring are alone.

Herr Weiring Listen. The whole thing is a mistake. I've thought about it. You're so young.

Christine Why are you saying this? What has changed?

Herr Weiring It's all wrong. It's delusion. Listen to me – it's best to forget all about it. It's just you and me again.

Christine Stop talking like this. I confided in you. You can turn me out if you like but don't tell me it's a mistake –

Herr Weiring Turn you out? How can you say that? You only have me to protect you, and I failed you. We'll start again. You'll take singing lessons. There's a lot more to life. Being together. You and I. And summer's coming – we can go out to the country –

Christine *What are you talking about?*

Herr Weiring *Listen,* damn you! You get more than one chance of happiness, don't you? You don't think everything stops the first time you get it or lose it?

Christine Why should I have to lose it?

Herr Weiring And it was never happiness anyway – do you think that I don't know? It was misery.

Christine You've heard something.

Herr Weiring No – nothing. But that man was playing with you, believe me, you've lost nothing. What do you know about him? Nothing. What did he know about your feelings? Did he appreciate you? Forget him. You'll meet someone decent, someone of your own kind and be happy.

She breaks away.

Where are you going?

Christine To find him. He can tell me himself.

Herr Weiring Don't be stupid. He's not there –

Christine I'll sit on his doorstep –

Herr Weiring I won't let you – for God's sake –

Christine Then tell me what you know.

Herr Weiring What is there to know? I know that I love you, that you're my only child, that you belong with me – and I should never have let you –

Christine That's enough! – Let go of me!

They see that Theodore has entered, with Mizi behind him. Theodore is wearing his Dragoons uniform.

Theo . . .? What's happened? Where is he? Tell me.

Theodore Christine, he . . .

Christine Tell me, can't you.

Herr Weiring He's dead.

Christine (*ignoring him*) Don't you dare say that, Theo. Tell me really.

Herr Weiring He's dead, my darling . . .

Christine Theo . . .

> *Theodore nods.*

Theodore Yes, he is.

Christine For God's sake tell me, Theodore.

Theodore He's dead.

Christine Yes. Of course he is. Don't touch me. Tell me.

Theodore What else is there to tell?

Christine I don't know *anything*. I don't know what's happened.

Theodore It was an accident. Well, a sort of . . .

Christine What? – Come on, Theo, do you think you have to spare me now? What difference does it make? How did it happen? Father . . .? (*to Mizi*) You know, don't you?

Mizi He was killed.

Christine What do you mean he was?

Theodore He was killed in a duel.

Christine Oh, my God –

> *Herr Weiring motions the others to leave.*

Stay here. Do you think I'm not going to get it out of you. Who killed him?

Theodore No one you know.

Christine I know *that,* Theo. I know Frau Binder didn't kill him – Damn you, Theo – I'm entitled to know – he loved me and I have a right to know who killed him.

Theodore What does it matter? He fought a duel. A matter of honour. He was killed.

Christine Honour?

Theodore The usual thing. Well, what I mean is –

Christine What you mean is what? A woman?

Herr Weiring Christine . . .

Christine Of course. For a woman. (*to Mizi*) That woman in the box. And her husband killed him. The usual thing. (*cries out*) He died for *her*? He loved *her*?

Theodore Love? No, he was – it was just a madness.

Christine Oh yes – mad about her, crazy for her, driven insane by her. I know about that, it's what love is, Theo, didn't you know that?

Herr Weiring Love isn't that – true love is something else, you'll find out, Christine –

Christine What was I, then?

Mizi You were a bit of fun on the side, Chrissie, like me for Theo –

Theodore I say, look –

Christine Theodore, have you nothing for me? Didn't he write anything for you to give me? A message? Nothing at all?

Theodore shakes his head.

And when he came to see me that evening, he already knew. He knew then that he probably wouldn't ever . . .

68

He amused himself with me and then went off to get himself killed for the woman he loved. Didn't he know that I would die for *him*?

Theodore (*remembering with relief*) He spoke of you! He really did. In the morning when we drove out together at dawn he also spoke of you.

Christine Also of me! Oh, good. He spoke of her, and him, and you, and his parents, his friends, and me.

Theodore I'm sure he loved you too.

Christine Like you love Mizi? I worshipped him. He was God and salvation and I was his day off.

Theodore (*to Mizi*) Honestly, you could have spared me this – I've had enough upsets these last couple of days.

> *The Conductor and the Musicians reappear, crossing the stage towards the pit.*

Christine Theodore, take me to him – I want to see him for the last time.

Theodore I can't –

Christine Please – I want a proper last time, you can't deny me that.

Theodore It's too late. They buried him this morning.

Christine Buried him? Without even telling me? They shot him and put him in a coffin and took him away and buried him and you didn't even tell me?

Theodore Listen, I haven't had a minute! These last two days, you've no idea . . . Don't forget I was the one who had to tell his parents, I had a lot on my mind, and consider my own feelings too, I was his best friend . . . and anyway it was all done very quietly, only the relatives and people closest to him –

Christine Only the closest? And what am I, then?

Mizi That's what they would have wanted to know.

The orchestra is heard tuning up. The Tenor and the Soprano return to the stage. The Tenor is wearing a different tunic. The Stage Manager tries to get the attention of Herr Weiring, indicating that the rehearsal must continue.

Herr Weiring (*to the Stage Manager*) Yes . . . yes.

Christine Take me to his grave.

Herr Weiring No, please – Christine –

Stage Manager (*generally*) Please, ladies and gentle-men . . . Herr Weiring.

Herr Weiring leaves down the steps, followed by the Stage Manager.

Mizi Don't go, Christine – you may find *her* there, praying.

Christine I'm not going there to pray.

Theodore Perhaps later when you're . . .

Christine When I'm calmer?

Theodore Yes.

Christine Tomorrow? Or in a month when I'm over it? Or six months when I'm in love again? *Damn* you, Theo.

Theodore I'm very sorry. I thought you understood. Everyone else did. How was I to know that . . .

Christine What? That I loved him? You shit-bucket, Theo. You fat, ugly, ignorant, lecherous, dirty-fingered God's gift to the female race, your breath stank of stale women when you kissed me, I was nearly *sick*!

The duet has now started again. The Tenor and the Soprano are now singing together and alternately, and the music and the dialogue are organized together so as to leave the end of the chorus still to be sung after Christine's exit. The last words of the play are thus the sung words:

Sweetheart, won't you dally, do
Or I'll die,
Or I'll die for love of you.

Christine leaves, pausing on her way to listen to the duet for a few moments. Mizi and Theodore remain, immobile, listening as the duet continues. Slow curtain.

UNDISCOVERED COUNTRY

Das weite Land
by Arthur Schnitzler
in an English version
by Tom Stoppard

Characters

Genia Hofreiter
Friedrich Hofreiter
a businessman, Genia's husband
Erna Wahl
Dr Franz Mauer
Mrs Wahl
Erna's mother
Mrs Meinhold von Aigner
an actress, Otto's mother
Adele Natter
Otto von Aigner
a lieutenant in the navy, Mrs von Aigner's son
Dr von Aigner
divorced husband of Mrs von Aigner
Paul Kreindl
a young man
Mr Natter
a banker, Adele's husband
Rosenstock
porter of the Lake Vols Hotel
Gustl Wahl
Mrs Wahl's son
Mr Serknitz
a hotel guest
Albertus Rhon
a writer
Penn
a guide
Mrs Rhon
Albertus Rhon's wife

Demeter Stanzides
a captain in the Hussars
First Hiker
Second Hiker
Kathi
the Hofreiters' maid
Italian Girl
Spanish Girl
French Girl
Bellboy
Head Waiter
The Natters' Two Children
French Nanny

Hotel Guests, Hikers, Waiters

*The action takes place at the Hofreiter villa
in Baden, near Vienna, and at the Lake Vols Hotel
in the Dolomites*

Undiscovered Country was first performed at the Olivier Theatre, London, on 20 June 1979. The cast was as follows:

Genia Hofreiter Dorothy Tutin
Friedrich Hofreiter John Wood
Erna Wahl Emma Piper
Dr Franz Mauer Michael Byrne
Mrs Wahl Sara Kestelman
Mrs Meinhold von Aigner Joyce Redman
Adele Natter Anna Carteret
Otto von Aigner Greg Hicks
Dr von Aigner Michael Bryant
Paul Kreindl, John Harding
Mr Natter Brian Kent
Rosenstock Peter Needham
Gustl Wahl Adam Norton
Mr Serknitz Roger Gartland
Albertus Rhon Dermot Crowley
Penn Martyn Whitby
Mrs Rhon Marjorie Yates
Demeter Stanzides Glyn Grain
First Hiker Elliott Cooper
Second Hiker William Sleigh
Kathi Janet Whiteside
Italian Girl Susan Gilmore
Spanish Girl Fiona Gaunt
French Girl Anne Sedgwick
Bellboy Mark Farmer
Head Waiter Nik Forster

The Natters' Children Graham McGrath,
  Sandra Osborn
French Nanny Marianne Morley

Directed by Peter Wood
Designed by William Dudley

Act One

Conservatory and garden of the Hofreiter villa.
    Late afternoon, after the rain.
    Genia Hofreiter, dressed simply and respectably,
stands listening to a Chopin record on the gramophone.
    Kathi, the maid, comes in with a tray to clear away
the tea things, but hesitates.

Kathi Shall I clear away, madam? Herr Hofreiter will no
doubt have taken tea in town.

    Genia nods, barely paying attention.

Shall I bring something to put round you, ma'am? It's
turned quite chilly.

Genia Mm . . .

    Genia notes the approach, beyond the fence and
    mostly hidden by it, of a funereal parasol and two
    elegant but equally funereal head-dresses.

. . . my white shawl.

    Kathi completes her business and leaves with the tea
    things on her tray. Mrs Wahl and Erna approach.
    Genia waves her hand gracefully and moves to greet
    them. Mrs Wahl, slim and lively, about forty-five, has
    an air of self-conscious dignity. She speaks through
    her nose in an aristocratic manner which is not quite
    convincing. In expression and speech she is languid
    and vivacious by turns. Erna, taller than her mother,
    slim; outspoken without being offensive; a cool, self-
    possessed expression. Genia greets them, shaking hands.

79

Do come in. Safely back from town?

Mrs Wahl As you see, my dear Genia. The weather was frightful.

Genia It rained out here, too, until an hour ago.

Mrs Wahl You did quite right to stay at home. We nearly went under at the cemetery. It was only Erna made me go. In my opinion, the church service would have been quite sufficient. What good does it do anyone, after all?

Erna Mama is quite right there – we certainly didn't bring poor Korsakow back to life.

Genia Many there?

Mrs Wahl *Tout le monde*. The Natters rolled up in their new scarlet motor.

Genia (*smiling*) It's seen all over the place, I hear.

Mrs Wahl Well, it certainly made a lively impression at the cemetery . . .

> *Kathi comes out of the house with a white shawl, which she puts around Genia.*

Kathi Good evening, madam. Good evening, miss.

Erna Good evening.

Mrs Wahl (*friendly*) Bless you, Kathi, dear . . .

> *Kathi exits.*

Genia Did you speak to Friedrich out there?

Mrs Wahl Only in passing.

Erna He was quite upset.

Genia I'm not surprised.

Erna I was, as a matter of fact. He doesn't normally let things affect him so easily.

Genia (*smiling*) How well you seem to know him.

Erna Well, why not? (*very simply*) I've loved him since I was seven years old. I loved him before you did, Frau Genia.

Genia (*chiding her affectionately*) Oh . . . *Frau* Genia, am I?

Erna (*almost tenderly*) Genia. (*She kisses Genia's hand.*)

Genia Friedrich was very fond of Alexei Korsakow, you know.

Erna Obviously. And there was I thinking that Korsakow was just . . . his pianist.

Genia How do you mean, 'his pianist'?

Erna Well, just as Dr Mauer is his best friend, Mr Natter is his banker, I'm his doubles partner, and Captain Stanzides is his . . . his second . . .

Genia Oh . . .

Erna In theory, I mean . . . So I thought Korsakow was Friedrich's pianist. Friedrich takes from each according to his needs, you see . . .

Mrs Wahl Do you know, my dear Genia, what my late husband used to say about those remarks? – 'There goes Erna, pirouetting along the psychological tightrope.'

Erna Lieutenant!

Otto von Aigner arrives at the edge of the garden.

Otto (*as he arrives*) Good evening.

Genia Good evening, Lieutenant von Aigner. Won't you come in for a moment?

Otto With your permission, ma'am. (*He enters the garden. He is a young man of twenty-five, modest and charming. He is wearing the uniform of a naval lieutenant.*)

Genia How is your mama? We haven't seen her today.

Otto Didn't she come yesterday, ma'am?

Genia Yes, she did. And the day before, too. (*smiling*) You see she's been spoiling me.

Otto My mother has gone into town. She has a perform-ance tonight. (*to Mrs Wahl and Erna*) I believe you ladies were also in town today . . .?

Mrs Wahl We went to Korsakow's funeral.

Otto Of course . . . Does anybody have any idea why he killed himself?

Erna No.

Mrs Wahl Somebody at the funeral said they thought it was an artistic tantrum.

Genia What . . .?

Mrs Wahl Yes. Because he was forever being told he could only play Chopin and Schumann, but not Beethoven or Bach . . . I must say I thought so too . . .

Otto Seems a bit extreme. Didn't he leave a note?

Erna Korsakow wouldn't be seen dead with a suicide note.

Mrs Wahl There she goes . . .

Erna He was far too intelligent and he had too much taste. He understood what it means to be dead, and so cared nothing for what people made of it next morning.

Otto I read in the papers that on the evening before he killed himself he was dining with friends . . . and was in excellent spirits . . .

Mrs Wahl The papers invariably say that.

Genia This time it happens to be true – my husband was one of the friends he dined with.

Mrs Wahl Ah . . .

Genia (*casually*) When Friedrich has to work late in town he always dines at the Imperial Hotel. Korsakow was staying there. After dinner they went to the café and played billiards.

Mrs Wahl Just your husband and Korsakow?

Genia Yes. They even had a bet on – a box of cigars – and Friedrich lost. Next morning he sent Josef, his manservant, round from the flat with the cigars . . . and – didn't you know? – it was Josef who made the discovery.

Mrs Wahl What happened?

Genia Well, he knocked a few times – no reply; so finally he opened the door, and . . .

Erna There lay Korsakow, dead . . .

Genia Yes, with the revolver still in his hand . . .

Pause.

Mrs Wahl Awful moment for the manservant. What did he do with the cigars? Did he leave them?

Erna Mama believes in historical precision.

The sound of a car approaching.

Mrs Wahl It's stopping here.

Genia That's Friedrich's car.

Erna Good – we can arrange a game of tennis straight away. Is the court set up?

Otto Oh yes – Mr Hofreiter and I played singles for two hours yesterday.

Mrs Wahl You mean he was in the mood for tennis?

Erna Why shouldn't he be in the mood, Mama? When it's my turn to go, people can knock up against my gravestone if they like.

Dr Mauer arrives. He is thirty-five, with a blond full beard, pince-nez, sabre scar on his forehead; plainly, though not carelessly, dressed in a dark lounge suit.

Mauer Good evening, dear friends.

Genia Oh, it's you, Doctor . . .

Mauer (*taking her hand, kissing it*) Greetings, dear lady. (*to Mrs Wahl*) Good evening, Mrs Wahl. (*and to Erna*) Ah . . . Miss Erna. Good evening, Lieutenant. (*to Genia*) Friedrich presents his compliments, Frau Genia, but he's held up at the factory. He was kind enough to lend me his car to visit a couple of patients I've got out here. He's coming on by train.

Mrs Wahl Alas, we must go. (*to Mauer*) I hope we'll soon see you *chez nous,* Doctor. Although, thank God, we enjoy perfect health.

Erna You must come soon though, Doctor. We're off to the mountains in two weeks or so, to Lake Vols.

Mauer Ah!

Mrs Wahl We're going to rendezvous with Gustl . . . (*to Otto*) That's my wanderlust *Wunderkind* . . . He's been everywhere . . . India, last year.

Erna And I'm keen to go climbing again.

Mauer Then there's a chance we'll meet up on some mountain peak. The fact is I'm also being drawn to the Dolomites. (*to Genia*) And this year, dear Genia, I very much want to borrow Friedrich for the occasion.

Mrs Wahl I thought Friedrich had given up climbing since the accident . . .

Mauer Not for ever, surely.

Mrs Wahl (*explaining to Otto*) Seven years ago a friend of Friedrich's, his name was Doctor Bernhaupt, crashed right past him on a rock-face . . .

Erna . . . and lay dead where he fell.

Otto (*to Genia*) So it was your husband who was on that climb?

Erna (*thoughtfully*) It has to be said, he doesn't have much luck with his friends.

Genia (*to Otto*) You've heard about it, Mr von Aigner?

Otto Well, naturally . . . it happened on the Aigner-turm . . . which my father was the first to climb more than twenty years ago.

Genia That's right, it was the Aignerturm.

Mauer The Aignerturm . . . One quite forgets that it was named after a man who's still alive.

Short pause.

Erna Well, Lieutenant, it must be an extraordinary feeling to know that there is a mountain in the Dolomites to which you are, in a sense, related.

Otto Not really, Fraulein. Both the mountain and my
father are more or less strangers to me. I was a boy of
four or five when my parents separated . . . and I haven't
seen him since.

Pause.

Erna (*encouraging her to leave*) Well, Mama . . .

Mrs Wahl Yes, indeed! If we're ever going to get
unpacked . . . (*to Mauer*) We only moved out of town
on Sunday. We haven't yet sat down to a proper meal . . .
We have to eat in this awful park. Well, see you before
long, Genia . . . (*to Otto*) Will you come with us part
of the way?

Otto If I may accompany you as far as the tennis
courts . . . Goodbye, ma'am, please give my respects
to your husband.

Erna Goodbye, Genia. *Auf Wiedersehen*, Doctor.

They take their leave. Genia and Mauer remain.

Mauer (*after a short pause, looking after Erna*) Looking
at the daughter, one could almost forgive the mother.

Genia A son-in-law could do a lot worse than Mrs Wahl
. . . I should think it over, Doctor.

Mauer (*half joking*) I don't believe I cut enough of a
dash for Erna.

Genia By the way, I had no idea that Friedrich was
going to have to work late.

Mauer Yes, I was meant to tell you, he had to wait for
an important telegram, from America.

Genia Yes?

86

Mauer Yes. Really. About that business of a patent for his latest invention, the incandescent light.

Genia (*drily*) That was Edison. (*She sits down.*)

Mauer Well, his improvement then. Anyway, as always, business seems to be booming. He's got a meeting with his banker first thing tomorrow.

Genia (*slightly wary*) With Mr Natter?

Mauer Natter *is* his banker.

Genia They were at the funeral too, I hear, the Natters.

Mauer Yes.

Genia The scarlet motor car made an impression.

Mauer (*shrugs*) So it's scarlet.

   Short pause. Genia watches Mauer with a faint smile.

By the way – your husband's affair with Mrs Natter is over.

Genia (*still calm*) Oh really?

Mauer Absolutely.

Genia That's good. Did Friedrich tell you?

Mauer No, he wouldn't. But my diagnoses rarely call for a second opinion. In all honesty, there was never any cause to take it too seriously. Adele is very flighty.

Genia Oh yes, she's harmless. I'm not worried by her at all. But I think Mr Natter, for all his apparent friend-liness, is a brutal man. Spiteful, too, in some ways. And sometimes I've been afraid for Friedrich; like a mother being worried about a son – a rather overgrown son – who's got himself into some scrape. You can understand what I mean?

Mauer (*sitting opposite her*) Yes, of course – the mark of a good wife, mothering her husband.

Genia I haven't always felt so. More than once I thought of leaving him.

Mauer Oh!

Genia Once I even thought of killing myself. Mind you, that was a long time ago. And perhaps it only seems like that to me now . . .

Mauer Quite so. You would never have done it . . . you wouldn't have wished to cause him the inconvenience.

Genia Do you think I'm so considerate? You're quite wrong . . . There was even a time when I thought of inconveniencing Friedrich as only a wife can, especially a wife with a possessive husband. I wanted revenge.

Mauer Revenge?

Genia Well, let's say I wanted to get even.

Mauer That would have been the rational thing to do. Well, never mind . . . The fateful moment may still be waiting for you, Frau Genia.

Genia I don't necessarily have to wait for it.

Mauer (*seriously*) But you will – alas. My sense of justice has long been affronted by my old friend Friedrich getting off scot-free.

Genia Oh, Friedrich pays. Not in the same coin, but he pays all right. Sometimes I even feel sorry for him. Sometimes, Doctor, I really think there's a demon driving him.

Mauer A demon? Well, well! Even so, there are women we know who would tell their husbands to go to hell and take their demon with them.

Genia looks at him inquiringly.

I was thinking of our local celebrity, Otto's mother.

Genia Mrs von Aigner?

Mauer Yes, her husband was a bit of a devil with the ladies, and she wasn't as resilient as you. Perhaps after all those years in the theatre, real life took her by surprise.

Genia Perhaps she loved her husband more than I love Friedrich. Perhaps the highest form of love leaves no room for forgiveness.

Friedrich Hofreiter enters. He is slim, with a thin, distinguished face, a dark moustache clipped in the 'English' style, blond hair, with the parting on the right and a touch of grey. He wears pince-nez without a cord, and sometimes removes them. Tends to stoop a little. Small eyes, a little pinched. He speaks in a gentle, almost caressing way, which can change to biting sarcasm. His movements are graceful but suggest energy. He dresses elegantly but not foppishly: dark lounge suit, a black coat (not buttoned up) with wide satin lapels, a round black hat, a slim umbrella with a simple handle.

Friedrich (*at the door*) Good evening. (*coming in*) Hello, Mauer.

Mauer (*stands up*) Hello there, Friedrich.

Friedrich (*kisses Genia lightly on the forehead*) Good evening, Genia. How are you? Do you want to come to America?

Genia No. Do you want some tea?

Friedrich No . . . I had tea at the office. Pretty awful it was, too. Didn't Mauer tell you I was at the office?

Genia Yes . . . Did you get your telegram?

Friedrich I did . . . There are sailings to New York on August the 29th from Liverpool and on September the 2nd from Hamburg. North German Lloyd. The captain of the *King James* is a friend of mine.

Genia I expect we'll have another chance to talk about it before then.

Friedrich I hope to have that pleasure. I say, what a downpour that was. Did you have it out here? The cemetery was awash. But that was partly the speeches. An inch of slush fell in half an hour. You were well out of it . . . (*Pause.*) Well, Mauer, did the motor behave itself? How fast did you drive? Ten miles an hour, what? Safety first, that's you.

Mauer Pull my leg if you like. I've had three cases of injury from car accidents in the last week.

Friedrich Oh yes – how *is* Stanzides?

Mauer I'm just going to see him, as a matter of fact. He's very impatient, considering he ought to be grateful he didn't break his neck.

Friedrich Not to mention mine. I was thrown thirty feet up the road. But it's certainly true that the insurance companies will soon be turning down anyone who is acquainted with me.

Mauer Yes, as Erna Wahl was saying, you're not very lucky with your friends.

Friedrich So Erna's been here?

Genia Yes, with her mother. They have just gone off with Otto.

Friedrich Otto too? (*to Mauer*) What did you think of him?

Mauer (*slightly surprised by the question*) A nice enough fellow.

Friedrich Remarkable how like his father he is.

Mauer Is he? . . . Dr von Aigner was never my type, as a matter of fact. Had too many affectations.

Friedrich What he had was style. They're often confused. It's a long time, too, since I saw him. Do you remember, Genia?

Genia Oh yes. (*to Mauer*) I liked him very much.

Friedrich Yes, he was in fine fettle then. That's more than I was. (*to Mauer*) It was just a few days after the Bernhaupt thing. Yes, and Aigner had just come back from an election campaign. They say he's got at least one child in every village in the Tyrol. And not just in his own constituency either.

Mauer All right then, let's call it style. But I really must be going now. Stanzides will be expecting me.

Friedrich You will come back here for supper afterwards?

Mauer I don't know.

Friedrich Of course you will.

Mauer (*hesitatingly*) Thank you. But I must catch the 10.20 back to town. I have to be early at the hospital.

Friedrich Are you superstitious, Mauer?

Mauer Why?

Friedrich I thought perhaps you didn't want to spend the night in our guest room since poor Korsakow slept there

91

a week ago. But I don't think the dead are allowed out round their old haunts on their very first night.

Mauer How can you talk like that?

Friedrich (*suddenly serious*) You're right, it's really awful. A week ago he slept up there, and the evening before that he played the piano in there . . . Chopin – the Nocturne in C sharp minor – and something by Schumann . . . and we sat on the veranda there, Otto was here too, and the Natters . . . who would have dreamed . . .! If only one had an idea why . . . Genia – didn't he say anything to you either?

Genia Me?

Mauer (*helping out*) Well, artists are all more or less unhinged, aren't they? For one thing, the way they take themselves so seriously. Ambition is a disturbance of the balance of the mind. All that banking on immortality . . .!

Friedrich What are you talking about! You didn't even know him. None of you knew him. Ambitious . . . Korsakow? No, he'd got that handsome head screwed on all right. Bashing the ivories was just something to do. Do you know what he was really interested in? He had Kant and Schopenhauer and Nietzsche at his fingertips, and Marx and Proudhon . . . He was amazing. And twenty-seven years old!! And kills himself. Dear God, a fellow like that, with so much before him! Young and famous, and with that profile, too . . . and he shoots himself. If it was some old ass, for whom life had nothing more to offer . . . And the evening before, there we were sitting down to supper with a man like that . . . playing billiards with him . . . What is it, Genia? What is there to laugh at?

Genia Mrs Wahl wanted to know what became of the cigars.

Friedrich Ha! . . . She's really priceless. (*Takes a box of cigars from his pocket, offers them to Mauer.*) Josef brought them back to me, of course. Go on, have one. Korsakow has given them up.

Mauer Thank you. One shouldn't really, just before supper.

> *He takes one. Friedrich lights it for him. Kathi enters with letters. Genia takes them from her.*

Genia Postcard from Joey.

Friedrich 'Dear Mother'. For you, just a postcard, once again. Lazy devil.

Mauer Well, I'll be off. I'll be back in half an hour. By the way, this cigar is just about ready to join Korsakow, and that's no superstition. Don't get up. (*He leaves.*)

Friedrich Yes, it was just as well that you didn't go, Genia. Between the drizzle and the drivel . . . (*He flicks through the letters and the newspapers.*) . . . oh yes, as the coffin disappeared the sun suddenly came out. (*Pause.*) Isn't it Thursday today? He was going to have supper with us today. Here, let's have a look at Joey's card.

Genia (*passes it to him*) He'll be here in four weeks.

Friedrich (*reading it*) Yes. Hm . . . top in Greek. Well, not too bad. Perhaps he'll be a philologist, or an archaeologist. By the way, did you see the article in yesterday's London *Times* about the latest excavations in Crete?

Genia No.

Friedrich Very interesting.

Genia Why? Did they dig up a light bulb? (*Pause.*)

93

What was that about America – were you serious?

Friedrich Of course. Well, wouldn't you like to, Genia?

Genia slowly shakes her head.

Genia But I was thinking, while you're over there,
I thought I'd go to England – stay with Joey.

Friedrich Where did this notion suddenly come from?

Genia It's not so sudden. And since you seem determined to let him stay over there for years to come . . .

Friedrich Well, you can see how famously he's getting
on. It would be damned selfish to interrupt all that
fagging and cricket and bring him back here where they
educate you in every kind of sentimental brutality.

Genia If it wasn't for missing him so . . .

Friedrich Yes, of course . . . I suppose you think I don't
yearn for him? But in my opinion, yearning is a necessary
part of the soul's economy. Relationships are all the
better for it. In an ideal world more and more people
would see less and less of each other. Anyway we can go
back with Joey to England, and you can decide then if
you want to come with me or stay with the boy through
the winter.

Genia I'd rather you took it as final.

Friedrich Final? Look, what's the matter with you,
Genia? You're behaving very oddly.

Genia What's so odd about it? Soon he won't be mine
any more. It's not enough – two months in the summer,
a week at Christmas and Easter – I've borne it long
enough – I can't go on any longer!

*Genia moves into the garden. Friedrich looks after
her. Genia walks along the lawn, moving upstage.*

Friedrich follows her. He pauses by a rose bush. He smells a flower.

Friedrich The roses have no scent at all this year. I don't know why it is. Every year they look more gorgeous, but they've stopped bothering. Genia . . .

Genia What?

Friedrich No, I'll wait till you get here. Tell me something. (*looking her in the eye, quite calmly*) I was wondering whether perhaps you knew why Korsakow shot himself . . .?

Genia (*calmly*) You know I was just as surprised as you were.

Friedrich That's the impression one got, of course. Well, tell me why you want to leave me . . . at a moment's notice.

Genia I don't want to leave you. I want to visit Joey. And not at a moment's notice, but in the autumn. To be with Joey.

Friedrich Yes, otherwise it would almost look as if you were running away.

Genia I'm under no such necessity – we could hardly be further apart than we are.

Friedrich Look, Genia! He's dead and buried – Herr Alexei Korsakow.

Genia Then I suggest you stop digging him up!

Friedrich Don't get excited, my love, calm at all costs . . . I'm only trying to say that it can't make the slightest difference to him now if you . . . not that anything would happen to him if he were still alive, of course . . . no more than to you . . . Don't misunderstand me, Genia.

Nothing much need have happened between you. It could have been just a flirtation. Yes. Because if there had been anything more to it – why shoot himself? Unless (*seizing on it*) there *was* more to it – and you . . . ended it. (*He has been speaking quite quietly but now takes her arm.*)

Genia (*almost amused*) A jealous scene? Really! . . . You ought to take something for your nerves, Friedrich, I don't know . . . but I can't help it if Adele Natter is finished with you and you haven't yet found a replacement.

Friedrich Ah, you are very well informed. Well, I won't inquire as to the source of that knowledge. Besides, it's not my fault that you never asked me straight out – I wouldn't have told you you ought to take something for your nerves. That isn't like you at all. I really don't understand you. It's as though you didn't trust me, Genia. But I promise you, Genia – don't think I'm being devious – I would understand completely. You can't imagine how unimportant certain things become when you have just left a cemetery. So come – tell me. You can lie if you want, but answer you must. If it's true I'll find out anyway. Well . . . yes or no?

Genia He was not my lover. Unfortunately, he was not my lover. Does that satisfy you?

Friedrich Perfectly! So you were lovers. Well, if you say 'unfortunately', ergo you loved him and because you loved him, naturally you . . . What was there to stop you? And when you – put an end to it, he killed himself. And I can tell you why you put an end to it, too. Firstly because these things have to come to an end anyway. Especially in the case of a younger man – who is usually away on some concert tour. And then Joey's coming back soon, and when he does you'd like to feel – how shall

96

I put it? – unsullied . . . Well . . . all very respectable.
All very clear so far. Except for this idea about a trip
to England. No, come to that, that makes sense too.

Genia Friedrich! Read that. (*She takes a letter from her
belt.*)

Friedrich What do you want me to. . .?

Genia Read it.

Friedrich What is it . . . a letter? A letter from him? Ah,
keep it. I don't want it.

Genia I said read it!

Friedrich Anyway, why should I have to? You can tell
me what's in it. It could well be in Russian . . . and tiny
handwriting. One could do irreparable damage to one's
eyesight.

Genia Read it.

*Friedrich turns the wall light on, sits under it, puts on
his pince-nez and begins to read.*

Friedrich (*reading*) 'Farewell, Genia.' (*Looks up at her,
in astonishment.*) When did you get the letter, then?

Genia An hour before you brought the news of his death.

Friedrich So when I came home, you already knew . . .?
I'm just . . . Well, at the risk of your thinking me a
complete idiot, I didn't notice a thing, not a thing . . .
(*Reads to himself for a while, then looks at her in
surprise again, then reads half to himself.*) 'Perhaps it
was as well you rejected my presumptuous advances.
Neither of us was made for deceit . . . I was, perhaps,
but not you . . . in spite of everything . . .' In spite of
everything . . . You must have complained about me a
good deal. (*reading*) 'Now I do understand why, in spite

97

of everything, you don't want to leave Him . . .' With a capital H, very flattering. 'You love him, Genia, you still love your husband, the mystery is resolved. And perhaps what I refer to by that stupid word . . .' I can't read this bit at all . . .

Genia 'That stupid word faithfulness . . .'

Friedrich Thank you . . . 'is nothing more than the hope that he will one day come back to you.'

Genia That's his interpretation. You know I hope for nothing – and want nothing.

Friedrich (*looks at her. Then –*) 'When I spoke to you yesterday I had already made up my mind . . .' Yesterday? . . . Was he here on Sunday then? Yes, that's right, you were walking up and down the path together, back there . . . yes . . . (*reading*) 'When I spoke to you yesterday I had already made up my mind that everything would depend on your yes or no. I have told you nothing about it because I was afraid that if you had suspected that I just couldn't go on living without you . . .' He writes in considerable detail, does Herr Alexei Ivanovitsch . . . Would you have said yes if you had known it was a matter of life or death?

Genia If I had *known* . . .? Could one ever . . .?

Friedrich Well, let me put it another way . . . though it's six of one and . . .

Paul Kreindl, elegant, young, dreadfully smart, appears at the gate, interrupting Friedrich.

Paul Good evening!

Friedrich Whom have we here?

Paul My compliments, ma'am.

Friedrich . . . Ah, Paul, it's you. (*He comes down from the veranda.*)

Paul Forgive me. (*He approaches Friedrich.*) Don't let me disturb you. The thing is, I've come as an ambassador from the park – from Mrs Wahl and Miss Erna and Lieutenant von Aigner and Captain Stanzides . . .

Friedrich He's abroad already?

Paul Would the present company care to come to the concert?

Genia I'm afraid we have a guest for supper – Dr Mauer.

Paul Well, do bring him along too, ma'am!

Friedrich All right then – perhaps we'll come on later . . . but no promises.

Genia Thank you all the same.

Paul Oh, not at all. We would all be delighted. I take my leave, ma'am. Adieu, Mr Hofreiter. A thousand pardons for disturbing you.

He exits. Pause.

Friedrich . . . and half a dozen of the other, but I'll put it another way. I mean, suppose you could bring him back to life by telling him you were prepared . . . to be his mistress.

Genia I don't know.

Friedrich You can't have been that far from it . . . Come on, you *did* love him . . .

Genia But not enough, as you see.

Friedrich You say that as if it was *my* fault.

Genia No. It was mine.

Friedrich But you do reproach yourself that you . . . drove him to kill himself.

Genia I'm sorry he's dead. But what should I reproach myself for? – my faithfulness?

Pause.

Friedrich Here's your letter, Genia.

Genia takes the letter as Mauer arrives.

Mauer Here we are again . . . I hope I haven't kept you from supper?

Genia I'll go and see how it's getting on . . .

Friedrich Look, I've got an idea . . . Let's go to the park right away. I'm damned if I'm not in the mood for music and company. It's all the same to you, Mauer, isn't it?

Mauer Me? What about your wife?

Genia (*reluctantly*) I'd have to change . . .

Friedrich Hurry up and change then, we'll be waiting for you in the garden. (*to Mauer*) What do you say? (*nervily*) All right then, let's stay at home then, fine . . . that's an end of it.

Genia I'll be right back . . . I'll just put my hat on.

She exits. Pause.

Mauer I really don't understand you . . .

Friedrich Oh, nothing wrong with the park, you can get a good meal there. (*Pause.*) By the way – it's probably just as well that you're not stopping the night. The chances of a ghostly apparition in this house have considerably increased.

Mauer What?

Friedrich Actually, you don't deserve my confidence, you blurt out everything you know, even things I never told you . . .

Mauer What do you mean?

Friedrich Well, how did Genia find out that I've finished my affair with Adele Natter?

Mauer You ought to be thankful that for once it is possible to say something to your credit . . . What was that about a ghost?

Friedrich What . . .? Oh, that – Well, why do you think Korsakow killed himself? Go on, have a guess! – Because of a hopeless love – for my wife. Yes. A hopeless love! Now we know there is such a thing . . . He left a letter for her. She made me read it . . . quite a remarkable letter . . . not at all badly written . . . for a Russian.

Genia comes in with her hat on. The music from the park can be heard.

Genia Here I am. Well, dear Doctor, let me tell you that it's only for your sake that I've abandoned our nice supper. Erna is in the park.

Friedrich Ah? Erna! (*to Mauer*) Yes, that would be quite a match. Well, dear chap, gird yourself. I wouldn't let anybody have her.

They all leave the garden.

Act Two

The Hofreiter villa. Another part of the garden. The back of the house, with doors opening directly on to the garden. A small balcony on the first floor. A tree, a bench, table and chair. A partly obscured tennis court in the background, with wire netting around it. A hot, sunny, summer's day.

Genia is sitting in the garden, in a white dress, a book in her hand, but she is not reading. On the tennis court a game in progress, involving Friedrich, Adele, Erna and Paul. One may see the bright white tennis clothes but not much of the people. From time to time one can hear the sounds of tennis.

Otto von Aigner arrives, wearing tennis clothes with a panama hat, and carrying a tennis racket. He is on his way to the tennis court, but catches sight of Genia. He goes up to her. She greets him with a friendly nod.

Otto Good morning, ma'am – you're not playing?

Genia As you see, Lieutenant. I'm no match for that company.

Otto They're not all athletes either . . . I don't speak for your husband, of course. I mean . . . (*Pause.*) . . . Forgive me, ma'am, I'm disturbing your reading.

Genia You aren't disturbing me at all. We haven't seen your mother. Does she have a performance today?

Otto Oh, no.

Genia It must be nice for your mother to have you with her again.

Otto And for me . . . Especially since this is my last leave for some time to come. I've been ordered to a ship that's going to the South Seas for three years.

Genia (*conventionally*) Oh.

Otto The War Ministry has attached us to a scientific expedition.

Genia The South Seas . . .? I dare say you will fill up your free time with all kinds of studies, eh, Lieutenant?

Otto How do you mean, ma'am?

Genia I wouldn't imagine that official duties cover all your interests?

Otto (*smiling*) Permit me to observe that in the navy we undertake all sorts of things which could, without presumption, be described as showing the flag.

Genia That's what I thought.

Otto Actually, I hope to learn more about a subject which up to now I have studied only superficially . . . Our expedition is equipped for deep-sea exploration, and one of the technicians . . .

  Mrs Wahl approaches.

Genia (*rising*) You must tell me more another time, Lieutenant . . . about these deep waters . . .

Mrs Wahl Good day to you, Genia. Good day, Lieutenant. (*She puts her lorgnette to her eyes to look at the tennis court.*) The young generation already hard at play . . .?

Genia If you include Friedrich.

Mrs Wahl Friedrich especially. Who's still playing, then? Adele Natter, for one . . . I saw the scarlet motor car

outside. It doesn't look so out of place in the country –
compared with the cemetery.

Genia (*smiling faintly*) It seems to have made a lasting
impression on you.

Mrs Wahl Well, it's only a fortnight . . .

> *Friedrich and Erna come from the court with their
> rackets in their hands.*

Friedrich (*in his laughing, mischievous mood*) What's
only a fortnight? How are you, Mama Wahl? Hello
there, Otto!

Mrs Wahl Poor Korsakow's funeral.

Friedrich Oh yes . . . Was it as long ago as that? How
did you get on to this black-bordered subject, anyway?

Genia Mrs von Wahl saw the Natters' motor car outside
– the scarlet one – it reminded her.

Friedrich Ah ha –

Erna Who else would go from a scarlet motor to a dead
piano player on such a beautiful summer's day?

Mrs Wahl Did you ever see such a deep-thinking girl?
Another of her performances on the philosophical flying-
trapeze, as her late father used to say.

Erna No, he didn't.

Mrs Wahl Must have been someone else.

Friedrich She'd best take care she doesn't fall off one
fine day, our little Erna . . .

> *Adele Natter and Paul Kreindl come from the tennis
> court with their rackets. General greetings. Adele is
> pretty, plump, wearing white with red belt and
> floating red scarf.*

Adele What's happening then, aren't we going to play any more?

Paul kisses Mrs Wahl's hand.

Friedrich You could have carried on with singles.

Adele But I play too badly for this gentleman here.

Paul What do you mean, ma'am? (*whining*) I'll soon have no one bad enough to play with me. Honestly I've been playing like a pregnant sow. Pardon me, but honestly it's true. It's exactly as though I'd been put under a spell. Or perhaps it's just that I've got a new racket. Would the distinguished company excuse me – I'm going to rush off home and get my old one. (*He takes his leave to general laughter.*)

Friedrich What is there to laugh at? He at least takes it seriously. In my opinion a good tennis player is a nobler specimen of humanity than a mediocre poet or general. (*to Otto*) Well, aren't I right?

Adele (*to Genia*) Well now, when is Master Joey returning, Frau Genia?

Genia In a fortnight. And then you must bring your children along one day, won't you?

Adele Gladly, if you'd let me. Although whether your big boy will deign to play with my little rascals . . .

Dr Mauer arrives, with Stanzides in uniform.

Stanzides My compliments!

Genia (*to Stanzides*) Ah, Stanzides, it's nice to have you with us again.

Friedrich How's the arm?

Stanzides Thanks for asking. My medical adviser has just given it a final prod. But I still can't play tennis yet.

Mauer But you will.

Stanzides (*to Adele*) Are you ready for the fray too, ma'am? I just had the pleasure of meeting your husband in the park.

Friedrich Now, Mauer – you've been keeping yourself well out of sight. I thought you were already over the hills and far away.

Mauer I leave tomorrow.

Genia Where are you going?

Mauer To Toblach. From there I'll walk the passes – Falzárego, Pordio . . .

Friedrich Will you take me with you, Mauer?

Mauer Can you? And do you really want to?

Friedrich Yes – why not? . . . You start tomorrow?

Mauer First thing, I'm taking the express.

Erna (*to Mauer*) And when will we have the pleasure of welcoming you to Lake Vols?

Mauer In a week or so, if that's all right.

Friedrich (*frankly put out*) Ah . . . everyone planning their assignations . . .

Erna And without asking your permission, Friedrich!

Mrs Wahl We're going the day after tomorrow – straight to Lake Vols.

> *During the following, Otto, Genia and Adele form a group to one side.*

My Gustl is already there. By the way, the things he's been telling me about in his letters . . . Do you know who the manager of the new hotel is? Otto's father, Dr von Aigner.

Friedrich Oh . . . Aigner!

Mrs Wahl And apparently all the ladies are in a spin over him, despite his grey hair.

Friedrich Yes, women have always been putty in his hands. So have a care, Mama Wahl.

Paul (*returning*) Back again! (*holding his racket up*) There's my old beauty! Now I feel I've got something I can volley with.

Friedrich Well, shall we start? (*to Paul*) But no more excuses! Or change your vocation – take up some local pastime – light opera – or psychoanalysis . . .

Friedrich, Otto, Erna, Adele and Paul go to play tennis. Mrs Wahl and Stanzides follow. Genia and Mauer remain.

Genia Shall we watch the game? Erna's particularly worth watching on the tennis court!

Mauer Can't you see, my dear friend, that she doesn't care two pins for me?

Genia Perhaps that's the best foundation for a happy marriage.

Mauer Oh yes, if I reciprocated her feelings, but in this case . . . (*breaking off*) By the way, Frau Genia, is Friedrich serious about coming with me?

Genia I don't know. I was taken by surprise myself.

Mauer What about this American trip?

Genia Friedrich is going over.

Mauer And you?

Genia I might.

Mauer You'll be travelling together. Bravo.

Genia Spare the celebration . . . I said I might.

Mauer But you'll go. It would really be too silly for Korsakow to have died entirely in vain. Yes, I'm convinced that Korsakow was destined by providence to . . . fall as a sacrifice.

Genia (*increasingly bewildered*) As a sacrifice?

Mauer For you – and your happiness.

Genia You believe in that sort of thing?

Mauer Generally speaking I don't, but in this case I feel something of the mysterious connection between things. Hasn't the same thought occurred to you?

Genia Me? I confess I forget to think about that sad business. I feel a slight pang – nothing more. Is there no way I can be better or less insensitive than I am? Perhaps I'll feel differently later. Perhaps when autumn comes. Perhaps the days are too bright and summery for sorrow – or indeed for taking anything too seriously. For instance, I can't even be angry with Adele Natter. It just seems pointless to bear her a grudge.

Mauer Well, now at last things will change between you. One can't stay angry with old Friedrich for long. I'm just the same where he's concerned. I may get absolutely furious with him – but as soon as he turns on the charm, I'm at his mercy again.

Kathi enters from the house.

Genia Well, I'm not! I need to be wooed – long and patiently.

Otto, Friedrich, Adele, Stanzides and Mrs Wahl come from the court.

(*Having received a word from Kathi*) If you're ready, ladies and gentlemen . . . Tea! Ice-cream is available too. No one need feel obliged . . .

Mrs Wahl and Stanzides, Genia and Otto, and Mauer go into the house. Friedrich and Adele remain behind.

Friedrich (*as Adele is about to go into the house*) I'm afraid, Mrs Natter, I haven't yet had the opportunity to inquire after your health. How are you then, Addy?

Adele I'm extremely well, Mr Hofreiter. And may I suggest that you address me with a little less familiarity? What's over is over. I like straightforward relationships.

Friedrich Really? – I had the impression you like ambiguous ones.

Adele Don't. We should be glad that it ended without mishap. We're both of us too old for youthful follies. My children are growing up. And your boy, too.

Friedrich What difference does that make?

Adele And if you would allow me to give you some advice, I think the way you're flirting with Mrs Wahl's little girl is frankly disgraceful. And for heaven's sake don't think this is jealousy. I'm not thinking of you at all . . . more of your wife . . .

Friedrich (*amused*) Ah!

Adele . . . who really is the sweetest, most touching creature I've ever met. When she asked me to bring the children round – did you hear her? – I wanted the earth to swallow me up!

Friedrich I assure you it didn't show.

Adele Truly, you don't deserve her.

Friedrich I can't say you're wrong about that. But I can't imagine what you're suggesting. Erna! A girl I have dandled on my knee.

Adele What difference does that make? There are girls of all ages of whom that can be said.

Friedrich Very true, Adele. It's not a bad idea . . . oh, Addy, it would be wonderful to be young again!

Adele You've been young quite long enough.

Friedrich Yes, but I was young too soon . . . these things are so badly arranged. One ought to be young at forty, then you'd get something out of it. Shall I tell you something, Adele? It really does seem to me that everything that has happened up to now has only been a preparation. And that now life and love are just beginning.

Adele There is more to life than – women to make love to.

Friedrich Oh, yes – there are the spaces between them. Not uninteresting. If one has the time and if one is in the mood, one builds factories, conquers nations, writes symphonies, becomes a millionaire . . . but, believe me, all that is merely to fill in the time. Life is for you! for you, for you! . . .

Adele (*shaking her head*) And to think that there are people who take you seriously!

> *Mr Natter arrives. A tall, rather robust man, in a very elegant summer suit: mutton-chop whiskers, and monocle.*

Natter Good evening, Adele! How are you, Hofreiter, old man?

Friedrich (*extending his hand*) Natter! Why are you so late?

Adele (*very affectionately*) So, what have you been up to?

Natter Forgive me, my love. I've been sitting in the park reading – it's the only chance I get. Tell me, Hofreiter, is there anything nicer than sitting under a tree with a book?

Friedrich That depends . . . on the book . . .

> *Paul and Erna come from the court. Mauer comes out of the house.*

Paul Honestly, Miss Erna, true as I stand here! Your service – absolutely terrific!

Friedrich Yes – and what about her backhand return? She learned that from me, too.

Erna A dubious boast.

Friedrich See what I mean?

Erna (*to the others, especially Paul*) He was merciless! And at the first sign of slacking off one was treated like a miserable sinner . . .

Friedrich (*casually*) Yes – these things are all a matter of character, in my opinion . . . (*to Natter*) Will you have some tea with us? We were just about to . . .

Natter Love to . . . By the way, is Stanzides still here?

Friedrich Oh, bound to be.

Natter I want to ask him to come to the theatre with us. (*to Adele*) If that's all right with you. I've taken a box in the Arena.

Mauer and Erna have moved to one side.

Friedrich Does that trash amuse you?

Natter And why not?

Adele There's nothing on earth that doesn't amuse him. My husband is the best audience anyone could have.

Natter Yes, that's true. I find life entirely amusing.

Friedrich, Adele and Natter enter the house. Mauer and Erna are already in conversation.

Mauer Shall I come, then?

Erna Of course you must. I'll engage you as our guide, for the usual fee, naturally.

Mauer I never imagined that I could lay claim to anything more.

Erna Was that in earnest, Dr Mauer, or in jest?

Mauer Shall I come to Lake Vols, Fraulein Erna, yes or no?

Erna I can see no reason at all why you should alter your plans.

Mauer Is it really impossible for you to give me a straight answer, Erna?

Erna It's not easy, Doctor. You know I'm very fond of you. You ought to come anyway. It would be the best way for us to get to know one another better. But naturally, you mustn't feel any more committed than I do.

Mauer Neatly spoken.

Erna And there's more. Listen. Naturally you have a favourite lady friend or some such – all unmarried gentlemen have. Well, don't be hasty. I mean, don't go away after our conversation thinking that you owe me your faithfulness.

Mauer Alas, your kind concern comes too late. Of course, I can't deny that, like all men, as you say . . . but not any longer . . . in my case. A squalid affair has no appeal to me. I would disgust myself.

Erna What a gentleman you are, Dr Mauer! I feel that if one put one's fate in your hands . . . one would have reached harbour.

Mauer Don't think me a fool, Miss Erna, if I venture that at my side you may find, if not perhaps the best that life can offer, at least much that is worthwhile.

Erna To be frank, Dr Mauer, I sometimes feel that I need something more from life than security and peace.

Mauer There is more to life than adventure . . . Well, shall I say, adventures of a certain kind.

Erna Have I suggested . . .?

Mauer You haven't said so, Miss Erna, but that's what you are thinking. And who's to wonder – in the very air we breathe! But I tell you, I could show you another world – where the air is purer.

Erna You're not a fool, Doctor. I like your frankness. I like you very much. Come to Lake Vols. We'll see.

Adele, Natter and Stanzides come out of the house, followed at intervals by Genia, Otto, Paul, Friedrich and Mrs Wahl.

Stanzides Sometimes in the old days I didn't watch the show from the auditorium at all, but from way above – a bird's eye view from the hill behind the Arena.

Adele That must be fun.

Stanzides I don't know about fun. It's certainly strange. You can only see a little bit of the stage-setting, of course. A corner of a crag, or a statue, or something. And of course you see nothing at all of the actors, you just hear the odd word every now and then . . . but the strangest thing is when without warning, among all those voices, one floats up to you and you recognize it – for example if you happen to be a friend of one of the actresses. And then all of a sudden you can understand the words too. Nothing of what the others are saying – only the familiar voice of the actress with whom you have been friends.

Adele (*laughing*) Or the friendly voice of the actress with whom you have been familiar!

Friedrich To speak of being familiar with a loved one is a contradiction in terms . . . Lovers should be referred to as constant unfamiliars . . .

Adele Or members of the fair sex, if you're being discreet.

Friedrich Or unfair sex.

Erna If you're not.

Mrs Wahl Erna!

Natter It's getting late. We must be going if we want to see anything of the show. Please don't let us disturb you.

Natter, Adele and Stanzides leave.

Paul (*to Otto*) Once – last year – Dr Herz and I took a set to 28 games to 26. After the first four hours we had an omelette . . .

Otto What sort of omelette? (*He continues listening to Paul.*)

Mauer Time for me as well . . . (*to Genia*) Dear lady . . .

Friedrich Look, why be in such a hurry? Give me a quarter of an hour and I'll drive in with you.

Mauer What – are you serious then?

Friedrich Of course . . . you'll wait then?

Genia You mean you're going into town with Dr Mauer? Now?

Friedrich Yes, that's the most sensible thing. I've got all the things I need for the mountains at the flat. Josef can pack them for me in an hour, then I'll be able to set off with Mauer first thing in the morning.

Mauer All right.

Genia But . . .

Friedrich So you'll wait? – Fifteen minutes.

Mauer Yes, I'll wait.

Friedrich goes quickly into the house. Erna, Paul, Otto and Mrs Wahl are standing together. Genia's gaze follows Friedrich.

Paul Come on, then, let's not waste the last of the light . . .

Mauer (*to Genia*) He's a man of quick decisions.

Genia doesn't reply. Erna, Otto, Paul and Mrs Wahl move off towards the tennis court. Mauer follows after a brief pause. Genia still stands motionless, then moves suddenly to go into the house, but meets Mrs von Aigner coming out. Mrs von Aigner is about forty-four, and looks it, her features being somewhat worn, though her figure is still youthful.

Mrs von Aigner Good evening.

Genia Oh, Mrs von Aigner, so late? I was afraid you weren't going to come at all today. Now I'm doubly happy that you're here. Come, won't you sit down, dear Mrs von Aigner? Perhaps over there – it's your favourite spot.

Mrs von Aigner (*noticing Genia's distracted air*) Thank you, thank you.

Genia Or shall we go to the tennis court? They're playing heart and soul over there, and you enjoy watching Otto, don't you?

Mrs von Aigner (*smiling*) But it's not Otto I've come to see, I've come to see you, dear Mrs Hofreiter. Only aren't I disturbing you? You seem to me a little . . . perhaps you'd rather go into the house?

Genia Not at all. It's just that . . . my husband is going to town with Dr Mauer. Actually, he's going away with him tomorrow. They're going on a walking holiday together. Just imagine, an hour ago he didn't know himself. And now he's just off. (*She looks up at the balcony.*)

Mrs von Aigner Then I've certainly come at a bad time for you.

Genia Oh no, it's not for long. We're not sentimental about being parted, believe me.

Mrs von Aigner Yes, I see. But what about Joey – won't he be back soon?

Genia Oh, Friedrich is bound to be back by then. Joey isn't coming for a fortnight.

Mrs von Aigner You must miss him very much.

Genia As you can imagine, Mrs von Aigner. You know what it means to see so little of your son.

Mrs von Aigner I do indeed.

Genia Your son will be leaving you now for . . . years?

Mrs von Aigner Yes.

Genia In the South Sea Islands, he was telling me.
I wonder whether you are not more fortunate than
I am, Mrs von Aigner. You have your career, and you
are such a celebrity. It must be so fulfilling.

Mrs von Aigner Yes, one would think so.

Genia Isn't it? For a woman to be only a mother . . .
it isn't right, it seems to me sometimes. If that had been
your only role in life, just Otto's mother, you'd never
have allowed him to join the navy.

Mrs von Aigner And if I hadn't allowed it?

Genia Then he would have stayed at home with you.

Mrs von Aigner I have the impression, my dear, that
I'd be lucky to see more of him at home than when he's
on the high seas. What do you think?

Genia Oh . . .!

Mrs von Aigner In fact, Mrs Hofreiter, the sooner we
free ourselves of the illusion that we can ever possess our
children, the better. Particularly sons! They have us, but
we don't have them, even when they are under the same
roof. While they are small, they would sell us for a toy.
Later on . . . for even less.

Genia (*shaking her head*) That is just . . . no, that . . .
Can I tell you something, Mrs von Aigner?

Mrs von Aigner (*smiling*) Why not? It's just idle chatter.

Genia Actually, I'm just asking myself, when you made
that very – forgive me – melodramatic remark about

people in general – whether that doesn't have something to do with the roles you have to play, so that life and melodrama sometimes seem a little difficult to separate.

Mrs von Aigner (*smiling*) Melodrama – do you think so?

Genia Because I have obviously got a lighter view of life than you have, Mrs von Aigner. Your son seems to me to be especially tender in his – I'm sure he thinks the world of you. And if he ever were to 'sell' you, as you say, it certainly wouldn't be over anything unworthy.

Mrs von Aigner (*after a short pause*) He's a man. One has to look to the future . . . even sons, they all turn into men, don't they?

Friedrich appears on the balcony.

I would have thought you had some idea of what I mean.

Friedrich A familiar voice floats up to me and – yes, I thought as much . . . How are you, Mrs von Aigner?

Mrs von Aigner Good evening, Mr Hofreiter.

Genia Do you need anything, Friedrich?

Friedrich Oh, no thank you. I've almost finished. I'll be right down. I'm going away, you see.

Mrs von Aigner Yes, Mrs Hofreiter was telling me.

Friedrich See you in a minute then.

He leaves the balcony. Pause.

Genia Mrs von Aigner, everything you say seems so right, so unanswerable, but aren't you being just a little unfair?

Mrs von Aigner Perhaps so, Mrs Hofreiter . . . But after all, being unfair is our revenge.

Genia looks at her in surprise.

Our only way of getting even for the wrongs done to us.
Oh, I know what you're thinking – what does she want,
this old actress? – Her marriage broke up aeons ago, and
ever since, so they say, she's lived her life simply to please
herself . . . She doesn't seem to have shed any tears for
her husband . . . so what does she want? Isn't that what
you think, Mrs Hofreiter?

Genia (*somewhat embarrassed*) No one would deny that
you had the right to live as you pleased . . .

Mrs von Aigner Quite so. And I'm not trying to say I feel
anything like pain any more about those events which
took place so long ago . . . or resentment either! But –
I don't forget . . . that's all. Think of all the other things
which I've forgotten since then! Happy things and sad
things . . . all forgotten – as if they had never been! But
not that. That remains as sharp and as complete as it
was on that first day – not to be denied – that's what
I'm trying to say, Mrs Hofreiter . . .

Otto comes from the tennis court.

Good evening, Otto . . .

Otto Mother! Good evening.

Mrs von Aigner My darling! (*to Genia*) Permit me . . .
I've come to see you play.

Mrs von Aigner and Otto go to the tennis court.
Genia moves quickly to the house, but meets Friedrich
in the doorway. He is dressed in a grey travelling suit.

Genia Why – why – are you going away? (*Pause.*)
You're not answerable to me, indeed you're not. But
I really can't see why you should want to avoid the
question.

Friedrich I need a change of air, a change of surroundings. In any event, I must get away from here.

Genia From here? . . . From me!

Friedrich Very well, from you!

Genia But why? What have I done to you?

Friedrich Nothing . . . who said you'd done anything to me?

Genia You must explain, Friedrich . . . I'm completely . . . I was prepared for anything except that . . . you should . . . so suddenly . . . from one minute to the next – I mean . . . I've been expecting us . . . to discuss things . . .

Friedrich I think it's not yet time to . . . talk . . . I've still got to get myself clear about all kinds of things.

Genia Clear –? What can be unclear? Listen . . . you had his letter in your hand! You've read it, haven't you? If you had doubted me before . . . which I simply don't believe . . . since that evening, for God's sake, Friedrich, since that evening you had his letter in your hand, you must have had some idea – Friedrich, some idea what you mean – what I feel – God – do I really have to tell you?

Friedrich No, of course not . . . That's just it. That evening. Yes. Ever since then I've felt – forgive me, of course you didn't mean to – but I felt that you were somehow playing off Korsakow's suicide against me . . . without knowing it, of course . . . And that – that makes me just . . . a little upset . . .

Genia Friedrich! Have you gone . . . ?

Friedrich Without knowing it. I know you didn't see it like that – Absolutely. I'm not saying you took any pride

in the fact that for your sake he . . . that you, so to
speak, drove him to kill himself . . . by rejecting him
when he – yes, I know all that . . .

Genia Well, if you know it –

Friedrich Yes, but the fact that it did happen at all –
just think about it . . . just think that poor Korsakow is
now rotting underground and you were the cause of it!
The innocent cause, and innocent in both senses, as I
said. Another man might go on his knees before you for
that very innocence, worship you . . . but I am not like
that . . . no, it has distanced me from you.

Genia Friedrich!! . . .

Friedrich I would have understood it if you had been
repelled by him. But you were not. On the contrary he
attracted you . . . One might even say you were a little
in love with him. Or if I had deserved your fidelity, if
you had felt honour-bound to be faithful, as they call it,
to a faithful husband – but I did not have that right . . .
So the question I keep asking myself over and over again
is: what did he die for?

Genia Friedrich!

Friedrich And, you see, the thought that your virtue . . .
that something so abstract – at least compared to the
terrible and irreversible fact of death – that your
virtuousness drove a marvellous man to his grave, that
to me is ghastly. Yes . . . I can't put it any other way . . .
it'll pass, of course, this feeling . . . in time . . . in the
mountains . . . and if we are apart for a few weeks . . .
but at the moment, it is there – and I can't do anything
about it . . . Yes, Genia, there you have me – Other men
would feel differently, perhaps . . .

Genia is silent.

I hope you won't take it badly that I – since you asked me – have brought it into the open. So much so, indeed, it hardly seems true again . . .

Genia It's true all right, Friedrich . . .

The others are approaching, from the court.

Paul Don't even ask me how I got on – tomorrow it's back to coaching for me.

Mauer I'm sorry, Friedrich, but it's high time . . . Perhaps you could come on a later train . . .

Friedrich I'm all ready . . . (*calling up*) Come on, Kathi – be quick! My overcoat and my small tan bag, on the divan in my dressing room.

Mrs Wahl Safe journey then, and all being well we'll see each other again.

Erna At Lake Vols.

Mrs Wahl I'll tell you what would be fun, Mrs Hofreiter – if you came too.

Erna Oh yes, Frau Genia.

Genia That's not possible, unfortunately – what with Joey coming . . .

Friedrich He's not coming all that soon. (*to Mauer*) When will we get to Lake Vols?

Mauer In eight or ten days, I should think.

Friedrich Yes, Genia, that's an idea. Do think it over –

Genia All right, I'll . . . think it over.

Kathi comes out with the overcoat and the small bag.

Mauer Goodbye then, Mrs Hofreiter. (*He takes his leave of the others.*)

Friedrich Farewell, dear friends. What are you all going to do with yourselves today?

Paul This might be an idea – a moonlight trip to Holy Cross!

Erna I'm game.

Mrs Wahl On foot?

Friedrich That's not necessary. I'll send you the car back from the station.

Paul Three cheers for our noble benefactor!

Friedrich No demonstrations, I beg you. Adieu then. Enjoy yourselves, everybody. Goodbye, Genia. Come along, Mauer, we haven't got all day.

Friedrich takes Genia's hand, which she then lets fall limply. Friedrich and Mauer leave through the house. Genia stands still. Paul, Erna and Mrs Wahl are standing together. Otto and Mrs von Aigner catch each other's eye.

Otto (*taking leave of Genia*) Ma'am, we must also . . .

Genia (*quickly, pulling herself together*) You're going? And you, Mrs von Aigner? There's plenty of room in the car for everyone.

Erna Of course. Mr Kreindl can sit in front with the driver.

Paul Only too delighted.

Otto I feel I ought to point out that this moonlight drive will have to transcend the absence of a moon.

Erna We'll manage with the stars, Lieutenant.

Mrs Von Aigner (*looking at the sky*) I'm afraid you'll have to do without those, too.

Erna Then we'll take a leap into the dark.

Genia Yes, Erna, that might be the most exciting thing of all.

Genia starts to laugh. They all move off.

Act Three

*The lobby of the Lake Vols Hotel. The entrance is a
glass revolving door. There is a lift, stairs, a view of
mountains, forests, etc. A curtain hangs over the
entrance to the corridor leading to the dining room.
By the entrance is the reception desk, behind which are
the pigeon-holes for letters and keys, etc. Hotel lobby
furniture.*

*There is a certain amount of movement in the lobby,
which, without interrupting the action, continues
through the act at appropriate moments. Hikers and
summer visitors come in from outside, guests go up in
the lift, others use the stairs, occasionally a waiter.
People read the papers or chat. A bellboy by the lift.
Behind the reception desk stands the porter, Rosenstock,
a ruddy, quite young man with a small black moustache,
black hair, sly, good-natured eyes, friendly and shrewd.
He hands newspapers to a bellboy who runs up the stairs
with them and disappears. Two men in alpine clothes
come in from outside and go straight into the dining
room. Rosenstock makes notes in a book. Two young
hikers enter from outside, with rucksacks, climbing
jackets, sticks, etc.*

First Hiker (*full of beans*) Morning, all! – No, I'm a
liar – good evening.

Rosenstock Your humble servant.

Second Hiker Tell me, do you have two rooms with one
bed?

First Hiker Or one room with two beds?

Rosenstock What is the gentleman's name?

Second Hiker So, one has to introduce oneself here.

First Hiker Bogenheimer, student at law, from Halle. Born at Merseburg, of Protestant stock, and this . . .

Second Hiker Archduke Ferdinand, travelling incognito.

Rosenstock (*smiling slightly*) I only wished to inquire whether the gentlemen had booked rooms.

Second Hiker Nay, lad, that we 'aven't.

Rosenstock (*very politely*) Then I'm very sorry, but unfortunately we have nothing at all available.

First Hiker Not even a straw mattress to cling to?

Rosenstock Not even a palliasse.

First Hiker We've been on the hoof for fourteen hours.

Rosenstock That's a long time.

Second Hiker I'm not moving.

First Hiker Did you hear that, Cerberus? My friend isn't moving.

Rosenstock *Bitte*. In our hall there's room for all.

First Hiker Ah, you're a poet, then?

Rosenstock Only in a crisis.

First Hiker What are we going to do then?

Rosenstock If the gentlemen would perhaps like to try the Alpenrose . . .

First Hiker Is that a hotel too?

Rosenstock In a manner of speaking.

First Hiker Do you think they'll have something there?

Rosenstock They always have something there.

First Hiker Very well. We'll take a sniff at the old Alpenrose. Up you get, old son.

Second Hiker I'm not moving. If you get a room send a sedan chair.

First Hiker Kindly see that my friend is not disturbed. (*as he goes, singing the Schubert song . . .*) 'Das Wandern ist der Müllers Lust . . .'

> *Second Hiker makes himself comfortable and soon falls asleep. As First Hiker exits . . . Paul Kreindl arrives, in an elegant travelling suit, large top coat, green alpine hat with a chamois tuft, tan gloves, tennis racket and bag in his hand. A bellboy follows him with his luggage.*

Paul Good day.

Rosenstock Your servant, Mr von Kreindl.

Paul Ah, who's this! You, my dear old Rosenstock! Are you here now? How will the Alpenrose get on without you?

Rosenstock I'm going up in the world, Mr von Kreindl. From a thousand metres to fourteen hundred . . .

Paul You received my telegram?

Rosenstock Of course. Yes . . . You'll find numerous acquaintances here, Mr von Kreindl, sir. Mr von Hofreiter is here . . .

Paul Know him . . .

Rosenstock Mrs von Wahl with her son and daughter . . .

Paul Know them . . .

Rosenstock Dr Mauer . . .

Paul Know him . . .

Rosenstock Then there's Rhon the poet, who's here resting on his laurels.

Paul Ah, him too.

Rosenstock We had to put you on the fourth floor, I'm afraid.

Paul The sixth will do me. (*to the bellboy*) Take that stuff up. (*retrieving his tennis racket*) Ah no, I'll hang on to that.

Rosenstock Mr Hofreiter has been on a climb since yesterday.

Paul One of the big ones?

Rosenstock Oh no. They were only going as far as the Hofbrand Hut. There were ladies with them. Mrs Rhon and Miss von Wahl.

Paul My dear Rosenstock, don't tell anyone I'm here. I'm going to give them a surprise!

Mrs Wahl comes down the stairs in a summer dress which is a little too young for her.

Mrs Wahl (*casually*) Oh, hello Paul. (*to Rosenstock*) Are they still not back?

Rosenstock Not yet, madam.

Paul (*disappointed*) How do you do, ma'am.

Mrs Wahl (*to Paul*) I'm distraught. Erna has been out climbing since yesterday. She should have been back for lunch, now it's five o'clock. I've just been to her room – she's living as close as you can get to heaven already . . . her all over! – and she isn't back yet. I'm beside myself.

Paul It's quite a large party, I gather.

Mrs Wahl Gustl's there, of course, and Friedrich Hofreiter, and Dr Mauer and Mrs Rhon.

Paul Well, then, nothing can have happened. By the way, please, ma'am, don't tell anyone I'm here, if they happen to return while I'm changing.

Mrs Wahl Why?

Paul I'd like to surprise them, you see. (*regretfully*) In your case, I'm afraid I didn't succeed.

Mrs Wahl You really have to forgive me that today, dear Paul, with all this worry.

Paul Well, perhaps some other time. Goodbye for now, ma'am, and don't say anything. (*He goes up in the lift.*)

Rosenstock (*to Mrs Wahl*) Madam really need not be concerned. After all, the party took a guide with them.

Mrs Wahl A guide just to go to the Hofbrand Hut? I say, I don't like the sound of that.

Rosenstock Only to carry the haversacks. And besides, your daughter is an excellent climber . . .

Mrs Wahl So was Dr Bernhaupt. And look what happened to him.

Rosenstock Yes . . . In the midst of life we are in death . . .

Mrs Wahl Look – would you please mind! . . .

Rosenstock Oh, sorry . . . I need hardly say that that does not apply to your daughter.

Mrs Wahl Rosenstock, I left a book with you, can I have it, by Rhon . . . with a yellow cover . . . Yes, that's the one . . . I'll sit here and read for a bit, if I can.

Rosenstock Ah, that's a book which will take your mind off anything, madam. He's a clever writer, Mr Rhon.

Mrs Wahl sits down at one of the tables. Serknitz comes down the stairs, wearing woollen clothes and a hiking shirt.

Serknitz (*to Rosenstock*) Letters here yet?

Rosenstock Not yet, Mr von Serknitz. In about half an hour.

Serknitz What a shambles!! The postman left ages ago.

Rosenstock But it has to be sorted, Mr von Serknitz.

Serknitz Sorted!! You sit me down there, and I'll sort the whole lot for you in a quarter of an hour. Typical Austrian slovenliness. And then you complain about the poor tourist trade.

Rosenstock We're not complaining, Mr von Serknitz. We're overflowing.

Serknitz The Austrians don't deserve the place.

Rosenstock But we've got it, Mr von Serknitz.

Serknitz You may dispense with the von, Porter. I'm not impressed by that ploy. In fact it's not the post I've come about – I've come about the laundry.

Rosenstock Please, Mr Serknitz, I have nothing to do with . . .

Serknitz Nor anybody else. The maid upstairs tells me to go to the desk. I've been waiting for my laundry for three days.

Rosenstock I'm really very sorry. However, here comes the manager.

Serknitz Not alone – as usual.

*Dr von Aigner has just arrived from outside with
a very beautiful Spanish girl. He takes leave of her
and she goes up in the lift. Dr von Aigner is a man
of over fifty, still very good looking. Elegant alpine
knickerbocker suit; black hair flecked with grey,
twisted moustache, monocle; amiable but a little
affected.*

Ah, Manager . . .

Dr von Aigner (*barely polite*) Be with you in a moment
. . . (*to Rosenstock*) My dear Rosenstock, His Excellency
Wondra is arriving tomorrow instead of Thursday, and
requires, as you know, four rooms.

Rosenstock Four rooms, sir, for tomorrow . . . How am I
supposed to do that? That means people will have to . . .
pardon me, sir, but that means I'll have to kill people.

Dr von Aigner Fine, Rosenstock, just be discreet about
it. (*to Serknitz, introducing himself*) Dr von Aigner . . .
How can I be of service to you?

Serknitz (*with some embarrassment, which he seeks
to conceal by his assured manner*) Serknitz . . . I was
just . . . I must express my irritation, or at least my
dismay . . . To put it bluntly, the way this hotel is run
is a disgrace.

Dr von Aigner I'm dumbstruck. What is your complaint,
Mr Serknitz?

Serknitz I can't get my laundry back, you see. I've been
asking for it for three days. It puts me in an awful spot.

Dr von Aigner Yes, I see. But why don't you ask the
chambermaid . . .

Serknitz You're the manager! My principle is always
to go to the top. Really, I get very little pleasure in

appearing in this get-up among your countesses and dollar princesses.

Dr von Aigner Forgive me, Mr Serknitz, but we have no rules here about how one must dress.

Serknitz No rules!! . . . Do you really think it isn't noticeable how different people are treated here?

Dr von Aigner My dear sir –!

Serknitz I will tell you to your face, my dear sir! – if the King of England, or His Excellency Wondra stood here instead of plain Carl-Maria von Serknitz you would adopt a very different tone. Yes indeed. You would be well advised to put a notice over the entrance: 'Some hope, all ye who enter here, unless you're a baron, a bank director, or an American.'

Dr von Aigner That would not correspond to the true state of affairs, Mr Serknitz.

Serknitz Just because I didn't arrive here by limousine I haven't the right to the same consideration as any trust magnate or minister of state? – is that your attitude? The man hasn't been born who can get away with treating me in that high-handed fashion . . . Whether he wears a monocle or not.

Dr von Aigner (*as calm as ever*) If anything about my manner is a personal affront to you, Mr Serknitz, I am of course at your disposal.

Serknitz Ha ha! So now it's swords or pistols, is it! That's a good one. You must take out a patent on that – one complains that some shirts haven't been delivered, and they shoot you dead to boot. Listen, Herr Direktor, if you think that sort of thing is going to be particularly good for business, you are labouring under a massive delusion. I would leave this joke hotel, this Eldorado of snobs, swindlers and stockbroker Jews, on the spot, by special express, but for the fact that I don't intend to make you a present of my laundry. For the moment, I will go and see if it has been returned. In the meantime, your humble servant, sir. (*He leaves up the stairs.*)

Dr von Aigner Good day, Mr Serknitz. (*to Mrs Wahl, to whom he has already nodded during the conversation*) Good afternoon, madam.

Mrs Wahl I wish I had your self-control.

Dr von Aigner Why? What's the matter?

Mrs Wahl I'm in a terrible state. Our party isn't back yet.

Dr von Aigner Oh, but I beg you, madam . . . No one has ever failed to come back from the Hofbrand Hut. It's only a stroll . . . (*sitting down next to her*) May I?

Mrs Wahl *May* you? One must be grateful if for once you aren't frantically – or romantically – busy.

Dr von Aigner Frantically . . . romantically . . .? That doesn't sound like you – a nice lady like you couldn't be that wicked.

Mrs Wahl No . . . it's Rhon.

Dr von Aigner Yes, I thought so . . . he's a poet, Mr Rhon, yes. What a lovely brooch you have there.

Mrs Wahl Yes, it's quite pretty, isn't it?

Dr von Aigner Peasant baroque.

Mrs Wahl And not at all dear.

Dr von Aigner Quite delightful.

Mrs Wahl Not that it was exactly cheap. Swaten in Salzburg always puts these things by for me. He really knows my taste.

Albertus Rhon comes downstairs.

Rhon Good day, madam. Good evening, Herr Direktor. Well, aren't our mountaineers back yet?

Mrs Wahl They are not!

Rhon They'll be here soon . . . Perhaps they've break-fasted too well . . . My wife, anyway.

A very pretty Italian girl comes up to Dr von Aigner, speaks with an Italian accent.

Girl Signor . . . Herr Direktor . . . one can speak with you?

Dr von Aigner *Prego* . . . Signorina . . . (*He goes upstage with her.*)

Rhon (*to Mrs Wahl*) His latest conquest.

Mrs Wahl What, her? You pointed out a different one yesterday.

Rhon It was a different one yesterday. Oh yes, what a man! You have no idea of the swathe he has cut through the district. Haven't you been struck, for instance, by the similarity between Aigner and the head waiter?

Mrs Wahl You think the head waiter is his son?

Rhon His nephew anyway. Yes, the way he gets about, even his nephews look like him.

Mrs Wahl How can you be in any sort of mood to make jokes! They should have been back for lunch. It's half-past five now. I blame myself for not going with them.

Rhon You're quite wrong to do so. It would only have made rescue more difficult, and added to the casualty list.

Mrs Wahl I find your jokes in horribly bad taste.

Rhon Well, I'm writing a tragedy.

Dr von Aigner has come forward again.

Still, they ought to be back by now. My wife at least. I'm accustomed to being received by her when I re-enter the real world *entre actes*. We like to spend the interval together.

Dr von Aigner Usually at the buffet.

Rhon (*clapping him on the shoulder good-humouredly*) True, true. Tell me, anyway, is it really such a straightforward business, this Hofbrand Hut.

Dr von Aigner As I told you, a stroll. Even I could manage the Hofbrand Hut.

Mrs Wahl Why didn't you go with them, Dr von Aigner? I wouldn't have worried then.

Dr von Aigner Yes . . . unfortunately I have my hands full here, as you were remarking, dear lady. Furthermore, since the Hofbrand Hut is about as far as I can go I'd rather not go at all.

Rhon Very good. But another thought has just occurred to me, Herr Direktor – doesn't the climb to your peak start from the Hut? To the Aignerturm, I mean?

Dr von Aigner Yes, it was mine once! No longer. But no one else's either.

Rhon It must be an extraordinary feeling, to sit at the foot of a peak one was the first to go up and find oneself no longer able even to . . . yes, one might venture a simile here . . .

Mrs Wahl gives a little scream.

No, I see what you mean.

Mrs Wahl So what it comes down to, they're all up the Aignerturm.

Rhon (*also somewhat alarmed*) Why do you think that?

Mrs Wahl Of course they are. Otherwise they'd be back by now. They've got a guide with them, too. Dr von Aigner, you're all in it together –

Dr von Aigner I promise you . . .

Rhon Isn't that a guide?

Mrs Wahl Where?

The guide Penn is standing by the Porter. Rhon and Mrs Wahl rush over to him.

Penn! Were you with the Hofreiter party?

Penn Aye.

The next five lines overlap.

Mrs Wahl Where's my daughter?

Rhon Where's my wife?

Mrs Wahl Say something.

Rhon When did they get back?

Mrs Wahl Where are the others? Why are you alone? What's happened?

Penn (*smiling*) They're all back here with me, Mrs. The young lady managed splendidly.

Mrs Wahl What do you mean?

Rhon Where were you, then?

Penn We've been up the Aignerturm.

Mrs Wahl (*with a quiet shriek*) Oh my God!

Rhon My wife up the Aignerturm? It's not possible.

Penn No, the little fat one didn't go up. Just Miss Erna, Hofreiter and Dr Mauer.

Rhon And what about my wife?

Mrs Wahl And my son?

Penn They waited for us in the hut, till we got back.

Mrs Wahl So where are they, then?

Penn The ladies and gentlemen came in by the tap room, so's not to cause a flap.

Mrs Wahl I must go upstairs, I must see Erna. (*to Dr von Aigner*) Oh, you . . . (*She goes to the lift; because the lift is upstairs she rings in despair. To Aigner*) Why does your lift spend all its time at the fourth floor? That's another funny thing about this hotel. (*to Rhon*) Aren't you coming up?

Rhon I can wait.

The lift comes down with the bellboy. Rhon draws Mrs Wahl aside.

Psst! Just look at that lift boy.

Mrs Wahl Why?

Rhon Amazing similarity.

Mrs Wahl enters the lift. Gustl Wahl arrives, in an elegant summer suit, speaking with a kind of affected drawl, at times with a calculated air of significance. He's always good humoured.

Gustl Good evening, Mr Rhon. (*to Dr von Aigner*) How do you do, Mr Aignerturm.

Rhon Gustl!

Dr von Aigner (*to Penn*) So, you got to the top?

Penn Yes, Mr Aigner. It wasn't easy.

Dr von Aigner I can imagine.

Penn We had to duck sharpish a few times. And as for the last hundred feet, God knows . . .

Dr von Aigner But up top was good.

Penn Mr Aigner knows right enough. It's always good up top, especially on the Aignerturm.

Gustl (*to Rhon*) Must congratulate you on your wife. Plays an excellent game of dominoes.

Rhon You played dominoes the whole time? While the others were suspended between life and death? I'm not surprised about my wife. Women have no imagination. But you should know better.

Gustl We didn't play dominoes all the time. At first I tried to engage your wife in conversation.

Rhon About Buddhist philosophy, I presume.

Gustl Mainly.

Rhon My wife isn't interested in Buddha.

Gustl Yes, I got that impression too. That's why I suggested dominoes.

Dr von Aigner Since when have they had a domino set up there?

Gustl One can always find a domino set. On this occasion one found it in one's rucksack. I never take a step without a set of dominoes. I've spent years in the study of the game.

Mrs Rhon arrives, a small, pretty, rather plump woman. She throws her arms round her husband's neck.

Mrs Rhon Here I am again!

Rhon Come, come, that'll do. We're not alone . . .

Dr von Aigner Please don't mind us.

Rhon (*coolly*) Well, did you enjoy it?

Mrs Rhon It was glorious.

Rhon I hear you played dominoes.

Mrs Rhon Are you cross with me? I won.

Rhon Well, it's better than trying to climb the scenery anyway.

Mrs Rhon Do you know, I really was tempted for a moment. Only, they didn't want to take me.

Rhon Now listen, don't start getting ideas like that. I'm not going to have the pleasure of my solitude ruined by having to worry about you. When you're not with me, I don't want to have to think about you at all.

Gustl That's why she doesn't think about you either, Rhon old man. Take my word for it, you're going to get an awful shock one day. It was sheer luck that I wasn't your wife's type.

Rhon Tell me, Gustl, why are you so tactless?

Gustl I do it to impress. And anyway – what is tact! A third-rate virtue. Even the word is quite new. You won't find it in Latin, nor Greek, nor – most significantly – in Sanskrit.

Mrs Rhon (*to Rhon*) Well then, what have you been doing in the meanwhile? Did you get any further?

Rhon End of Act Three, the audience rushes deeply moved into the bar.

Mrs Rhon Then I've come back at the right moment.

Rhon Yes, only this time it's a short interval. First thing tomorrow I'm locking myself away again so that I don't have my mood disrupted by having to look at all those stupid face at lunch. And you'll be free to play dominoes.

Gustl Madam, get a divorce. How can anyone marry a poet? They're a subspecies. It was much better in the olden days, when one kept a poet like a slave or a barber – a tradition, incidentally, which survives in Isfahan – but to let a poet run around loose is plain silly.

Friedrich (*entering in an elegant hiking suit*) Good evening, ladies and gentlemen, how's the lovely poet's wife? What, you've changed already? You've been quick.

Dr von Aigner (*who is now standing near Rosenstock*) Hallo there, Hofreiter.

Friedrich Good evening, Aigner. (*to Rosenstock*) Nothing for me? Telegram? Letter? That's odd. (*to von Aigner*) Well, I can tell you that nothing has changed in the least up there, not on top anyway. Of course, the route has got more difficult. If it keeps on crumbling, it'll be certain suicide.

Dr von Aigner Yes, Penn told me.

Friedrich You know when you come to that gully, three hundred metres below the summit . . .

Dr von Aigner (*interrupting him*) I'd rather not hear about it. How did the little lady get on?

Friedrich Erna? Simply splendidly.

Dr von Aigner Taking her with you . . . I must say . . .

Friedrich She took *us*. I hadn't the slightest intention of climbing that mountain again. Where's Mauer, by the way?

Dr von Aigner I haven't seen him yet.

Rhon Tell me, Hofreiter, how did you actually feel when you passed that place . . .

Friedrich What place? . . . My God, seven years is a long time. I've forgotten most things that lie much closer in the past.

Rhon Well, yes . . . I suppose one often passes by a place where someone fell down, and fails to recognize it. Don't you think . . .?

Friedrich If only you knew how little I feel in the mood for philosophizing, Mr Rhon . . .

Paul (*coming rapidly down the stairs*) Your humble servant, Mr Hofreiter!

Friedrich (*rather offhand*) Ah – hello there, Paulie.

Paul Good evening, Mr Rhon. I've had the pleasure once before . . . Well, first of all, I've got loads of greetings for you. First from your good lady, then from Captain Stanzides, the Natters, from Mrs von Aigner, and from young Mr von Aigner . . .

Friedrich Allow me to introduce you . . . Mr Paul Kreindl – the manager, Dr von Aigner.

Paul Ah . . . most pleased . . . (*He stops, disconcerted; then, collecting himself, to Dr von Aigner:*) Actually I have the pleasure of knowing your son.

Dr von Aigner Unfortunately, I haven't.

Friedrich So what's new in Baden? (*quietly*) Do you know – if perhaps my wife is coming?

Paul Your wife, coming here? Sorry, she said nothing to me.

Friedrich Are they amusing themselves all right?

Paul Wonderfully! Just the other day we were all together at the Arena Theatre. No doubt your good lady has written you all about it.

Friedrich Yes, of course.

Paul And before that a travelling fair set up in the field by the house. We joined in with the people. We danced.

Friedrich My wife too?

Paul Yes, absolutely – with the Lieutenant . . . By the way, at the Arena we caused a great sensation when the actors suddenly spotted the famous Mrs von Aigner in our box. After that they more or less played to us, actually.

Rhon What was the play?

Paul I never noticed. Lot of Frenchmen in wigs. I think it rhymed. Yes . . . people in wigs rhyming . . . The girl had consumption. Wasn't that your dear wife? Excuse me, gentlemen. (*He exits.*)

Rhon One pours out one's life's blood for people like that.

He follows Paul. Friedrich remains with Dr von Aigner. Friedrich lights a cigarette and sits down.

Dr von Aigner I had no idea that my former family had the run of your house.

Friedrich Yes, one sees them from time to time. In particular, your wife – as was – has become great friends with mine. And I sometimes play tennis with Otto. He plays very well. In fact he does you credit altogether. Perhaps he's a future admiral of the fleet.

Dr von Aigner You're telling me about a young man who's a stranger to me.

Friedrich Tell me, Aigner, have you really no desire to see him again?

Dr von Aigner Again? The most you could say is, be introduced to him. That naval officer has nothing to do with the boy I saw twenty years ago when I kissed him for the last time. (*Pause.*) Actually, it is an extraordinary coincidence.

Friedrich What is?

Dr von Aigner That you should start talking to me about my son . . . just after you've come back from up there . . . Do you know when I took on that climb? It was just after I . . . separated from my wife.

Friedrich Do you mean there was a connection?

Dr von Aigner In a way . . . I'm not quite claiming that I was flirting with death – there are simpler deaths available – but at that time life didn't mean very much to me. And perhaps I wanted to provoke a kind of divine retribution.

Friedrich Listen, if every erring husband started climbing up the nearest cliff . . . the Dolomites would afford a very quaint spectacle. Anyway, you didn't do anything worse than a lot of others.

Dr von Aigner The measure is in the effect on the other person. My wife loved me very much.

Friedrich All the more reason for her not to be so unforgiving.

Dr von Aigner Possibly. But I loved her very much too. That's the trouble! I loved her inexpressibly . . . like no other woman, before or since . . . It was because I loved her so much – and was still capable of deceiving her – that's what made it irreparable. You see, my dear Hofreiter, that left her utterly confused, about me and about the whole world. After that there was absolutely nothing on earth she could count on . . . no possibility of trust, that's what drove her away from me. And I could understand that. I should even have been able to foresee it.

Friedrich Well, that being the case, I have to ask why . . .

Dr von Aigner Why I betrayed her? *You* ask *me*? Haven't you ever thought what a strange uncharted country is human behaviour? So many contradictions find room in us – love and deceit . . . loyalty and betrayal . . . worshipping one woman, yet longing for another, or several others. We try to bring order into our lives as best we can; but that very order has something unnatural about it. The natural condition is chaos. Yes, Hofreiter, the soul . . . is an undiscovered country as the poet once said . . . though it could equally well have been the manager of a hotel.

Friedrich The hotel manager wasn't so far wrong . . . yes. (*Pause.*) The pity of it is that your wife had to find out . . .

Dr von Aigner . . . I told her.

Friedrich What? – You told her? –

Dr von Aigner Yes. I had to. I worshipped her. I owed it to her and to myself. It would have been cowardice not to. One shouldn't try to have things so easy. Don't you agree . . .

Friedrich Shows great nobility – or affectation. Or tactics . . . or convenience . . .

Dr von Aigner Or all three, which would also have been possible. Because the soul . . . and so forth.

Mrs Wahl (*coming down from upstairs*) Ah, there he is!

Friedrich How are you, Mrs Wahl?

Mrs Wahl I'm never going to say another word to you, Friedrich. What if she'd fallen? Could you ever have faced me again? And I've finished with Dr Mauer, too. Where is he then? It's quite monstrous.

Friedrich But, Mama Wahl, Erna would have climbed up with or without us.

Mrs Wahl You should have tied her up.

Friedrich But she was, Mama Wahl. We were all tied up together, on the one rope.

Mrs Wahl It should have been a strait-jacket.

Erna (*entering in a white summer dress*) Good evening.

Dr von Aigner Greetings, Erna. How are you? (*He takes both of her hands and kisses her on the forehead.*) May I . . .?

Friedrich Like the aged Liszt and the young lady pianist.

Erna More like quite a young lady pianist with a not yet particularly aged Liszt.

Dr von Aigner Nevertheless, Erna . . .

Mrs Wahl Yes – I should think so!

Erna It was the most wonderful experience I've ever had.

Dr von Aigner Ah yes – at the summit! Even so, I hope that there are some even more wonderful experiences ahead of you, Fraulein Erna.

Erna That would scarcely be possible. Oh – life might well seem wonderful again, no doubt – but that death should seem so completely unimportant – that's the true wonder, and it could only happen at such a moment.

Meanwhile, the post has arrived. Rosenstock sorts letters, guests arrive, take their correspondence, etc. And Paul returns, followed by Rhon, Mrs Wahl, Gustl.

Paul Miss Erna, allow me to lay out my admiration at your feet!

Erna Hello there, Paul, how are you?

Paul Oh God – damn it – sorry . . . isn't *anyone* surprised to see me?

Friedrich (*sitting down*) Look, Paul, it's much more surprising that *we're* here.

Dr von Aigner is standing to one side with a beautiful French girl.

Rhon (*to Mrs Wahl*) Look at that, ma'am, that's tomorrow's. He's stocking up.

Erna (*to Mrs Wahl, who has collected her letters from Rosenstock*) Well, Mama?

Mrs Wahl From home. (*to Friedrich*) Ah, there's a card from your wife. She sends her best wishes to you, Friedrich.

Friedrich (*rising*) Really? Ah, there's one for me, too.

Mrs Rhon (*to Gustl, who has laid his correspondence on his forehead*) What are you doing?

Gustl I never read letters any more.

Mrs Wahl He simply presses them to his forehead and absorbs the contents. (*to Friedrich*) Well, is she coming after all?

Friedrich No.

Rhon (*sitting and reading his letters*) just listen to this. It's unbelievable. Queries from correspondents! At what age did you first experience the joys of physical love? Have you ever been aware of any perverted inclinations?

Friedrich And have you?

Rhon I should have been a businessman – they never get asked. Alas, I never had a head for business, so I became a poet.

Friedrich I often wonder if it's only because of their shortcomings that poets become poets.

Rhon What do you mean?

Friedrich I imagine that many poets are born criminals, only they lack the necessary courage; or libertines who shrink from the expense . . .

Rhon And do you know what manufacturers of incandescent light bulbs usually are, Mr Hofreiter? Incandescent-light-bulb manufacturers, that's all.

Friedrich If only that were true . . .

> *A bellboy brings Friedrich a letter. He opens it, smiles and bites his lip. Erna has noticed this.*

Mrs Wahl Well, you must excuse me, I still have to change . . . come, illustrious poet . . . (*to Mrs Rhon*) with your muse . . .

Mrs Rhon (*as Gustl opens one of his letters*) But you're reading it.

Gustl I have to verify my gift ... yes ... yes ... yes ... I am amazing.

> *Mrs Rhon and Gustl go upstage and leave. Dr von Aigner goes to Rosenstock, then leaves. Rhon goes likewise. The lobby is almost empty.*

Erna (*looking over Friedrich's shoulder*) Love letter?

Friedrich Guess who from? Mauer. He's just received an urgent telegram from Vienna. Had to leave immediately ... he's gone ... asks me to convey his respects ...

Erna I thought it would be something like that.

Friedrich So did I ... Yes, Erna, one really oughtn't to roll around on the grass fifty feet from a hut with twenty windows.

Erna You think he saw?

Friedrich Probably.

Erna And do you think it would have made any difference if he hadn't? We wouldn't even have had to look at each other for him to notice, just as the others noticed ...

Friedrich What is there for them to notice?

Erna Our feelings for each other.

Friedrich But, Erna, how can these people . . .?

Erna Perhaps we have a sort of lovers' glow around our heads, like a halo.

> *Friedrich laughs.*

Yes, it must be something like that – I've often thought so.

Friedrich It should have been me who left, Erna.

Erna Yes, that would have been much more sensible.

Friedrich You shouldn't be such a flirt.

Erna I really am not.

Friedrich Then what are you?

Erna I'm just the woman I am.

Friedrich There you have the advantage of me. I am not the man I was. I've gone mad since that kiss yesterday . . . Come closer, Erna. (*He takes her hand.*) Sit down here by me.

Erna Now don't get carried away.

Friedrich Erna, I didn't close my eyes last night.

Erna I'm sorry. I slept splendidly. I took my blanket out into the meadow – our meadow – and slept in the open . . . wrapped in your coat.

Friedrich Erna, Erna! I'm in a state to do something madly foolish. I suddenly understand all that nonsense I used to mock in other people . . . the faithful vigil under a lady's window . . . the serenading of one's mistress . . . (*with gestures*) I understand how one might duel with naked blades for love's favour, or throw oneself off a precipice for love unrequited.

Erna Unrequited?

Friedrich (*seriously*) Don't deceive yourself, Erna. Yesterday evening . . . the whole thing, the moment up there on the summit, pressing each other's hands, the sense of belonging together, the overpowering feeling of joy, it was all just a kind of tipsiness – drunk on altitude. I mean for you. It all comes from being three thousand metres up in the sky, with the thin air, and the danger. It was very little to do with me personally.

Erna Why do you say that? I've loved you since I was seven. Not counting interruptions, of course. But recently I've got it very badly again. Seriously. And then yesterday and today – and up there – and now! Oh God, Friedrich, all I want to do is to get hold of your hair and run my fingers through it.

Friedrich Careful – that really isn't necessary. Listen, Erna – I want to ask you something.

Erna Then ask me.

Friedrich All right – what would you think if . . . listen – pay attention! – I'm quite sensible again. I want to get a divorce from Genia . . . and marry you, Erna.

Erna laughs.

Why . . . are you laughing?

Erna Because you were only just saying that you were in a state to do something madly foolish.

Friedrich Perhaps it wouldn't be if we just took it for what it is. I know, Erna, you won't always love me.

Erna But you will always love me!!

Friedrich That is more probable. Anyway . . . as for eternity! What does it mean? Next year one climbs up another little peak, and that's the end of eternity! Or another beginning. All I know is this. I know with absolute certainty that I cannot exist without you. I'm faint with longing for you, I won't be able to think or work any more, or occupy myself with ordinary life until . . . until I hold you in my arms, Erna.

Erna Why didn't you come out and fetch your coat last night?

Friedrich I beg you, Erna, don't tease me. Look, just say no, and that's an end of it. They can still get Mauer back. I have no interest in making a public spectacle of myself.

A gong sounds. The Hiker who has gone to sleep at the beginning of the Act wakes up from a dream, gets up, screams, howls and crashes out across the full width of the stage. Mrs Wahl comes down the stairs. Other guests gather, moving to the dining room, Dr von Aigner among them.

Heavens, the way we've chatted on . . . now I haven't got time to change.

Mrs Wahl You're handsome enough as you are. Where's Dr Mauer, by the way?

Friedrich Oh yes, that's right – he sends his respects, he had a telegram and had to leave at once.

Mrs Wahl A telegram – Dr Mauer? That's odd . . . someone's keeping something from me. He's fallen! He's dead!

Friedrich Now look, Mama Wahl, do you believe we could all be sitting around chatting if . . .

Mrs Wahl With you one can never tell.

Friedrich At the very least we'd be chatting in black gloves.

Serknitz enters in white tie and tails. He goes to Dr von Aigner.

Serknitz I have the honour, sir, to present myself, Herr von Aigner. Serknitz. My laundry has arrived, and I immediately took the liberty of attiring myself in the costume appropriate to the pretensions of your hotel.

Dr von Aigner Mr von Serknitz . . . You look absolutely ravishing.

TOM STOPPARD

Serknitz goes into the dining room. Mrs Wahl, Dr von Aigner, Mrs Rhon, Gustl, Rhon and others likewise go into the dining room. Erna and Friedrich are left.

Friedrich Do you want to be my wife?

Erna Wife? – No.

Friedrich Right, fine.

Erna Perhaps later on.

Friedrich Later –?

Erna Go on reading your letters.

Friedrich What for? The whole factory can go up with an incandescent bang for all I care. Everything can go to hell. What does that mean – later! Life isn't long enough. I'm not giving you time to consider. A kiss like yesterday's is binding. It binds you to an immediate parting or to an unconditional surrender. I can't wait. I won't wait. Say no, and I leave today.

Erna I'm not teasing you. I know what our kiss bound me to.

Friedrich Erna, think about what you are saying. If your door is locked tonight, I'll smash it down and that'll be the end of us.

Erna It will not be the end of us.

Friedrich Erna!

Erna Haven't you always known that I belong to you?

Friedrich Erna . . . Erna . . .

Erna I love you!

They enter the dining room.

Act Four

*The same scene as in Act Two. A summer afternoon. In
the garden sit Mrs Natter's two children, a nine-year-old
girl and a seven-year-old boy, with their French nanny,
who is showing them pictures in a book. From the house
drift Genia, Natter, Mrs Wahl, Stanzides, Gustl, Paul,
Erna, Otto and Adele Natter.*

Genia Do you like the pictures?

Children Oh yes.

Genia You must ask your Mama to bring you back on
Sunday because Joey's bound to be here by then. Well,
what would you like to do now?

Gustl I'll show them a marvellous game that the good
little Hindu boys and girls play on the banks of the River
Ganges. Would you lend me your parasol, Mademoiselle?
Thank you very much. Watch carefully. So – I draw three
concentric circles on the ground

Natter Well, I must say the welcome-home dinner for
our distinguished host was first rate. What a pity he
couldn't be here.

Genia He must have been held up at the factory.

Natter Small wonder after three weeks away.

Gustl One has a diameter of a metre . . .

Mrs Wahl Did you telephone the office, Genia?

Genia I didn't think it was necessary.

153

Gustl The middle one three-quarters of a metre

Genia I was sure he'd be back by noon after yesterday's telegram from Innsbruck.

Gustl Please! – The inside one half a metre. The Hindu children hit it to a millimetre. Now watch carefully. You draw one tangent along the outer circle.

Erna Let's go and play tennis.

Paul With the greatest of pleasure.

Gustl A second tangent at right angles to that one, along the middle circle.

Paul Ma'am? Lieutenant?

Gustl A third parallel to the first tangent along the inner circle.

Adele I won't play straight after a meal.

Gustl Thus you get segments, like so.

Otto I'm sure you'll permit me to finish my coffee.

Gustl Now in the outermost segment to the east . . . (*He takes a small compass out of his pocket.*)

Mrs Wahl He always carries a compass.

Gustl Well, it's beyond me how anyone with a sense of propriety if not of direction could go around without one. So . . . East is there. In the outermost segment one places a baby tortoise . . . (*He takes a tortoise from his pocket, and places it on the ground.*) In the west segment a scorpion . . .

> He brings his closed fist from his pocket. The children begin to cry.

Adele You just stop that, Gustl! Ma'm'selle – s'*il vous plaît* – Oh lord! (*She abandons French.*) Please, Nanny, would you take the children to play in the meadow. (*to the children*) You'll be safe there from scorpions and tangents.

Nanny goes off with the children. Stanzides picks up a paper and starts reading.

Stanzides Listen to this! 'We have a report from the Lake Vols Hotel that a few days ago a young lady from Vienna, Miss Erna Wahl, accompanied by two Viennese climbers, the manufacturer Friedrich Hofreiter and the well-known physician Dr Mauer, climbed the Aignerturm, known as one of the most notoriously dangerous . . .'

Erna Come on, Paul.

Paul Yes – today we'll only play singles. A singles tournament; I hope Mr Hofreiter comes in time to take part. Today we must settle the positions once and for all . . .!

Mrs Wahl (*to Stanzides*) How does it go on?

Stanzides (*continues reading*) '. . . known as one of the most notoriously dangerous peaks in the south-western Dolomites. It was there that seven years ago Dr Bernhaupt . . .'

Mrs Wahl Yes, my dear Genia, those two dragged my Erna up mountains like that. I've never been so angry in my life as I was with Dr Mauer and your husband.

Gustl The two of them took one look at Mama and packed their bags.

Genia (*looking at Erna, smiling*) Yes, it seems that Friedrich's guilty conscience made him restless. I got a postcard from a different place every day – Caprile, Pordio and heaven knows where.

Paul and Erna leave for the tennis court. Mrs Wahl has got hold of the newspaper and is leafing through it.

Natter You must be very proud, Mrs Wahl, now that Erna is a celebrity.

Mrs Wahl Proud? – me? What is this paper, actually?

Genia I don't know. I haven't seen it before. Who brought it?

Mrs Wahl There's an item underlined in red ink.

Stanzides I wouldn't pay any attention to anything underlined in red in a paper like that.

Mrs Wahl But this is extraordinary.

Adele, Gustl and **Genia** What is?

Mrs Wahl (*reading*) 'During the past few days a curious rumour has gathered force – and an accumulation of detail – in Viennese society. We pass it on with due discretion. It concerns the suicide of a world-famous pianist, who, at the beginning of the summer, was much in the limelight and then came under the shadow of what was not very satisfactorily explained by the hallowed phrase 'a sudden brainstorm'. According to the above-mentioned rumour the cause of the suicide was "an American duel"; with a difference. This was not, as is usual, a case of a black ball, but two white and one red . . .'

Adele Two white and one red . . . what does that mean?

Stanzides Billiards. And a black ball is obviously a bullet.

Genia (*calmly, after a nervous pause*) But Friedrich lost that billiard game with Korsakow. So it couldn't have been an American duel . . . because in an American duel it's the loser who has to shoot himself; so it would have been Friedrich, wouldn't it?

Pause.

Mrs Wahl (*understanding at last*) Ah, that billiard game. Your husband sent the cigars round to Korsakow at the hotel the next morning . . . That's right! I'd swear to that in court!

Gustl Mama, you won't be needed to swear. No one bothers about this sort of thing.

Stanzides It is unbelievable that one is more or less helpless against this sort of outrage. Especially as no names are mentioned.

Natter They're too careful for that.

Stanzides and Adele move towards the tennis court, and unhurriedly depart.

Mrs Wahl All the same . . . How does something like that get into the papers? And why should Friedrich and Korsakow . . .

Gustl Mama!

Mrs Wahl What a good idea. Yes. Let's go and watch the tennis.

Mrs Wahl, Gustl and, just behind them, Natter also leave for the court. Otto and Genia remain behind.

Genia Do you believe it?

Otto This absurd nonsense about a duel? Of course not.

Genia But there could be something behind it . . . In a word, that I – was *Korsakow's* mistress, too.

Otto No. I don't believe it.

Genia Why not? Because I deny it? That's no reason. In your place . . . I'd believe it. (*She makes as if to go to the court.*)

Otto I don't believe it, Genia. I swear to you, Genia, I don't believe it. Why are we talking about it? Please don't go! Please! – who knows if we'll have another moment alone together. First thing tomorrow I've got to go to town, and I'm going to Polla by the night train.

Genia (*looking at him*) Is it tomorrow . . .?

Otto How will I be able to let you know what's happening to me?

Genia You can write. My letters aren't opened. And if you wanted to be especially careful, then simply write to me just as you are talking to me now – as to an old friend.

Otto I couldn't do that. Don't ask it of me.

Genia Then – don't write at all.

Otto Genia . . .

Genia Wouldn't that be the most sensible thing? After all, we won't be seeing each other again.

Otto Genia! I'll be back in three years.

Genia (*smiling*) In three years!

Otto And how am I to live . . . without you?

Genia You'll live. It was lovely. Let's call it a day. Pleasant journey, Otto, and good luck for the future.

Otto Will you remember me, Genia?

Genia Oh, yes. And I'll forget you too.

Otto Do you enjoy hurting me?

Genia Why do you think me better than I am? I'm not better than other people. Haven't you noticed? I lie, I'm a hypocrite. I act out this farce for everybody – for Mr

158

Natter and for Mrs Wahl . . . for your mother just as for my own housemaid. I act the part of a respectable married woman – and at night leave my window open for my lover. I write and tell my son he can stay longer with his friends, to my darling boy I write that . . . just so that he won't spoil my fun – and then I write to tell my husband that Joey absolute insists on staying on in England so that *he* doesn't hurry back either. And when he comes back today and shakes hands with you, I'll be standing by with a smile on my face and probably enjoying my cleverness. Do you find all that particularly attractive? Do you think – there's a person you can trust –? Believe me, Otto, I'm just like the others.

Friedrich appears on the balcony, speaking as he appears.

Friedrich Friends, Romans and countrymen! Hello there. I'm just changing.

Genia (*not alarmed*) Friedrich!

Otto Good evening, Mr Hofreiter.

Friedrich Hello there, Otto.

Genia (*cheerfully*) When did you get back?

Friedrich Got here ten minutes ago. (*to Otto*) I'm pleased to find you are still here. I was afraid you'd already be in Polla . . . or even on the high seas.

Otto I'm leaving tomorrow, Mr Hofreiter.

Friedrich So . . . tomorrow? Well, I'll be right down.

He leaves the balcony. Otto and Genia move across. The following is very quick.

Otto You can't stay here.

Genia Be reasonable, Otto.

Otto I know it now. You weren't made for deceit. I was, perhaps, but not you. You would give yourself away. Or just blurt it out deliberately.

Genia Possibly.

Otto (*suddenly deciding*) I'm going to tell him.

Genia For heaven's sake!

Otto Yes – it's the only thing to do – anything else would be cowardly –

Genia I'll tell him as soon as you've gone. Tomorrow.

Otto And what will happen?

Genia Nothing, probably. I don't want you to come here again, ever. Promise me . . . never . . . not even in three years . . . never . . .

Otto (*understanding*) You love him – you still love him!

Mrs Wahl, Natter, Adele, Stanzides and Gustl come from the court. Erna and Paul carry on playing. Friedrich meets them amid greetings and rejoicing.

Friedrich Hello there, Genia. (*Kisses her on the forehead. To Mrs Wahl, who refuses him her hand*) Come, come, Mama Wahl, are you still cross with me?

Mrs Wahl I'm not speaking to you. And I'm not speaking to Dr Mauer either.

Friedrich We'll have to see about that.

Genia He hasn't shown up at all yet.

Friedrich Really? – I hope he'll come today. I've written him a note. Well, Paul and Erna naturally refuse to be put off their game.

Genia Tell me, when did you arrive in Vienna?

Friedrich Last night. Yes – I would very much have liked to come out here earlier. But unfortunately it was quite impossible.

Genia We gave a luncheon party in your honour.

Gustl It was a great success none the less.

Friedrich Indeed . . .? Well I'll have a cup of black coffee anyway. (*He sits and lights a cigarette.*)

Natter You stayed away longer than you intended, my dear Hofreiter?

Friedrich Yes. (*He looks sharply at Natter.*) Yes. Aren't those your children leaping about in the field over there?

Adele I thought young Joey would be here by now.

Stanzides and Mrs Wahl have meanwhile moved upstage.

Friedrich Well, when is he coming? Getting himself invited to English country houses . . .

Erna and Paul come from the court.

Paul My compliments, Mr Hofreiter.

Friedrich Paul! How is everything?

Paul I can't get my service right.

Erna Good evening, Friedrich.

They shake hands.

Friedrich And did you continue to have a pleasant time at Lake Vols?

Erna Yes – imagine it – very pleasant, even without you.

Incidentally, that really wasn't very nice of you to
disappear so suddenly. Oh yes, by the way, thank you for
your postcards . . . You certainly had a lovely trip.

Friedrich Your fame has reached the papers today, Erna.

Mrs Wahl We've already seen it.

Friedrich So, you've already – you mean this newspaper
has found its way here too? – An interesting rag – isn't it?
(*Pause. He is amused by the others' embarrassment.*) Oh,
where's Otto? –

> *Otto is standing somewhat aside.*

. . . I have to pass on remembrances – or more precisely.
lack of remembrances – but I've spoken to your father.

Otto Your wife told me.

Friedrich It's a shame you're going away tomorrow.
Your father wanted to come to Vienna for a few days.
That you should sail off into the blue, without seeing
him, it doesn't seem right . . . does it?

Otto Perhaps – but now it's too late.

> *Paul, who has been standing with Erna and Mrs
> Wahl, comes forward.*

Paul Well then, Lieutenant, our singles match, if you
don't mind. I quite understand if none of you want to
watch.

Otto I'll go and get changed.

Paul You see, we're only playing singles today. You
are not exempt. Mr Hofreiter; the Lieutenant is leaving
tomorrow and so the position must be settled once and
for all.

Friedrich I am at your disposal. When I've finished my coffee.

Natter, Stanzides, Genia – after Friedrich's first words to Otto about Dr von Aigner – and Gustl, have already moved somewhat apart and are now followed by Paul, Adele and Otto. This leaves Erna and Friedrich. Erna remains standing behind his chair.

Oh Erna . . . (*He remains seated.*)

Erna I'm so glad to have you back.

Friedrich Really? (*He kisses her hand over the back of the chair.*) So am I.

Erna And now I'd like to know your real reason for going away.

Friedrich You are a funny girl. I told you. If I'd stayed, in a few days – oh God, on the same day – the whole hotel would have known about us. You know why . . . the sinner's halo, you called it.

Erna Lover's.

Friedrich Exactly! We'd done enough to earn it.

Erna And what if someone *had* noticed?

Friedrich Dear girl . . . that's not something to be given away to the world. And the less you think of the world, the less you should give it away. You should be grateful to me for not compromising your reputation. Later you would have come to blame me for it.

Erna Later? Oh, I see . . . But I'll never marry, Friedrich.

Friedrich Don't speak too soon, my darling. You should never try to look into the future. Not even into the next moment. Believe me.

Erna And do you think that if I ever loved anyone after you, I'd be able to keep silent about us?

Friedrich Of course you could. And you would be right to.

Erna Another man might think differently – a better man.

Friedrich You think so? (*He stands up.*)

Erna What's the matter with you? Why are you so nervous? Are you expecting somebody?

Friedrich Yes, Mauer.

Erna Dr Mauer? What do you want from him?

Friedrich A business matter.

Erna He's a doctor of medicine.

Friedrich He's also a friend.

Erna Do you think he still is?

Friedrich Yes. Friendship is above incident. These things don't depend on . . . events. He could shoot me dead and it would still be his friend he'd shot.

Erna What is this business that's so important?

Friedrich Come on, my sweetheart! A wife couldn't be more inquisitive. Anyway, it's just boring business.

Erna It seems to make you very nervous.

Friedrich Do I give that impression? Far from it. It's probably that I'm just rather short of sleep. I was keeping a vigil under someone's window.

Erna Last night?

Friedrich Yes, last night. Why are you so surprised?
I told you one evening . . . I suddenly understand all
those things – serenades . . . duels . . . suicide . . .

Erna I don't understand you. Who were you . . . whose
window . . .?

Friedrich Well, yours of course.

Erna Mine? What a romancer you are –

Friedrich You don't believe me? Then listen. Yesterday
evening I did come on out here. Straight after arriving
in Vienna. It was almost midnight when I was beneath
your window. You still had a light burning. I saw your
shadow glide past the curtains. If your room had been
on the ground floor . . . who knows . . .

Erna And then?

Friedrich And then I went away again. Back to town.
I had been near you. That's all I wanted.

Erna You were beneath my windows! . . . Friedrich!

Friedrich Would I tell you if it weren't true? . . .

Erna You were underneath my window! . . . My lover.

Friedrich Ssh . . . ssh . . .

*Friedrich moves to the door of the house. Mauer
comes out.*

Mauer Hello, Friedrich. Good evening, Miss Erna.

Friedrich I'm glad to see you, Mauer.

Erna (*calmly*) Good evening, Doctor.

Mauer (*quite collected*) Have you been back long, Miss
Erna?

Erna Just for two days . . . (*to Friedrich*) You want to speak to the doctor, I'll see you later. (*She goes towards the tennis court.*)

Mauer You wrote to me, so here I am.

Friedrich It was good of you to come. I hope I'm not keeping you from anything important.

Mauer Your note said you needed my advice. I take it you're not feeling well.

Friedrich (*looks at him*) I see! – No, it wasn't the doctor I wanted to see, it was the friend.

Mauer The friend, I see . . . Well, here I am.

Friedrich Actually, it's about an absurd rumour which perhaps you've already heard about or read about.

Mauer That Korsakow died in an American duel? Heard it, to tell you the truth.

Friedrich Well then, what am I to do?

Mauer What are you to do? You've got Korsakow's letter to your wife which shows that he had other reasons to kill himself.

Friedrich What good is that to me . . . I couldn't possibly . . . it would be very bad form . . .

Mauer All right then . . . just don't worry about it. The rumour will disappear as it came.

Friedrich Someone opened his mouth to put this libel about. I want to nail him.

Mauer Whoever it is, you'd have a job to find out.

Friedrich As far as I'm concerned I've found him. It's Natter.

Mauer You think so?

Friedrich It's his revenge . . . After all . . . he knew . . .

Mauer (*quickly*) Everything, I'm sure.

Friedrich Yes – there aren't anything like as many deceived husbands around as their wives like to think.

Mauer Have you any proof that he planted the rumour?

Friedrich Proof, no.

Mauer Then there's nothing you can do.

Friedrich I could accuse him to his face.

Mauer Naturally he'd deny it.

Friedrich Give him a good hiding.

Mauer That wouldn't help.

Friedrich Might help my mood.

Mauer As a means to an end, it would be somewhat disproportionate.

Friedrich I don't think so. A good mood is very important.

Mauer I would let the matter drop. With the best will in the world I can't advise you differently – so now I'll say good evening to your wife and then be on my way.

Friedrich You can damn well do that later! For the moment you'll be kind enough to stay here – All right, I kissed Erna once . . . I don't deny that. A kiss like that in the open air, on a beautiful day, at ten thousand feet, doesn't mean a thing. I'll call it vertigo.

Mauer Well . . . if that's what you'd call it . . . then everything's all right.

Friedrich Do you think there are lots of unkissed girls running around the world? It's even been known to happen at sea level! A kiss! – For a chap to think he's too good for a girl . . . just because . . . forgive me, but that's megalomania.

Mauer You get great pleasure out of lying, don't you?

Friedrich Enormous – at times. But on this occasion I'm denying myself. And let me tell you something else. Even if there'd been anything more to it . . . more than this kiss . . .

Mauer I haven't asked you. And I assure you it makes no difference to me how far things have gone between you.

Friedrich Ah, but it does, my dear Mauer.

Mauer Oh . . .?

Friedrich It might have been better for you if we had become lovers. The affair would have been over and done with. In a way you'd be more secure.

Mauer I'm beginning to find you amusing.

Friedrich Well, that's something. Since certainty is unattainable, entertainment value is the only justification for conversation.

Mauer I'd be able to get the truth from Erna herself.

Friedrich You think so?

Mauer I think that lying is the one thing left she is incapable of.

Friedrich You could be right. And that's worth a thousand times more than so-called respectability. Look at Genia.

Mauer I beg your pardon?

Friedrich My wife, Genia. Her affair with Otto.

Mauer Your wife?

Friedrich Didn't you know? Well, what have you got to say about that?

Mauer If it is true . . .

Friedrich Then it serves me right. I know. But let me tell you that your satisfaction is misplaced – for I'd have to find the affair hurtful, or at least irritating. But that is not the case. On the contrary. It's more like a happy release. I'm no longer the guilty party in this house. I can breathe freely again. It's almost as if she's atoned for Korsakow's death, and indeed in a most rational and painless way. She's begun to close the distance between us, as human beings. We are once more living, as it were, on the same planet.

Mauer I congratulate you on your poise. Clearly you don't believe a word of it: since one can never know for certain . . .

Friedrich I could be jumping to conclusions. All I've got to go on is seeing Otto climbing out of my wife's bedroom window at one-thirty in the morning.

Mauer Which morning?

Friedrich This morning. I in fact arrived last night, you see.

Mauer Really? And where were you until half-past one in the morning?

Friedrich Ha ha . . . You can't think of anything but Erna, can you? Well, just to reassure you, I came out here to Baden on the last train from Vienna; walked here from the station and came, as I sometimes do, through the little gate from the field into the garden. And then to my surprise, I hear voices. I creep nearer and I see a gentleman and a lady sitting under the tree there. Genia and Otto. At midnight, here in the garden. Of course I can't catch what they are saying. I keep my distance. After a few minutes they both get up and disappear into the house. I quickly leave the garden, go up through the back gate again, go around the house and position myself so that I'm bound to see anyone leaving the house by the front gate. No one comes. No one comes for half an hour. The lights in the house go out. I quickly retrace my steps, go round the fence and into the field, where I can keep my eye on Genia's bedroom window. (*Pause.*) It was dark. It was a beautiful night. I lay down on the grass in the shadow of the tree by the fence. And I waited. I waited until half-past one. At half-past one the window opened, a gentleman climbed out, disappeared from my view in the darkness of the garden. I heard the garden gate close, and immediately afterwards the slender figure of Lieutenant Otto von Aigner floated right past me.

Mauer I hope you're not thinking of making him and Genia pay for it. The only thing for you to do now – the thing that you ought to do – is to make a complete break. It could be done now with very little fuss. You need only go to America a little earlier than you had planned.

Friedrich Genia's coming to America with me.

Mauer Oh yes?

Friedrich Yes.

Mauer (*shrugging*) Allow me to take that, for the time being, as the ultimate expression of your self-regard. Now . . . if you'll excuse me, I'll say good evening to your wife.

Friedrich She'll be so pleased.

Mauer goes to the tennis court, passing Natter.

Natter (*entering*) Oh, good evening, Dr Mauer, how are you? Forgive me, dear Hofreiter, I just wanted to ask you . . . as we can't stay any longer, alas . . . if I could come to see you at your office tomorrow. That syndicate has shown up again. They're offering . . .

Friedrich Business tomorrow, Mr Natter.

Natter As you wish.

Friedrich Today we'll chat.

Natter With pleasure.

Friedrich Tell me, Natter, what do you make of Demeter Stanzides?

Natter Stanzides? A nice enough fellow. A bit soft-hearted for a captain in the Hussars. But a decent chap on the whole.

Friedrich Hasn't he got debts?

Natter Not to my knowledge.

Friedrich Doesn't he mistreat his subordinates?

Natter I've never heard anything like that.

Friedrich Does he perhaps cheat at cards?

Natter Do you have reason to think so, Hofreiter?

Friedrich No. I just wanted to make it easier for you to get something on him later on, when his affair with your wife is over.

Friedrich and Natter are standing face to face.

Natter I'm glad you don't think me a fool, Hofreiter.

Friedrich No . . . I think you're a . . .

Natter I warn you not to call me a scoundrel. I may not find it convenient to settle this business over a game of billiards.

Friedrich There are other ways.

Natter If I had wanted to challenge you . . . I would have had better cause not so long ago.

Friedrich Why didn't you? A man doesn't change . . . As a young man in uniform you risked your precious life for less than that.

Natter For less? For something else.

Friedrich If it meant so little to you – why do you stay with your wife?

Natter So little? To me life without Adele would mean absolutely nothing at all. The fact is I'm hopelessly in love with her. It does happen, Hofreiter. There's nothing I can do about it. You have no idea how many ways I've tried to break free of my need of her. In vain . . . all in vain . . . I love her despite everything. Ridiculous, isn't it? – But there it is.

Friedrich And you revenge yourself by inventing ridiculous tales about me?

Natter It could be the truth.

Friedrich God! – Do you really believe that? . . . that I . . . an American duel . . .

Natter Prove you didn't.

Friedrich I could do that – I know the reason for Korsakow's suicide. I happen to know that . . . Oh, what have I come to? Justifying myself to you, you –

Natter Careful now.

Paul and Otto enter from the tennis court.

Otto Time for our singles match now, Mr Hofreiter.

Friedrich Just coming.

Paul You see if you can beat him.

Paul and Otto return to the tennis court.

Friedrich I swear to you that you're wrong. I swear to you on . . .

Natter On your wife's virtue, perhaps?

Friedrich Sir – (*He goes up to Natter.*)

Natter Calm down, we don't want any fuss. I'm not going to brawl with you. But just one word more and . . .

Friedrich So I am to be at the mercy of you, of someone who . . .

Natter Someone who finds life wonderfully amusing . . . dear Hofreiter – and no more than that.

Paul (*returning*) Sorry to interrupt . . .

Friedrich Yes . . . yes . . . I'm ready – let the position be settled once and for all . . .

Natter Once and for all – to the death, perhaps?

Friedrich Why not?

Natter Don't let me keep you.

Mauer and Genia come from upstage.

Friedrich (*to Mauer*) No, you simply cannot go. You must keep him here, Genia – use all your powers of seduction.

Friedrich, Paul and Natter go to the court.

Genia I'm afraid my powers will prove insufficient.

Mauer Unfortunately I'm afraid I must go, Gnädige Frau.

Genia Am I right in thinking we won't be seeing you here for some time? I don't want to force myself into your confidence. I can guess what is driving you away from us.

Mauer This time I cannot congratulate you on your perspicacity.

Genia I'm sorry to have lost a friend.

Mauer Now if you'll allow me, Gnädige Frau, I must take my leave.

Genia It's not for me to allow you or forbid you, still less as Gnädige Frau!

Mauer turns back to Genia and they embrace.

Goodbye, dear Doctor! – And . . . please let me give you one piece of advice to go with you – Don't take it too hard. It would be silly for you, who see life at its most truly serious, to take seriously these foolish games. Well, that's all that love affairs are, Doctor, believe me. And once you've accepted that, they're very enjoyable to watch – even to take part in.

Mauer Once you have accepted that . . .

Genia You will too, my friend. And all those silly, overblown words that fill your mind – you'll see how empty they really are. They just blow away.

Mauer And only the lies remain. Don't they matter either?

Genia Lies? Can one have lies in a game? That's called bluff, all part of the fun.

Mauer A game? Oh yes, if that's how it was played! I assure you, Genia, I would have nothing at all against a world in which love really was in fact nothing but a delightful game . . . But in that case . . . in that case let it be played honestly if you will, let it be rotten with honesty, then perhaps you have a point. But this hole-in-the-corner posturing, this bogus civility between people made wretched by jealousy, cowardice, lust – I find all that sad and horrible – This much-vaunted freedom one finds here lacks conviction. That's why the happiness it seeks eludes it . . . and why its laughter dies in a grin.

Genia Oh really, you're going too far. We all make an effort, though of course it doesn't always go as well as we would like. But we do have the best of intentions. Haven't you noticed? Adele Natter visits, I chat to Erna, Friedrich plays his game of tennis with the Lieutenant . . .

Mauer And why shouldn't he?

Genia Oh, Doctor! . . .

Mauer Yes, I know . . . Tread carefully, Genia.

The tennis game is over. The players are gradually coming back.

Genia Why 'tread carefully'? – Friedrich won't mind. After all, Otto might have killed himself too, if I hadn't . . . Like the other one. And one mustn't drive a young chap to blow his brains out over a trifle like one's own virtue. Friedrich will give me his blessing. Tomorrow when . . . my lover has gone . . . I'll tell him all about it myself.

Mauer That won't be necessary. He saw the Lieutenant last night . . . at half-past one.

Genia starts, then pulls herself together quickly. Paul, Stanzides, Gustl, Erna, Adele, Mrs Wahl, Natter, Otto and Friedrich come from the court.

Genia Well, who won?

Paul The old guard lives on. Mr Hofreiter won.

Stanzides Pity you didn't see it, ma'am. It was a fine game.

Friedrich So, Mauer, you stayed after all. That's nice of you!

Paul Next it's the game between Miss Erna and Mr Hofreiter.

Erna It's already too dark, we'll postpone it till tomorrow.

Friedrich What a shame that we couldn't have played another game tomorrow, Otto! I didn't really enjoy my victory today.

Paul Why ever not? The Lieutenant played very well and you played a blinder.

Friedrich I don't know. You weren't on top form, Otto. You had one stroke I've never noticed before in your armoury. Such a nervous indecisive stroke as if your mind was elsewhere. Upset to be going, I suppose.

Otto Well, when I return in three years, Mr Hofreiter, I hope to be a better match for you.

Friedrich Yes, if one could be sure we would see each other again! . . . I never look as far ahead . . . Think of all the things that can happen. We are not masters of our fate. Anything might happen to make all prediction useless . . . and all caution.

Natter And caution doesn't happen to be one of the Lieutenant's strong points.

Otto I'm only too aware of that myself, Mr Natter.

Friedrich There's no way you could know, Otto, whether or not you're cautious by nature . . . In a profession where so much depends on morale and discipline as in yours, you can't know what your nature really is, don't you think?

Mauer It's getting late for psychology. (*to Otto*) Shall we go together?

Friedrich (*ignoring this*) I don't doubt for a moment, of course, that you would be ready to lay down your life for king and country, but external pressures play a certain role in that. In the depths of your soul, in the very depths, Otto, you're a coward.

Long pause.

Otto I haven't understood you correctly, have I?

Friedrich I don't know what you understood. In any case I'll repeat it: you are a coward.

Otto takes a step towards Friedrich. Friedrich moves quickly to meet him.

Otto You will hear from me.

Friedrich I hope so – (*quietly*) – and soon.

Otto leaves. Paul speaks quietly to Gustl and they follow Otto. Erna and Genia stand motionless. Mrs Wahl looks round helplessly and turns to Adele.

Natter Well, I think that's everything.

Friedrich No, don't go yet. (*to Mauer, aside*) Mauer, I hope I can count on you.

Mauer No. I'll have nothing to do with it.

Friedrich As a doctor, Mauer. You can't deny me that, it's your duty.

Mauer (*shrugging*) Very well.

Friedrich Thank you. Dear Stanzides.

Stanzides I am at your disposal.

Friedrich I thank you. Natter, can I ask you?

Natter My dear Hofreiter . . .

Friedrich (*pulling Natter downstage*) I think we share the same view of life, don't we? Too funny for words.

Natter I've always said so.

Friedrich This latest joke would have one more twist for me – if you would be my second.

Natter Only too pleased – the Lieutenant is bound to be a good shot.

Genia (*suddenly decided, goes to Friedrich*) Friedrich . . .

Friedrich Later.

Genia Now.

Friedrich (*to the others*) Excuse us.

> *Friedrich moves downstage with Genia. Mrs Wahl goes over to Erna, tries to get her to leave. Erna gestures her away and stands by the wall of the house. Mrs Wahl turns to Adele, who is watching her husband. Natter and Stanzides move upstage. Mauer stands by himself.*

Genia What on earth are you doing? How can you . . .?

Friedrich Look, don't worry. I won't do much to him, probably nothing at all.

Genia Then why? If it had anything at all to do with your feeling for me . . . if it were hate . . . rage . . . jealousy . . . love . . .

Friedrich That's right – I couldn't give a damn about any of that. But I won't be made to look a fool.

Friedrich turns from Genia and follows Natter and Stanzides. Genia stands downstage motionless. Erna remains standing by the wall of the house. The two women look at each other.

Act Five

A room in the Hofreiter villa, adjoining the conservatory of Act One. Light and friendly. The French windows leading to the conservatory are open.

Genia is in the room, in an agitated state. Erna, hatless, in a summer dress, enters very quickly from the conservatory.

Genia (*rising, quickly composing herself*) Erna? . . . What's the matter?

Erna They aren't back yet? Isn't there any news?

Genia How could there be? Get a grip on yourself, Erna. Nothing can happen till this afternoon at the earliest. I should think they're still discussing formalities.

Erna (*looking at her*) Yes, of course. You don't mind my asking. . .? I know I have no right, but . . .

Genia You have as much right to tremble for someone as I have.

Erna I'm not trembling, Mrs Hofreiter. I never tremble. I simply wanted to ask if you had seen your husband today?

Genia My husband went into town yesterday evening. Arranging various matters with his lawyer, by all accounts. That's quite usual, even if it is superfluous. He will settle his affairs. Perhaps even burn some letters and papers. In brief, behave just as if it were a deadly serious business instead of this charade of a foolish vanity defending a travestied honour – which is what we all know it to be.

Erna I'm not convinced of that, Frau Genia.

Genia I am. Come on, Erna, let's go into the garden, it's such a lovely day. Let's have a chat. You haven't told me anything about your travels yet. You had an interesting time . . . at Lake Vols . . .

Erna Is it possible that you can mock me at such a time, Genia?

Genia I'm not mocking you. It's the last thing I . . . You love him very much – don't you . . .?! Well, it's only to be expected – There's nothing like the first time. Or doesn't even that mean anything nowadays? You must tell me about that, Erna. When I was your age, one still took certain things terribly seriously. Now, I don't know where I am any more.

Kathi enters with a telegram and then leaves.

(*Opening it quickly*) Joey's arriving at midday. It'll be lovely to see him again. Come on, why don't we go into the garden, Erna?

Erna Genia! At five o'clock this morning I saw Gustl leave. The duel took place at six. While we're talking it's all long since been over.

Pause.

Genia So, everything is over . . . Now nothing can be changed, isn't that so? Then they'll all be sitting down together at the convent, under the shade of a tree and toasting the reconciliation . . . Erna, do you think they'll be drinking our health? Why not? Perhaps they'll turn up here together arm in arm. Yes . . . we should go and meet them . . .

Mrs von Aigner is seen approaching from the conservatory.

181

Erna It's Otto's mother.

Genia (*starts*) What . . .?

Erna She's walking quite calmly. She doesn't know anything.

Genia What's she doing here so early?

Erna She certainly doesn't know anything. She's quite unconcerned. Why should she know, anyway? Get hold of yourself, Frau Genia!

Mrs von Aigner (*entering*) Good morning.

Erna Good morning, ma'am.

Genia It's you, Mrs von Aigner. Ah . . . (*She rises.*)

Erna Goodbye, then . . .

Mrs von Aigner You're going? I hope I'm not driving you away?

Erna Not at all, ma'am. I had just taken my leave. Goodbye, Frau Genia.

Genia (*with tremendous self-control*) I'm delighted to see you again, Mrs von Aigner. We missed you yesterday.

Mrs von Aigner There were so many of you. I don't like a large crowd. Today I'm here all the earlier, as you see, Mrs Hofreiter.

Genia Is it so early? Friedrich went into town hours ago. You know of course, Mrs von Aigner, that he got back yesterday.

Mrs von Aigner Of course I know. (*smiling*) Otto conveyed Mr Hofreiter's respects to me last evening.

Genia I see. Your son is leaving you today . . .?

Mrs von Aigner My son has in fact already left. He caught the last train yesterday. And this evening he's travelling to Polla.

Genia This evening, is it? Ah!

Mrs von Aigner Was I really the first to tell you that?

Genia No, I did know.

Mrs von Aigner Can you imagine, Mrs Hofreiter, how I felt this morning as I sat down to breakfast in my summerhouse, once again quite alone. My little house is suddenly so empty . . . I had become unused to that. I suppose I've been really spoiled for quite some while – in spite of everything. I wanted to go for a walk . . . a walk by myself in the woods. And now I'm here. I don't know how that happened. Something must have directed my steps. (*She looks at Genia for a long moment.*)

Genia (*returning her look*) Thank you.

Mrs von Aigner You mustn't thank me. I had the choice of being very angry with you – or of being very fond of you. And when I left home I was still far from decided. Because in these last few days – now that he's gone I can tell you, I suppose, Genia – I have sometimes really been afraid . . .

Genia Afraid –?

Mrs von Aigner I do know my son . . . And I've seen how much he's suffered recently. He wasn't made at all . . . for deceit . . . I was . . . afraid for him . . . You meant so much to him, Genia! More than his profession, or his future, or me or his life. Oh God, I was so frightened about where it would lead to! And I kept silent. I had to keep silent. I had seen it coming, of course, from the day Otto entered this house. In all my resentment,

my fear, my jealousy, I had to understand. You were so
alone, Genia, and so much wronged . . . for so many
years! And even if it hadn't been as good a man as Otto –
I couldn't have blamed you. And now – now that he's
gone, all my resentment and jealousy have gone too,
and I only ask myself how will she bear it? She – who
loved him!

Genia Mrs von Aigner, I truly am not worth such
sympathy. I will try to forget him. And I will succeed.
That is certain – as certain as that he will succeed too.
You mustn't worry. There was no understanding between
us. I promise you . . . We're not even going to write to
each other. You may count on that.

Mrs von Aigner You're so good, Genia!

Genia I'm merely practical, Mrs von Aigner, only . . .
practical.

Mrs von Aigner Can't you find any other name for me?
I'm his mother.

Genia No, no, no, I can't! (*She breaks down.*)

Mrs von Aigner Genia, Genia. Don't cry, Genia! (*She
strokes Genia's hair.*) Child, child – do calm yourself.
You can see, of course, that my choice is made . . . I
cannot hate you. We will bear his absence together.
We're going to be friends, Genia. It's all we can be.

> *Friedrich enters from the veranda. A dark greatcoat
> over his black frock coat. Quickly buttons his
> greatcoat, composes his expression. Genia stares at
> him inquiringly. Friedrich gives a fixed smile, without
> nodding. He speaks to Mrs von Aigner in his laughing
> mischievous vein, which is now mask-like.*

Friedrich How do you do, madam. (*He takes her proffered hand with only the faintest show of hesitation.*) How are you?

Mrs von Aigner Well. Back so early from town?

Friedrich From town? No. I'm just going there now. I've just been for my morning stroll. A . . . glorious day . . .

Mrs von Aigner You've had a nice trip?

Friedrich Yes, very nice. Very nice. No complaints. Good weather, interesting people, what more could one want?

Mrs von Aigner Oh yes, I have to send someone's regards to you.

Friedrich Regards? To me?

Mrs von Aigner You'll be somewhat surprised. Regards from Dr von Aigner.

Friedrich From your husband?

Mrs von Aigner Yes, early this morning. Before I left the house there was a letter from him, the first for many years. And in a few days he's coming in person. A conference with the Minister, so he writes.

Friedrich He'll be Minister himself one day, your husband. Altogether a remarkable chap, a most remarkable man. He still has a great future.

Mrs von Aigner Do you really think so?

Friedrich Why not?

Mrs von Aigner Well, he also mentions his poor health . . .

Friedrich Poor health! . . . He'll outlive us all. Forgive me, naturally I can, of course, only speak for myself, that's all anyone can do . . . (*laughs*) A very interesting chap . . . we talked a lot together . . . in those few days . . . I like him.

Mrs von Aigner And he seems to have taken you very much to his heart. Yes, it's a strange letter. Almost touching. And a little affected. But it's too late for him to change now.

Friedrich Much too late.

Mrs von Aigner Well, goodbye for now.

Friedrich Goodbye, ma'am. And when your husband comes here our house is naturally . . . *Les amis de nos amis* . . . and so forth. Adieu, madam.

Mrs von Aigner (*as Genia accompanies her for a few steps*) Goodbye, dear Mrs Hofreiter.

> *She leaves and Genia returns quickly. Friedrich is standing motionless.*

Genia Well? . . . Everything . . . all right –?

Friedrich (*looking at her*) Well . . . !

Genia He's wounded?! Friedrich! . . .

Friedrich He's dead!

Genia Friedrich, Friedrich . . . (*She goes to him and seizes him by the shoulders.*) You shook hands with his mother.

Friedrich (*shrugs*) I didn't know that she . . . would be with you. What was I supposed to do?

Genia Dead . . . dead! . . . (*suddenly, at him*) Murderer!

Friedrich It was a duel. I'm no murderer.

Genia Why, why . . .?

Friedrich Why? – Obviously . . . because I felt like it.

Genia That's just not true! Don't make yourself out worse than you are. You didn't want to do it. It was a terrible accident . . . You didn't want to . . . It isn't true . . .

Friedrich At the moment he stood facing me, it was true.

Genia You didn't even hate him and yet you killed him – You vain, contemptible monster . . .!

Friedrich It isn't as simple as . . . You can't look into my soul. No one can. I'm sorry for poor Mrs von Aigner. And for poor old Mr von Aigner, too. But I can't help them. Nor you. Nor help him. Nor me. It had to be so.

Genia Had to? –

Friedrich When he stood facing me, with the insolence of youth in his eyes, I knew then . . . it was him or me.

Genia You're lying, he wouldn't have . . . he wouldn't . . .

Friedrich You're wrong. He wanted it, as I did. It was life or death. Him . . . or me . . .

Erna and Mauer enter from the garden. Erna remains standing at the door. Mauer goes quickly to Genia, and presses her hand.

Ah, Mauer, you here already?

Mauer There was nothing more for me to do.

Genia Where is his body?

Mauer On its way.

Genia Where to?

Mauer His mother's house.

Genia Does she know . . . who will tell her . . .?

Mauer No one has dared to yet.

Genia I will tell her. It's my duty. I'm going to her.

Friedrich Genia . . . just a moment. When you come back, I probably won't be here. I can't ask you to give me your hand, but – are we just going to say farewell?

Genia (*remembering*) Joey's coming. Any time now.

Friedrich Joey? I'll wait for him . . . Then . . .

Genia What are you going to do?

Friedrich Go to town. Give myself up. Nothing will happen to me anyway. I have only defended my honour. Perhaps I'll get bail and they'll let me . . . though of course they might suspect me of fleeing the country . . .

Genia You can think of that!! And he's lying dead.

Friedrich Yes, I can. He's got it easier now. For him it's all over. But for me – I'm still in this world. And I intend to go on living in it . . . Please make up your mind. Which way is it going to be?

Genia (*staring at him*) It's over. (*about to go*) It's finished.

Mauer Frau Genia . . . You can't walk that road alone. Allow me to go with you.

> *Mauer and Genia leave. Erna at the door is motionless. Friedrich stands stiffly as before.*

Erna What will you do?

Friedrich I'll leave the district of course . . . clear out altogether.

Erna Wherever you want to go, Friedrich – I will follow you.

Friedrich Declined, with thanks.

Erna I know it more surely than ever, Friedrich, we belong together.

Friedrich You are mistaken. At the moment you are under the spell of these events. Perhaps you're even impressed that I . . . but that's an illusion. It's all illusion. I'll fold up like a pocket knife, soon enough. It's over, Erna, for us as well. You're twenty years old, and you don't belong to me.

Erna (*still where she was*) You are younger than any of them.

Friedrich Hush! I know what youth is. It's not an hour since I saw it. It glows, it laughs, it has an insolence in its eye. I know what youth is. And I can't shoot them all . . . Stay where you are, have as good a time as you can . . .

Erna (*listening*) A car.

Friedrich (*still motionless*) Joey.

Erna (*now a little nearer to him*) Believe me, Friedrich, I love you, I belong to you.

Friedrich I belong to no one on this earth. No one. Nor do I wish to . . .

A Boy's Voice (*in the garden*) Mother! Father!

Friedrich (*moans quietly, once*) Joey, I'm coming. Here I am.

He walks quickly out on to the veranda. Erna remains standing.

ROUGH CROSSING

adapted from
Play at the Castle
by Ferenc Molnár

Characters

Turai
Gal
playwrights and collaborators, of middle age

Adam
a young composer, aged 25

Natasha
an actress, aged 35 to 40

Ivor
an actor, aged 45 to 50

Dvornichek
a cabin steward

and the Ladies of the Chorus

The action takes place on board the SS Italian Castle
sailing between Southampton and New York
via Cherbourg

A Note on the Accents

Little or nothing hinges on the nationality of the
characters. In the original production Turai and Gal,
who retain their names from the Hungarian, spoke
virtually without an accent. Natasha spoke with
a Hungarian accent invoking the tradition of English-
speaking Continental stars, but this is not a vital matter.
More point is made of Adam's being French, so he
spoke with the appropriate accent. Ivor is English.
My assumption about Dvornichek is that whatever
his nationality his English is mysteriously perfect.

Rough Crossing was first performed at the Lyttelton Theatre, London, on 30 October 1984. The cast was as follows:

Dvornichek Michael Kitchen
Turai John Standing
Adam Andrew C. Wadsworth
Gal Niall Buggy
Natasha Sheila Gish
Ivor Robin Bailey

Chorus Cristina Avery, Tracy Collier, Elizabeth Davies, Chrissie Kendall, Gail Rolfe and Debbie Snook, with David Hitchen

Directed by Peter Wood
Designed by Carl Toms

Songs André Previn (*music*), Tom Stoppard (*lyrics*)

Act One

The private verandas of the two most expensive suites on the Italian Castle. *Turai's veranda is needed more than Natasha's veranda. Entrances on to this little deck are made from upstage through the interior, partly visible, of Turai's sitting room.*

It is late at night. There is enough moonlight and electric light around to ensure that we are not peering into the gloom.

Turai is standing by the rail.

Dvornichek approaches from within, balancing a silver tray on one hand, and also balancing himself as though the boat were in a storm.

(Later when the boat is in a storm, and when everybody else is staggering about, the boat's movements seem to cancel out Dvornichek's so that he is the only person moving around normally.)

Dvornichek *(entering)* Here we are, sir! One cognac!

Turai Oh . . . Thank you.

Dvornichek For those in peril on the sea there's nothing like a large cognac as a steadying influence.

Turai You could do with a steadying influence yourself. You'd better put it down.

Dvornichek Thank you, sir. Your health. *(He drinks the cognac.)* And may I say what an honour it is to serve you, sir! *(He stands swaying.)* Quite a swell!

Turai *(modestly)* Thank you.

Dvornichek Will there be anything else, sir?

Turai Perhaps a cognac.

Dvornichek I recommend it, sir. It calms the waters something wonderful.

Turai Thank you . . . er . . .

Dvornichek Dvornichek, sir.

Turai Dvornichek. But surely we're still in harbour.

Dvornichek (*surprised*) Are we, sir? I see no sign of it.

Turai It's on the other side of the boat.

Dvornichek By God, you're right. I thought the front end was *that* way, but that's the back end, is it?, and you've got a right-hand-side room.

Turai Starboard.

Dvornichek I beg your pardon, sir?

Turai Er . . .

Dvornichek Dvornichek.

Turai Dvornichek. So this is your first crossing?

Dvornichek (*impressed*) That's miraculous. I suppose in your line of work you can tell a character at a glance.

Turai It's a gift. I take no credit for it. Where was your last position?

Dvornichek Paris, sir. The George. (*French pronunciation*)

Turai Cinq?

Dvornichek No, it's a hotel. I'd be grateful if you didn't mention it to anyone. I told them it was the *Mauretania*. They suspect nothing in the basement.

Turai I should try to pick up a few nautical expressions.

Dvornichek That's a very good idea, sir. I shall start immediately.

Turai And could you find Mr Gal for me.

Dvornichek No problem. He went to the telegraph office.

Turai Where is that?

Dvornichek On the . . . starboard side, sir. Up by the chimneys. I'll be back with your drink in no time.

Turai Get one too for Mr Adam – his cabin is opposite mine on the other side of the boat.

Dvornichek Yes, sir.

Turai Port.

Dvornichek Yes, sir. And a cognac.

Turai Er . . .

Dvornichek Dvornichek.

Turai Dvornichek. Present my compliments and ask Mr Adam what he'd like to drink. And, by the way, be patient when you speak with him – he suffers from a nervous disability, in fact a speech impediment, which takes the unusual form of . . .

He sees that Adam has entered the cabin and is approaching. As Adam enters the deck:

Ah, dear boy, how are you! Come out here –

Dvornichek Good evening, sir.

Everything stops. Adam's nervous disability takes the form of a pause of several seconds before he can embark on a sentence. Once he starts, he speaks perfectly normally without stuttering. One result of this, in certain situations, is that Adam is always answering the last question but one. Later on in the play, unless otherwise indicated, Adam always hesitates before embarking on a speech but usually the hesitation is notional.

Adam (*finally*) Good evening.

Dvornichek Welcome aboard, sir. If there's anything I can do for you don't hesitate to ask.

Pause.

Adam Thank you, I won't.

Turai All unpacked? Found a place for everything?

Dvornichek I expect you'd like a drink, sir?

Adam Oh, yes, but I haven't brought much with me.

Dvornichek No problem, we've got plenty, you'll be all right with us.

Adam No, I don't think I will.

Dvornichek Course you will – I trust your cabin is satisfactory?

Turai How did you find your lady love?

Adam Most comfortable, thank you.

Turai Have you seen her yet?

Dvornichek Are you going to get one in?

Adam Not yet, she's still at dinner.

Dvornichek No, I mean a drink. A port, wasn't it?

Turai Why don't we wait for her together?

Adam No, really, thank you.

Dvornichek We've got a Rebello-Valente 1911, or there's the '24.

Adam Thank you, I'd like that very much.

Dvornichek Which?

Turai (*crossly, to Dvornichek*) What do you *want*?

Dvornichek Oh, thank you, I'll have a cognac.

Adam I don't drink port.

Turai We could send word to her table that we're on board.

Dvornichek Forget the port – we've got everything. Just name it.

Adam No, I'd like it to be a surprise.

Dvornichek A surprise. Right.

Turai Er . . .

Dvornichek Dvornichek.

Turai Dvornichek – go away.

Dvornichek Go away . . . right. No problem.

> *He goes away. If there are chairs, Turai and Adam make themselves comfortable. There is quite a long pause while Adam struggles into speech.*

Adam Let's not talk if you don't mind because my starting motor is behaving worse than ever no doubt from the excitement of seeing Natasha again and I feel so silly having to choose between on the one hand struggling to resume each time the flow is interrupted and on the other hand gabbling non-stop so as to give an impression of easy conversation which isn't in fact easy when you are trapped like a rat in a runaway train of ever more complicated sentences that shy away from the approaching full stop like a – like a – damn!

Turai (*waves him courteously to silence*) Like a moth shying at a candle flame. Too boring. At a lepidopterist, then. Too banal. Like a girl shying at her first compliment. Oh, I like that. Like a boy shying at a coconut, no, I've gone too far again. How ironical that tongue-trippery should come in my shape and tripped-uppery in yours. I should like a leading man, and you look like one, and between us we have to rely on clods like Ivor Fish to present the world with our genius. Oh, hello, Gal, your genius too, of course.

> *This is because Gal has emerged from inside the cabin. He is perhaps not as clothes-conscious as Turai but has at least an equal dignity. This is not impaired by the fact that he happens to be eating a stick of celery.*

Gal There you are, Turai. Good evening, Adam. Any sign of Natasha? Don't reply. And don't listen to Turai. He has no genius. He can write a bit but unfortunately writes a lot. I have no genius either. Economy of expression I have. I have cabled New York.

Turai We really would have taken your word for it.

Adam No, she's still at dinner.

Gal I've ordered a cognac.

Turai What did you say?

Gal 'Bring me a cognac.'

Turai This was the cable to New York?

Gal You have become confused. We have an excellent cabin steward. I forget his name. I asked him to bring me a cognac. The cable to New York was another thing altogether: 'Safely embarked *SS Italian Castle,* arriving Sunday with new ending, don't worry.' I thought it best not to mention the new beginning.

Turai What's wrong with the beginning?

Gal Won't do. Curtain up. Chaps talking. Who are they? We don't know. They're talking about something they evidently know all about and we know nothing about. Then another chap. Who is he? They know so they won't tell us. Five minutes have gone by. Everything must fall into place or we'll stop caring. They mention a woman. Who is she? We don't know. They know so they won't tell us. So it goes.

Turai *The Merchant of Venice* begins like that.

Gal There you are, you see. Won't do.

Turai What do you suggest?

Gal Introduce a character part, on board the boat but outside the main story; comes in at the beginning and recognizes *everybody,* knows exactly what they are up to and fills in the whole jigsaw with one speech. He could be an Irish policeman called Murphy.

Turai Yes . . . I don't know, though . . . an Irish policeman called Murphy right at the beginning of *The Merchant of Venice.*

Gal I'm not talking about *The Merchant of Venice.*

Turai Oh, I see. But why should the policeman *do* such a thing?

Gal Why shouldn't he?

Turai And why is he Irish?

Gal I had a reason for that but I've forgotten what it was.

Turai And what is an Irish policeman doing on the boat anyway?

Gal Emigrating.

Turai But it's a round-the-world cruise.

Gal *That's* what it was.

Turai No, no, no. I'm disappointed in you, Gal. Fills in the jigsaw indeed! From now on you just do the cables.

> *Dvornichek arrives with a tray on which there are a cognac and a revolting looking cocktail.*

Dvornichek Here we are, gentlemen! One cognac and a Mad Dog.

Turai At last.

> *Gal takes the cognac. Turai arrives at the tray too late.*

What is this muck?

Dvornichek That's the surprise.

Turai I don't like surprises, especially when one is expecting cognac. How would *you* like it?

Dvornichek Thank you, sir, most considerate – your health! But first – if I may be so bold – a toast! A toast to three passengers who have honoured the steamship *Italian Castle* by their embarkation at Cherbourg tonight bound for New York. To Sandor Turai and Alex Gal, world-famous playwrights and men of the theatre, friends and collaborators over twenty years and countless comedies, dramas, light operettas, revues, sketches, lyrics and libretti, on five continents and in as many languages, joint authors, as ever, of the new comedy with music, *The Cruise of the Dodo*! *And* to their discovery, friend, protégé, the young maestro, plucked from obscurity to imminent fame, their new composer, Adam Adam! – Coupled with their lovely leading lady in the room above (*or 'next door', depending on the staging*) – the darling of the gods, Natasha Navratilova, or as she is known among the readers of the society pages . . . Natasha Navratilova! – Oh, and her leading man in D4 the matinée idol, Ivor Fish! Both of whom are now at dinner having boarded at Southampton earlier this afternoon! I raise my glass to your success in New York and I'm only sorry you're not taking the romantic lead yourself, Mr Adam; I saw you last year at the Chapeau Rouge in *One, Two, Button My Cabbage* and you'd be better than Ivor Fish any *jour* of the *semaine* but let that pass, on behalf of the management I bid you welcome within the four walls of the *SS Italian Castle,* and may I say how thrilled I am personally that you have booked the Pisa Room for shipboard rehearsals! (*He drains his glass.*)

Turai This is outrageous.

Gal Thank you . . . er . . .

Dvornichek Dvornichek.

Gal Do you mind if I call you Murphy?

Dvornichek Not at all, sir. Will there be anything else, sir?

Gal Well, we're also having a little trouble with the ending.

Dvornichek I know what you mean.

Gal You do?

Dvornichek Miss Navratilova was kind enough to let me read your play.

Turai Look, what does one have to do to get a drink round here?

Gal Murphy, another cognac.

Dvornichek Yes, sir.

Gal And a little something to eat.

Adam is trying to speak to Dvornichek.

Dvornichek No problem . . . (*to Adam*) Dvornichek.

Gal (*to Turai*) That man could do a lot for *The Merchant of Venice*. He's got everything in except why Natasha isn't expecting us until the morning.

Dvornichek is in the process of misunderstanding why Adam is having difficulty addressing him.

Dvornichek Dvornichek . . .

Adam tries again.

Murphy.

Adam (*finally succeeding*) I *know* I would but unfortunately, shortly after appearing in that revue at the Chapeau Rouge, I was struck by this curious disability which has made it impossible for me to continue my career as a performer.

Dvornichek (*sympathetically*) Why, what's the problem?

Turai (*to Dvornichek*) Are you still here?!

Dvornichek (*turning away from Adam*) Yes, Sir –

Adam (*just too late*) Timing.

Dvornichek (*continuing*) Just off, sorry – you gentlemen caught me on the hop arriving by private launch in the middle of dinner. Miss Navratilova told me you were in Deauville working on the ending and would be joining the ship with the Cherbourg passengers in the morning after breakfast.

Gal Yes, well –

Dvornichek Don't tell me – you got tired of work, tired of Deauville, and Mr Adam couldn't wait another night to be reunited with his lady-love.

Gal (*gratefully*) Murphy – have a cognac.

Dvornichek Thank you, sir! I'll be back in no time. (*He leaves.*)

Turai (*exasperated*) Are you paying that man?

Gal (*to Adam*) You know, Murphy's quite right. It's tragic that you can't play the role of Justine Deverell. Especially as we've got Ivor Fish. Ivor's very popular with the public, of course, a couple of hours of Ivor's company every eighteen months being just about right, but they don't knowingly get on boats with him.

Adam has been gearing up to speak.

Adam (*finally*) I could play it all right if only this ridiculous hesitation were the same each time.

Turai How do you mean?

Adam All I'd have to do is anticipate my lines.

Gal That's a good idea. I see what you mean.

Adam Then I'd start speaking just as it's my turn.

Gal Of course you would! Do you see what he's getting at, Turai?

Adam Unfortunately I can't time it.

Gal But you're timing it perfectly!

Adam It's a matter of luck if I come in at the right moment.

Gal Luck? What luck? You've solved it.

Adam It could go wrong at any moment because sometimes my voice comes out in a couple of seconds, sometimes I seem to be hesitating for minutes on end, and I never know which it's going to be.

Gal (*ignoring him*) I'll cable New York. 'Fish overboard, a star is born.'

Turai Well, what is it normally, would you say?

Gal We'll need costume fittings. What's your hat size?

Adam It varies according to my state of mind.

Gal That's remarkable. What is it at the moment?

Turai (*to Gal*) Be quiet. (*to Adam*) Perhaps the other actors could fill in until you're ready to speak, though it would be an enormous problem if the hesitation is too long.

Gal What about your feet?

Adam Enormous.

Gal Enormous feet.

Turai He's not talking to you! (*to Adam*) What's the longest it's ever been?

Adam The longest was two days, that night at the Chapeau Rouge when it all began.

Turai Two days? The audience would have gone home.

Adam (*pause*) They did. (*Pause.*) I looked up in the middle of my first song and there at a table in the front row was my mother.

Turai And you fell silent for two days?

Adam I hadn't realized she'd got out of gaol. She'd been arrested in front of the Mona Lisa, which is where she'd spent a surprising part of her time since becoming convinced that she was the reincarnation of that lady, and I could tell by the enigmatic way she was smiling at me she hadn't changed a bit. I found I couldn't speak.

Gal It had happened before?

Adam From childhood, every time she got out of gaol.

Gal But why did they keep putting her in gaol?

Adam Assault, battery, attempted incestuous rape of a minor, and committing a nuisance in a public place, namely in front of the Mona Lisa.

Gal Remarkable woman.

Adam Terrifying.

Turai Well, you've given her the slip now.

Adam I hope so. But it's just as well we've got Ivor Fish, and I don't mind a bit who plays Natasha's lover so long as I'm her lover because Natasha is my muse and without her love I would fall silent truly and forever.

Gal How the papers would have loved it. Adam. Adam and Natasha Navratilova, the love birds on stage together every night, and it would have given the ending a wonderful quality, too, if we had an ending.

Turai We have four and a half days. We wrote *Lottie from Brest-Litovsk* in four and a half days.

Gal It also ran four and a half days. It was the first play ever to close after a matinée.

Turai That's because we didn't have Adam's music.

Gal That's true.

Adam tries to speak.

Don't say anything unless you have an ending.

Adam Or Natasha either.

Turai What?

Adam (*pause*) You didn't have my music or Natasha either.

Gal Also true.

Turai And, don't forget, even if Deauville let us down with the end, we have brought her a new song for the second act.

Gal All true. With Adam's music and Natasha and the new song and a new ending and an Irish policeman, we shall have a wonderful success in New York if we do a little work on the middle even if we *are* stuck with Ivor.

Turai (*hopefully*) Ivor and Natasha have been very good together in the past, that play where Ivor had the motorbike . . .

Gal Yes, they had a wonderful eighteen months in *Pauline Rides Pillion*, and a *slightly* disappointing three weeks in *Romeo and Juliet*. God that was a mistake, people do the silliest things when they're in the middle of an . . .

Turai (*hurriedly*) I've got a wonderful idea! Let's welcome her back from dinner with the new song! Adam, go and get the score from your cabin, and a piano or something of the sort –

Gal Yes, yes, and if she comes back we'll keep quiet as mice till you return and then we'll serenade her together with the new number. What do you think?

Adam tries to speak.

Just nod.

Adam nods and leaves.

I'm sorry. It slipped out.

Turai You know . . . we should have sent her a telegram: 'Arriving tonight.'

Gal Adam wanted to surprise her.

Turai He may succeed.

Gal Oh, come now, all that was years ago. She was just a young girl flattered by an older man's attentions. Ivor was the bigger name then, and naturally one thing led to another, but everything's different now – she's a star and he's a middle-aged clod with a wife and four children and anyway she's in love with Adam – no, it's out of the question. (*He reflects.*) We should have sent a telegram.

Turai (*nodding gravely*) Never surprise a woman. They love surprises so long as they've been warned.

Gal Look, I'm sure this isn't necessary but why don't I keep Adam busy until Natasha is safely back in her room? Then let us know the good news and we'll all surprise her. We must have a happy composer to compose and a happy actress to sing and then we'll have a happy ending when we have an ending.

Dvornichek enters with a cognac and boiled potato on a tray.

Dvornichek Here we are, sir, one cognac and a little something.

Gal What's this?

Dvornichek A boiled potato, sir.

Gal (*taking it and leaving*) Thank you, Murphy.

Turai What kept you?

Dvornichek You wouldn't believe it. I went up the wrong staircase and found myself on the roof.

Turai (*irritated*) The top deck.

Dvornichek And then I nearly fell down the trap door –

Turai (*exasperated*) Down the hatch, Murphy!

Dvornichek Down the hatch, sir! (*He knocks back the brandy in one.*) – and tripped over a rope strung between bollocks.

Turai Look, would you please try to learn the proper names of things –

Dvornichek Yes, sir. Will there be anything else, sir?

Turai (*faintly*) Perhaps a cognac.

Dvornichek No problem, sir. (*solicitously and innocently*) Is everything all right, sir?

Turai No. Everything –

> At that moment he hears Natasha's voice singing from within her cabin.

Turai Yes! Yes, everything is fine, Murphy. Go and fetch – no, I'll go and fetch them. Get a bottle of champagne. Perrier. Jouet '21.

Dvornichek Yes, sir.

Turai And four glasses.

Dvornichek No problem.

> Turai hurriedly follows Dvornichek out through the cabin. Natasha's voice still continues singing and she emerges on to her veranda, singing to herself.

Natasha (*sings*)
> This could be the time.
> Never been so fancy free
> Till I kissed you
> And you kissed me.
> Isn't it sublime?
> This could be the time.
> When I saw you
> My knees went weak
> My throat went dry.
> I could hardly speak.

Ivor Fish in evening dress and holding a bottle of champagne and two glasses appears in the doorway and joins her on deck.

Ivor Do you have to sing that song?

Natasha (*sings*)
> Isn't it heavenly?

I'm singing it because I like singing it, and because he wrote it for me to sing . . .

> (*Sings*) Turtle doves sang two for tea
> Yes, it's true, when I kissed you
> Wedding bells rang tea for two

. . . and if it bothers you, you have your own cabin.

> (*Sings*) La la la la la la.

In fact I don't know why you're not in it. I never invited you into mine.

Ivor Natasha, Natasha, how can you forget?!

Natasha I haven't forgotten – you barged in and started opening my champagne.

Ivor I *sent* you the champagne.

Natasha That's why it's mine.

Ivor How can you speak to me like that? I was the love of your life!

Natasha That was another life. Now please go to bed, Ivor – it's very thoughtless of you to risk compromising me like this.

Ivor I? I compromising you? I who discovered you? Is this the thanks I get? I who picked you for my pillion!

Natasha (*primly*) I've already thanked you for that.

Ivor I who climbed up to your balcony!

Natasha (*coldly*) Only for three weeks.

Ivor And what about this afternoon in that very cabin?

Natasha It's very bad form to dig up the past like this.

Ivor Natasha!

Natasha I weakened for a moment when you said you'd kill yourself.

Ivor You weakened for twenty-five minutes.

Natasha You said you'd exterminate your entire family. If you had any soul you would have understood that this afternoon was my farewell to that part of my life. I'm going to be a different woman from now on. My Adam will be here in the morning. He calls me his madonna. So there'll be no more of *that*.

Ivor You don't love me?

Natasha No.

Ivor I'll kill myself.

Natasha Now, now.

Ivor I'll kill my wife and children and then myself.

Natasha It's no good, I'm not in the mood. Anyway, your wife is much more likely to kill *you* if she finds out what you're up to. You remember your wife? Piranha?

Ivor Paloma. But she'd still kill me. (*heroically*) I'm willing to take the risk – do you want a man or a boy?

Natasha A boy.

Ivor I'll kill him!

Natasha That would not be very sensible. If I know Gal and Turai those three will show up in the morning with half the second act still to come.

Ivor (*unheroically*) Oh, how can you treat me like this when I love you so dreadfully.

Natasha Now don't be such a baby. I can't bear you to cry. Come on, you must go to bed.

Ivor All right, I'll go. Only let me wait till you're ready for bed so I can kiss you goodnight and then I swear I'll leave you.

Natasha All right. But you wait out here while I change, and no peeking.

Ivor Oh, thank you, thank you, every moment is precious.

Natasha I'll only be a minute.

Natasha disappears inside continuing to sing to herself. Ivor stands looking moodily at the sea.
    Below, Turai, Gal and Adam creep back into view and on to their deck. Gal carries sheet music and is eating a chicken leg. Adam is carrying a banjo. Turai takes charge in mime, getting the group into serenading position. Irritably he dispossesses Gal of his snack. He examines the manuscript score closely.

When he is satisfied and everything is ready, he takes up the stance of a conductor. Above, Natasha reappears having changed into a very beautiful but high-collared négligée. She pauses in the doorway as Turai's hand is about to descend.

Natasha There! I'm ready!

Ivor My darling!

The three troubadours freeze.

Natasha Now you may kiss me.

Ivor My angel!

The troubadours turn.

Natasha Now, you promised not to get carried away.

Ivor I can't help it.

Natasha You're not going to begin again!

Ivor Yes, again!

The troubadours recoil in silent confusion.

And again! And again!

Turai (*urbanely to Adam*) This doesn't necessarily mean –

Ivor I love you, I adore you, I worship you!

Gal (*thoughtfully*) He's always been a tremendous fan of hers.

Ivor I worship you as the moth worships the candle flame!

Turai gives a professional wince.

I love you as the Eiffel Tower loves the little fleecy cloud that dances around it in the summer breeze.

Adam sits down.

Natasha You'll soon forget me!

Ivor No, no, I'm mad about you. But you've plucked out my heart like the olive out of a dry Martini and dashed me from your lips!

Despite everything, Gal and Turai turn to each other in wonder.

Natasha Don't spoil everything we've had together.

Adam breaks a banjo string.

Give me your hands – I will remember your hands, such clever, wicked hands, too, when I think of what they have done.

Adam breaks two more banjo strings.

Please be a good boy – remember this afternoon.

Adam stands up.

Here, let me kiss you.

Ivor That's not a kiss. That's a tip!

Natasha Keep your voice down.

Ivor I don't care. Let the whole world know that I mean nothing to you. I'm a dashed Martini!

Turai (*quietly to Adam*) Come on –

Natasha That's not true – you will always be the first. I was a girl and you made me a woman. If I had *ten* husbands no one can take your place.

Adam takes the score from Turai and rips it once across, and throws it down.

But I'm engaged to be married so please be kind and leave me now.

Adam makes to leave but is given further pause by the next lines.

Ivor All right, I will. Only let me see you as I want to remember you. Lift your hair. Let me move your collar just a little.

Natasha Oh, you're impossible. What are you doing?

Ivor One last look, one touch, I beg you! Oh, that pink rounded perfection! Let me put my lips to its rosy smoothness.

Gal Her shoulder.

Ivor And the other one!

Gal Her other shoulder.

Ivor How beautifully they hang there!

Gal We should have sent a telegram.

Natasha Now stop it –

Gal I will throw myself overboard.

Adam leaves.

Turai (*to Gal*) Go with him.

Gal leaves.

Ivor Oh, forgive me.

Natasha I'll forgive you, you donkey, if only you'd go.

Ivor I'm going now. Goodbye, Natasha, goodbye forever.

Natasha See you after breakfast. I'm going to be up early to meet Adam. And those two old rogues.

Turai looks pained.

I do hope they've looked after my poor boy.

Turai looks even more pained.

Ivor One more kiss!

Turai almost loses patience.

Natasha Good night, Ivor. There. . . good night . . .

Ivor Good night. (*He leaves.*)

Natasha (*sings*)
This could be heavenly
This could be the one.

Natasha returns to her cabin.

Turai At last.

Turai collapses into a chair or against the rail. Natasha sings quietly for a few moments and then the soft light inside is extinguished. Turai picks up the torn score. Gal returns, eating.

Gal All quiet?

Turai nods.

Interesting silence?

Turai shakes his head.

Turai He's gone. (*bitterly*) Eiffel Tower . . . How's Adam?

Gal He's fine. The banjo isn't so well.

Turai Did he say anything?

Gal He was trying.

Turai Nodding his head, or shaking it?

Gal Banging it against the wall.

Turai Will you explain to me about you and food?

Gal No.

Turai I only eat once a day.

Gal That's going to be a very convenient habit from now on.

Turai It's the poor boy I'm worried about.

Gal You don't have to worry about him – young people can always get their hands on a sandwich.

Turai Look – we're being much too pessimistic. Natasha is a trouper and Adam will realize that his music means more to him than any woman.

Gal Meanwhile he's torn up the rest of the score.

Turai A gesture. Whish! – once across and tomorrow the glue. No?

Gal It looks like a honeymoon suite in there. Without of course, the bride. (*venomously*) Fleecy little cloud . . . she shouldn't be let out without a general alert. And as for that damned Martini . . .

Turai Dashed.

Gal *Dashed* Martini – Well, he certainly solved the problem of the ending: we won't be needing one.

Turai (*thoughtfully*) Yes . . . yes . . .

Gal I'll cable New York. 'Disembarked. Don't worry.'

Turai Wait! I've got the strangest feeling . . . that everything is going to be all right.

Gal I think you need to eat something.

Turai Sssh! . . . (*He freezes with intense concentration.*) We will have our première!

Gal With Adam's music?

Turai With Adam's music, with Natasha, with an Irish policeman if you like! I feel it. I see light . . . a vision I can't quite make it out but the edges are incandescent with promise! I see success – happiness – a wedding . . .

Gal Low blood sugar.

Turai (*excitedly*) Stay with the boy! All night! Don't leave his side. Give him a sleeping pill.

Gal I haven't got one.

Turai Don't be obtuse! Make him drunk! I want him asleep for eight hours at last. Tomorrow is going to be a day to test our mettle!

Gal (*getting up*) Whatever you say. Make him drunk.

He goes towards the door and meets Dvornichek coming in with the champagne and the four glasses.

Dvornichek Here we are, sir! Champagne!

Turai Excellent!

Gal Perfect! (*He takes the champagne and two of the glasses and departs. Leaving*) Good night, Turai!

Turai He took the champagne.

Dvornichek Sorry I was so long. I've been all over. You wouldn't believe the cellar in this place – the *noise* – the *filth* –

Turai (*angrily*) That's the engine room!

Dvornichek (*agreeing*) You don't have to tell me!

Turai Well, what were you doing there?

Dvornichek A misunderstanding. American couple in E5, asked for two screwdrivers. First off, I can't find the doorman. So I get on the house phone for what I thought was the *bell* captain. 'Are you the captain?' I say. 'I am,' he says. 'Would you know where to put your hands on a couple of screwdrivers?' I say. Then the conversation deteriorates.

Turai Look, I've been trying to get a drink since I came on board.

Dvornichek May I fetch you something, sir?

Turai Perhaps a cognac.

Dvornichek Very good, sir.

Turai By the way . . .

Dvornichek Yes, sir?

Turai Bring the bottle.

Dvornichek No problem.

> *Dvornichek leaves. Turai whips out a gold pencil and starts scribbling in a notebook. He paces up and down in deep thought, occasionally making a note. Dvornichek returns with a bottle of brandy and a glass on his tray.*

Shall I pour you one, sir?

Turai (*impatiently*) Yes, yes. Be quiet.

> *He continues making notes while Dvornichek opens the bottle and pours a glass of brandy. This empties the bottle. Turai is suddenly satisfied. He relaxes. He accepts the glass from Dvornichek, sniffs it and holds it up to the light. As he is about to drink –*

Dvornichek Will you be requiring early morning tea, sir?

Turai Yes.

Dvornichek What time?

Turai What time is it now?

Dvornichek Coming up to one o'clock.

Turai I'll have it at half-past one, three o'clock, four-thirty and six.

Dvornichek With milk or lemon?

Turai With cognac. Breakfast at seven.

Dvornichek Yes, sir.

Turai raises his glass again, but –

Dvornichek Tea or coffee?

Turai Black coffee. Half a grapefruit. Perhaps a little ham . . .

Dvornichek takes out a notebook and attempts to write down the order.

Sausage, scrambled eggs, kidneys, a potato or two . . . some cold cuts – chicken, beef, tongue, salami – oh, some kind of smoked fish, I'm not fussy – cheese, white rolls, brown toast, a couple of croissants . . .

Dvornichek is still trying to organize himself to write down the first item. Turai impatiently puts down his glass and snatches Dvornichek's notebook and continues, scribbling in the notebook.

Butter, strawberry jam, honey, pancakes and some stewed fruit.

Turai hands back the notebook. Dvornichek picks up the silver salver on which Turai has replaced his untouched drink.

Dvornichek Cream?

Turai (*sharply*) No. (*then relenting*) Well, a little. I only eat once a day. Do you know what is the most important thing in life?

Dvornichek Yes, sir.

Turai Good health.

Dvornichek Thank you, sir. Good health! (*He drains Turai's glass.*) Tea in half an hour. I'll make it myself.

Turai Thank you, er . . .

Dvornichek Murphy.

Turai Thank you, Murphy.

Dvornichek Thank you, sir.

> *Dvornichek leaves.*
> *Transition into interior of Turai's cabin. A silver tea service, cup and saucer, without any tray, are on the writing desk. Turai's impressive breakfast has arrived on a trolley and Dvornichek is laying out a breakfast table. Turai can be heard singing cheerfully offstage. Turai enters looking rejuvenated, showered, shaved, well scrubbed and in elegant yachting clothes. Dvornichek, laying out the breakfast, greets him cheerfully.*

Dvornichek Ahoy there! Seven bells and all's well! The sun's over the yardarm and there's a force three east-sou'-easterly with good visibility. Where do you want the vittles?

Turai Who are you?

Dvornichek Murphy, sir.

Turai I see you've picked up the lingo.

Dvornichek Speak it like a native, sir. Had to put in a

bit of spurt. They're getting suspicious about me being on the *Mauretania*.

Turai Really? What happened?

Dvornichek It's that captain again. Half-past five he phones down for a cup of Ovaltine and a chocolate biscuit. 'Where are you?' I say. 'On the bloody bridge, where do you think I am?' he says. 'Jump to it.' So I jump to it, and I'm looking both ways along the veranda but none of the bridges are out and by the time I find him pacing up and down the front balcony he's absolutely demented, threatened to have me ironed in the clappers. How was your night?

Turai Quite successful, thank you. (*He is lifting various silver domes on the table.*) I can't see the smoked fish.

Dvornichek Starboard of the coffee pot.

Turai Oh, yes.

> *Turai sits down and Dvornichek pours coffee. From now on he starts tucking into his breakfast. Dvornichek goes to clear up the teapot, etc.*

Dvornichek What happened to the tray?

Turai Never mind that. Would you lift up that telephone and speak to Miss Navratilova and then Mr Fish. Present my compliments, apologise for the hour and ask them to join me.

Dvornichek Aye, aye, sir. (*He lifts the phone. Into phone, conversationally*) Ahoy there. Please connect me with Miss Navratilova.

Turai And then see that we are not disturbed.

Dvornichek Not even by Mr Gal and Mr Adam?

Turai Especially not by them.

Dvornichek Aye aye sir. (*into phone*) Yes, miss. It's Dvornichek. Yes, miss, I'm speaking from Mr Turai's cabin. Yes, he's here and he presents his comp – (*She has hung up. He replaces the telephone.*) I think she's coming. (*He lifts the telephone again. Into phone*) Ahoy again. Connect me with Mr Fish in D4 please.

Turai You don't have to keep saying ahoy.

Dvornichek Aye, aye, sir. (*into phone*) Yes, he's rather hard to wake . . . no problem, I'll go and bang on his door. Bon voyage. (*He puts the phone down.*) Will that be all, sir?

Turai No. (*He hands Dvornichek a slip of paper.*) I want you to send this telegram for me. It's to go to Mr Adam Adam, c/o the *SS Italian Castle* en route to New York.

Dvornichek Fast rate or overnight?

Turai Fast rate. In fact he'll be joining me in here within half an hour: I want you to deliver it as soon as I ring that bell.

Dvornichek No problem.

Turai Are you sure?

Dvornichek Am I sure what?

Turai Nothing. The telegraph office, you'll recall, is on the starboard side.

Dvornichek Right.

Turai Up by the chimneys.

Dvornichek We don't call them the chimneys, sir. We call them the smokesticks.

Turai That will do.

Dvornichek Yes, sir.

Dvornichek goes to the door and meets Natasha coming in.

Good morning!

Natasha Hello, Dvornie.

She sees Turai. Dvornichek leaves, closing the door.

Sandor! Darling! How wonderful! Are you all here? Alex? And my Adam?

Turai All aboard.

Natasha You early birds! It must have been dawn.

Turai No, it was while you were having dinner.

Natasha What? – you've been there all night? For God's sake, why didn't you tell me? I would have ordered champagne! You idiot! I was up till midnight and my cabin is *literally* up *above*. You'd only have had to raise your voi-oi-oi-oi – No.

Turai Yes.

Natasha Oh no.

Turai Oh yes.

Natasha But only you.

Turai No.

Natasha You and Alex?

Turai No.

Natasha (*under sentence of death*) Adam?

Turai Every word.

He is placidly eating breakfast. She lunges at the table and grabs a knife.

(*Calmly*) That won't do any good.

Natasha You don't know me, Sandor! I have Romany blood in my veins.

Turai I mean it's a fish knife.

She throws the knife down and collapses into a chair, sobbing.

Natasha Where's Adam?

Turai Asleep, I trust. I made Gal stay with him.

Natasha He called me his madonna. Oh, Sandor, you're the only one who knows how I loved him.

Turai No, as I say, it was all three of us.

Natasha Don't be cruel! I'm the victim of my own generosity. Ivor is so pathetic – he keeps bursting into tears telling me to remember the old days on the pillion. (*viciously*) It was all that shaking up and down on the pillion which got me into this! I swear to you it's over – last night was the last flicker of the candle flame.

There is an angry knocking on the door.

Turai Here comes the moth.

The door opens and Ivor comes in wearing pyjamas and dressing-gown.

Turai Good morning, Ivor.

Ivor What the devil is going on – I was asleep. (*Then he sees Natasha.*) Oh – good morning, my dear.

Turai I'm sorry to wake you.

Ivor Actually I didn't close my eyes till dawn . . . tossing, turning, pacing the floor –

Natasha Oh, shut up.

Ivor Is everything all right?

Natasha No.

Turai Sit down. Our little show is in trouble.

Ivor You haven't done the ending. Honestly, Turai, one likes to give you writer johnnies a bit of leeway but –

Turai (*thunders*) Silence! (*He points witheringly at Ivor.*) Eiffel Tower! Dashed Martini!

Ivor When did you get here?

Turai Last night while you were having dinner, we got aboard, unpacked a few things and sat on the sundeck in the moonlight to wait for you.

> *Ivor goes out and inspects the geography of the adjacent sundecks. He comes back.*

Ivor You and Gal.

> *Natasha starts to weep again.*

And Adam. I'm a dead man if this gets out.

Turai Yes, how is Mrs Fish?

Ivor (*in panic*) He wouldn't tell her? What did he say?

Turai He said he was going to cut your part to ribbons and post it to her.

Ivor (*aghast but also surprised*) He said that?

Turai He was trying to.

Natasha Poor love, poor handicapped little love! See what you've done, you selfish monster – ruined his life, and mine! Oh, to die – to die!

Ivor (*heroically*) Together! Like Romeo and Juliet! (*He snatches up a piece of cutlery.*)

Turai That's a spoon.

Natasha (*to Turai*) How much did he hear? When I think of those silly things one says . . . Was it from the moment we got back until Ivor left?

Turai Not quite. Roughly from Eiffel Tower to pink rounded perfection.

Natasha (*cries out*) He knows about that one?

Turai And the other one. The question is, how can we repair the harm. I mean to the boy. My only thought is for the boy.

Natasha So young, so brilliant . . . so damaged!

Ivor If only it had been his *ears*.

Natasha Shut up, you brute!

Turai Yes, do be quiet, Ivor. I'm trying to get you both out of this mess.

Natasha There's no way.

Turai There is. I am about to pull the rabbit out of the hat.

Natasha You have a rabbit?

Turai I have.

Natasha Sandor, I'll be your slave for life, I'll put myself under contract – I'll – (*Caution intercedes.*) What is it?

Turai What you were doing in your cabin last night was learning your parts? Do you understand?

Natasha Yes! No.

Turai Your conversation, which we partly overheard, was not a conversation, it was a rehearsal.

Natasha (*awestruck*) That's *brilliant*! (*and immediately irritated*) That's *stupid* – where on earth are we ever going to find a play with lines like that in it?

Turai (*indicating the desk*) Over there.

Natasha goes to the desk.

Natasha Here?

Turai You hold it in your hands.

Natasha (*understanding*) Of course . . .! Sandor . . .

Ivor You found one?

Natasha Be quiet, Ivor. Sandor, how do you do it?

Turai Either one is a playwright or one is not.

Ivor You wrote it?

Turai I did. And never was anything written with truer purpose. Never! We each fight life's battle with the weapons God gave us. Mine is theatre. Alas. But today I feel like a Greek athlete at the Battle of Marathon. Yes, he thinks, yes, for once there seems to be something *to* this javeline business.

Natasha is looking through Turai's manuscript pages.

Natasha 'I love you as the Eiffel Tower loves the little fleecy cloud that dances –'

Ivor snatches the page from her. She reads from the next page.

Natasha 'You have plucked out my heart like the olive out of a dry Martini –'

Turai It reads better than it plays. But you've played it once so you can play it again.

Natasha What do you mean? Do we have to *do* it?

231

Turai Of course. Who will believe you otherwise? Rehearsal this afternoon, two o'clock sharp in the Pisa Room. Adam will be there so make sure you've learned it.

Ivor I can't learn all this in a morning.

Turai Why not? You knew it well enough last night.

Natasha I never said, 'No one can take your place.'

Turai Yes, you did.

Natasha Well, I didn't mean it.

Ivor You didn't?

Natasha Of course I didn't. A *budgerigar* could take your place!

Ivor You bitch!

Natasha I hate you!

Turai It's too late now – last night was the time for that. Off you go. There's a copy for each of you.

Ivor Excuse me – why are we rehearsing this new piece when we're supposed to be in the middle of rehearsals for *The Cruise of the Dodo*?

Natasha (*to Ivor*) Oh, don't be so – (*to Turai*) Why *are* we rehearsing this new piece?

Turai It's not a new piece, it's the new ending.

Natasha That's brilliant. That's stupid! We can't go on stage and say these stupid things! We'd be a laughing stock! 'I worship you as the moth worships the candle flame'!

Ivor (*hurt*) What's wrong with that?

Natasha (*to Turai*) And just to put your rabbit out of its misery, may I ask why we're rehearsing in my cabin at midnight?

232

Turai Quite simple. Gal and I were due to arrive in the morning. It was your last chance to polish up your surprise for us.

Ivor What surprise?

Turai Your new ending.

Ivor Mine?!

Turai Well, of course. Who's going to believe that I wrote that bilge? And anyway, I couldn't have written it because I would have recognized it. No, what happened was that you two knew damned well that Gal and I would get nowhere in Deauville so you thought you'd have a crack at it yourself.

Natasha I can't write.

Ivor I can't write.

Turai (*sadly*) I know. He has a certain gift for construction.

Ivor Oh, do I?

Turai He tells the story, but he doesn't understand character. (*squeezing Ivor's shoulder*) Touched, all the same, I'll let you down gently, count on me. The new scene takes off from the line, 'Mother is coming up for sale this afternoon.'

Natasha and Ivor 'Mother is coming up for sale this afternoon.'

Turai We will rehearse the old ending and when we all agree that it needs something, Ivor will say, 'Actually, Turai, while you were in Deauville I put pen to paper and Natasha and I have worked up a little scene which you may care to have a look at,' and I will say, 'My dear Ivor, I'm touched beyond measure, do let's see what you've been up to,' and then off you go from 'Mother is coming up for sale,' and Bob's your uncle, I don't see how anything can go wrong. Meanwhile you have a busy morning, so back to your cabins.

Ivor sighs.

Turai Don't sigh like that.

Ivor It was a sigh of relief. Paloma, you know.

Turai Don't worry about her. She has other fish to fry. Now, don't forget when next we meet you haven't seen me for a week.

Ivor Until two o'clock then. (*He leaves.*)

Natasha Sandor, you've done it. Did Gal help?

Turai No. He knows nothing. I thought after twenty years of marriage I'd treat myself to a night out. Until two o'clock, and don't forget you're my slave for life.

Natasha (*kissing him*) The things one says when one's back is to the rail.

Natasha leaves. Turai goes to the telephone and lifts the receiver.

Turai (*into phone*) Good morning. This is Sandor Turai. Would you please connect me with Mr Gal?
Oh really?
How kind of you to say so.
Well, it's just a gift, really.
Sometimes the words before the music, sometimes the music before the words.
I don't really have a favourite.
Actually, that was written by two other people.
It's perfectly all right.
Oh, have you?
Well, unfortunately I haven't got much time to read nowadays. Mr Gal would love to read it. Why don't

I ask him? Yes, why don't you, he is in Cabin B2 at the moment.

Thank you so much.

Pause.

Gal, are you awake?

Don't be a pedant.

Well, I'm sorry.

Half-past seven or so. Is Adam awake?

What do you mean?

Well, where is he?

You incompetent! – I said get *him* drunk!

Well, you'd better go out and find him! I don't know – look in the water. Do I have to do everything for you? I already do the plot, the characterization, the better jokes and binding contracts – if anything's happened to the boy I'll get someone else to do the cables!

There's a knock at the door.

Come in. (*continuing*) Don't you practise your economy of empression on *me* you drunken –

He sees that it is Adam who has entered.

My dear boy! Come in –

(*Into phone*) Adam has just come in. (*to Adam*) Would you like some breakfast – coffee? (*into phone*) So glad you had a good night's rest, dear chap, why don't you get up now and join us. The sun's over the yardarm and it's a beautiful day with fresh north-south-easterly breeze with good visibility.

He sees that Gal has entered.

Hello, Gal, come in –

He does a double-take at the telephone in his hand and puts it down. Gal is wearing last night's clothing and looking worse for wear. Adam is wearing what is clearly a disembarkation outfit – including hat and topcoat. He does not have his luggage with him but is carrying, perhaps, an attaché case, which Gal and Turai affect not to notice. Adam offers his hand to Gal in farewell. Gal shakes it casually.

Gal Good morning, Adam.

Adam . . .

Adam offers his hand to Turai, who shakes it vigorously.

Turai (*cheerfully*) Good morning! You're looking wonderfully refreshed. Been for a walk? Not much of a town, is it?

Adam . . .

Gal Had breakfast? I hardly bother with it myself.

Adam . . .

Turai Don't try to talk. Have some coffee.

Adam . . .

Turai I know, I know. But we can ring for a cup. (*He goes to a bell push and presses it long and firmly.*) I know what you're going to say. You've woken up a new man. You laugh at love like this – ha! ha! You snap your fingers at it like *that* (*Snap!*) – you are free of the tyrannies of the heart. Nothing else matters to you but to hear your music played. You are an artist. For you there are no more women, only Woman, the female spirit that remains constant while the Natashas and the Marias and the Zsa Zsas come and go, each seeming for a moment to embody the idea, each giving way to the next, illusory, inconstant, all too human, unequal to the artist's measure, unworthy of his lute.

Gal That gives you an idea of the sort of plays he'd be writing if he didn't have me to stop him. (*He has been picking at the ample leftovers of Turai's breakfast.*)

Turai Would you be good enough to order your own breakfast?

Gal It's as much as I can do to pick at something to keep my strength up.

Adam (*finally*) Goodbye! (*Pause.*) I'm sorry.

Turai Adam, I'm astonished. And yet, I understand. First love. The pain of it all. But take the advice of an older man.

Gal Try the kippers.

Turai Wait!

Gal Wait till you've tried the kippers.

Turai Wait! – because while you wait, fate's caravan moves on. Do nothing! Say nothing! Wait!

Gal It's no good. I can't swallow. My throat is constricted.

Turai Yes, I know. You want to kill yourself. Or her. Or Ivor. I understand, especially in the case of Ivor. But stay your hand – for an hour – two hours – where the hell is that steward? (*He presses the bell yet more firmly.*)

Adam My luggage is at the top of the gangway and when the boat sails in ten minutes it will sail without me for my muse is dead and as for me I will never write music again!

Gal My dear boy, you're talking nonsense. I know about writer's block. What you need is a cooked breakfast.

Turai Adam, sit down and keep calm!

Adam How can you speak of breakfast when it's the end of everything and my music is a thousand scraps of paper floating away on the tide, I thought you were my friends –

Gal We are, we really are – is there any cream?

Turai No!

Gal No *cream*?

Turai No! – Let the boy be. Adam, I'm sorry. I have no right. You must do as you wish. Your life is your own. If you must go, then go you must, and God be with you. And, by the way, there is something I would like you to have, a negligible piece of the Turai family silver which I was going to give you on the occasion of your American début – please, no argument – let it be a memento of happy days spent together in the vineyard of musical comedy. The fruit stayed on the vine but there will be other seasons, and ripeness is all.

> *Turai has detached himself to produce a flat parcel wrapped in tissue paper from which flutters a white envelope containing as it happens a white card. Turai presents the parcel with great dignity. Adam seems moved. Adam takes off the envelope and removes the card and reads it silently. He is even more moved. He embraces Turai and kisses him on both cheeks. Adam places the card on the table and begins to unwrap the parcel. Gal picks up the card and reads from it.*

Gal 'Homard, maestro.' Is it a lobster?

Turai (*taking the card from Gal*) Homage, maestro . . . all for one and one for all . . .

> *Adam has now revealed a silver tray.*

I hope you like it – made of silver washed from the upper Danube, one of the last pieces – the family silver is sadly depleted and dispersed. You see it's engraved with the Turai motto, *Festina lente*. Every lent a festival. That's us Turais I'm afraid! – irrepressible! Gal, press the bell, we must drink Adam's health before he goes.

Adam Wait! I cannot leave you like this . . .

Turai (*relieved*) My dear boy . . .

Adam (*changes his mind*) But I must. Goodbye.

Dvornichek enters with a telegram envelope borne ceremoniously on a silver tray.

Dvornichek Your telegram.

Turai Ah! Just in time.

Dvornichek It's for Mr Adam.

Turai So it is. Gal – a telegram for Adam. (*to Dvornichek*) You call this fast rate?

Dvornichek This boat was designed by a lunatic. When you're coming from the front starboard's on the left.

Adam is evidently taken aback by the telegram. He looks at the envelope carefully. Meanwhile Gal is studying Adam's tray.

Gal 'Festina lente.'

Dvornichek 'Make haste slowly.'

Turai Thank you, Murphy.

Dvornichek No problem.

Gal 'Festina lente C.L.' What's the C.L.?

Turai That's the date.

Gal One hundred and fifty. That's early.

Turai I mean the weight.

Dvornichek Castle Line.

Turai That will be all, Murphy. Champagne and four glasses.

Dvornichek (*leaving*) Four? You're too kind.

As Dvornichek closes the door behind him, Adam, who has opened the telegram and read it and gone into a freeze, starts to have a minor convulsion.

Gal Adam, what is it?

Turai Not bad news, I hope?

Adam collapses into a chair, letting the telegram fall to the floor. Gal picks it up and reads it.

Gal (*reads*) 'Arriving Cherbourg – disembark and embrace your ever devoted mother.'

Turai It seems your mother has tracked you down.

Adam stands, takes off coat.

Changed your mind? (*to Gal*) Telephone Natasha's cabin. Explain that we have arrived on board and ask her to join us. (*to Adam*) Sit down, Adam.

Gal (*into phone*) Good morning.

Turai Now listen.

Gal (*into phone*) This is Alex Gal. Would you connect me with –

Turai You can remain on one condition.

Gal (*into phone*) Oh really? How kind of you to say so.

Turai You must behave as though nothing has happened. Otherwise you might as well pack yourself off on the Paris train with your mother and leave us to start again with a new composer.

Gal (*into phone*) Mostly me. He works under my supervision.

Turai (*his attention caught*) Just a moment.

Gal (*into phone*) Oh, have you? All about a telephone operator, eh? What a good idea.

Turai (*resuming*) Because we have four and a half days. We can manage a musical comedy, but we can't afford a melodrama.

Gal (*into phone*) Well, unfortunately I haven't got time to read, but why don't I ask Miss Navratilova . . .

Turai In short, your score and your presence are worse than useless without your absolute discretion.

Gal (*into phone*) Natasha? It's Alex! I'm with Turai . . . yes and Adam of course. Come and – I think she's coming. (*He puts the phone down.*)

Turai So what is it going to be? On one side – courage, dignity, style and my respect. On the other side – mother.

Adam stands up. He screws up the telegram and then picks up the silver tray. He stands before Turai trying to speak.

Adam (*finally*) With this piece of silver you have made me of your family. I am a Turai and I will obey you.

Turai (*joyfully*) I knew you could do it! It will be as though last night never happened. In fact last night we were on shore. We arrived this morning with a precious gift, our new song for Natasha, and we shall present our gift when she enters and show her who can and who cannot be counted on when it comes to delivering the goods!

There is a knock at the door. Turai indicates that Adam should open it. Adam does so and Natasha steps into the cabin. Adam and Natasha look at each other for a moment and then kiss, a little warily despite the pretence which each has to maintain. Turai and Gal are poised to sing the song for Natasha. The three men start to do this, using cutlery to accompany themselves by setting up a percussion beat on the various pots and dishes and silver domes on Turai's breakfast table.

The song may be sung as a trio or distributed between the three men. The lines 'up and down' and 'round and round' may be given to Adam solo, in which case Adam's hesitation makes a momentary hiatus in the song.

After 'You have a volunteer' the ship's hooter sounds and Natasha says: 'You're here! And just in time!' (and she could plausibly join in on the last two lines).

'Where Do We Go From Here?'

We just said hello and how do you do,
And both of us know I'm leaving with you,
The signs are all too clear
But where do we go from here?

We'll sail through the night
And sleep through the day,
We're travelling light,
Let's go all the way.
It sounds a nice idea –
But where do we go from here?

242

This way, that way, up or down
We could go both ways.
Forward, backwards, round and round,
What do I care
So long as when we get together
And you're restless again
And closing your grip
And you need a friend
To help with the zip,
You have a volunteer
So where do we go –
When do we go –
Darling I'm so ready to go –
So why don't we go from here?

Act Two

A 'salon' aboard the Italian Castle *. . . this would be a moderately splendid public room available for private hire. There are entrances upstage Right and Left on a raised section, and the body of the room is approached down a short Central staircase, perhaps only a few steps. The space has been fairly cleared.*

One table, however, is preserved to accommodate a fairly elaborate buffet.

The salon contains a telephone.

There is also a baby grand piano. Adam is at the piano. Gal is at the buffet.

We are in mid rehearsal. Natasha and Ivor are singing a duet. They are not 'in costume'. After the first verse they go straight into the dialogue of the rehearsal.

Turai, who is nominally in charge, divides his time between watching placidly from one side and reading a newspaper.

'This Could Be The One'

Natasha and Ivor
This could be the one,
Never knew the sky so blue
Till you kissed me and I kissed you.
When all's said and done,
This could be the one.

Natasha Justin, I've been looking everywhere for you.

Ivor Have you?

Natasha Oh, Justin! I need your help. Actually it's mother.

Ivor Have you thought of asking Reggie Robinsod?

Natasha Reggie Robinsod? Why do you say that?

Ivor (*lapsing*) It's the way it's typed. (*Pause.*) Oh, right. (*resuming*) Have you thought of asking Reggie Robinsod?

Natasha It's Reggie who's the cause of the trouble. He has telegraphed the Italian police to arrest Mother as soon as the Dodo reaches Naples!

Ivor I'm sorry to say this, Ilona, but your mother's arrest is long overdue. I don't know why she is still at large.

Natasha Justin!

Ivor Your mother gives a chap pause, Ilona. As a matter of fact, your mother would give anybody pause, even two or three chaps working as a team. Pause, if we're going to be open about this, is what your mother would give Mussolini . . . so don't worry your pretty little head about the Italian police, and tell your mother not to worry her pretty enormous one either.

Natasha Justin!

Ivor It was the sight of your mother, Ilona, which made me hesitate to propose to you until fully three hours after I saw you standing here at this rail when I came aboard at Monte Carlo. I noticed her on deck when I was halfway up the gangplank. 'That's jolly nice!' I said to myself, taking her to be a small bandstand, and then I heard you say 'Good morning, Mother' and the words, 'Will you marry me whoever you are' froze upon my lips.

Natasha Justin! (*to Turai*) Look, is that all I get to say? He's walking all over my mother with his smart remarks and all I do is bleat 'Justin'.

Turai Well we can stop to criticize my work or we can get on to more important matters.

Natasha (*getting the point immediately*) Justin!

Ivor I feel I can speak freely about your mother now, now that you have evidently broken off our secret engagement.

Natasha Justin! (*to Turai*) Good.

Ivor I must have been blind! Last night when you kissed me on the stern (*lapsing*) . . . Do you think that might be misunderstood? I'll make it the poop, shall I? (*resuming*) Last night when you kissed me on the poop . . . (*lapsing*) well, how about the sundeck!

Gal In the moonlight.

Ivor Last night when you kissed me on the sundeck in the moonlight –

Gal Forget the sundeck.

Ivor Last night when you kissed me in the moonlight it was Reggie Robinsod who was in your thoughts.

Natasha Justin!

Gal Reggie.

Natasha Reggie! How could you think –?

Ivor How could I not? Ilona, last night when you kissed me I gave you a pledge of my love, a single emerald ear-ring which had once been worn by the Empress Josephine and has been in my mother's family since the day the Little Corporal tossed it from his carriage window to my maternal ancestor Brigadier Jean-Francois Perigord de St Emilion who had escorted him into exile. That jewel was our secret, but it has betrayed you. Here it is.

Natasha Where did you find that?

Ivor Where you left it – in Reggie's cabin!

Natasha Reggie!

Gal Justin.

Natasha Justin!

Ivor Yes. I looked in on him before breakfast to tell him I had booked the ping-pong table. He had already left. As I was closing the door something by his bed caught my eye. It was Empress Josephine's ear-ring. Say nothing, Ilona. There is nothing to be said. I know that Reggie Robinsod has money while I have nothing but the proud name of Deverell.

Natasha Not even that, Justin. Your name isn't Deverell and never has been.

Ivor Ilona!

Natasha It is Tomkins!

Ivor Ilona!

Natasha I wanted to give you the chance to tell me yourself. I would have forgiven you. Now it's too late.

Ivor But how –?

Natasha I thought I knew you the moment I caught sight of you coming up the gangplank. When I saw your forehand topspin it came back to me – Bobby Tomkins who won the ping-pong tournament at the Hotel des Bains on the Venice-Lido in '26. I confess I was a little in love with you even then.

Ivor Well! So neither of us is quite what we seem, Ilona. Perhaps we belong together after all.

Natasha There's one more thing I haven't told you.

Ivor What is that?

Natasha This! (*She sweeps back her lovely hair from one ear, dramatically.*)

Ivor (*gasps*) Josephine's other ear-ring!

Natasha Ear-rings come in pairs, after all, Justin.

Gal Bobby.

Natasha Bobby. Reggie Robinsod is the rightful owner of the emerald ear-rings. One of them disappeared years ago and ended up, God knows how, in the innocent possession of my mother, unregarded and unrecognized until last night when Reggie noticed it among her trinkets. He called my mother a thief and left to telegraph the Naples police, taking the emerald back to his cabin, where you found it! As for this one which you gave me, it was stolen recently from his suite in the Grand Hotel in Monte Carlo – wasn't it, Tomkins?

Ivor I cannot deny it.

Natasha (*passionately*) Oh, tell me it was just a moment of madness! You're not really a jewel thief.

Ivor I am. I have always been. I was the village jewel thief and I went on from there – regional – national – international! I've been stealing ear-rings, necklaces, bracelets and the occasional tiara all my adult life.

Natasha But why?

Ivor Who knows? Perhaps I was starved of affectation as a child. (*lapsing*) That's a typing error, is it? (*a hostile silence*) Oh I see. While we've stopped, how would some corporal get hold of the Empress Josephine's ear-rings? Does that seem odd to any body? (*Pause.*) Right. (*resuming*) I didn't go to Reggie's cabin to ask about ping-pong – I waited until he left and then went to steal whatever I could find. I might as well be frank.

Natasha Frank!

Gal Bobby.

Natasha Bobby! Oh what a fool you've been! You must have known something was up when you found the ear-ring in the cabin of the very man you stole it from!

Ivor The name Reggie Robinsod meant nothing to me. The hotel room which I burgled belonged to the shipping magnate Sir Reginald Sackville-Stew.

Natasha You mean Reggie Robinsod is Sir Reginald Sackville-Stew of the Sackville-Stew Line, owner of the Dodo?

Ivor (*lapsing*) They'll never follow this, you know. And we haven't even got to the complicated bit when it turns out that, after the child was stolen in Harrods while the Sackville-Stew nanny was buying sensible shoes, the first ear-ring was found in Ilona's potty.

Natasha What potty? The ear-ring was clutched in my little fist.

Ivor It was in your potty.

Natasha It's obscene, my script says fist.

Ivor All the others say potty.

Natasha (*leaving*) Right.

Gal Fist.

Natasha (*returning*) Thank you.

Ivor Well what are you going to do, Ilona?

Natasha I have no choice. My mother has been branded a common thief. I must clear her name and tell the Italian police everything I know, including, come to think of it, my suspicions concerning the several robberies at the

Hotel des Bains in Venice the year Bobby Tomkins won the ping-pong singles under his real name.

Ivor It wasn't actually. I've used many names.

Natasha Well, what is your name?

Ivor Gerald something. They'll have it at Haileybury if you really want to know. I still have the cups for cross-country and boxing somewhere. The police were called but they never suspected me. In fact I've never been caught for anything. I was always too careful . . . until I fell in love!

Adam, at the piano, picks up the tune again.

Natasha I wish I knew what to do, Justin!

Gal Gerald.

Natasha Gerald.

Ivor and Natasha go back into the song.

Ivor
When I saw you
My knees went weak
My throat went dry,
I could hardly speak,

Natasha
Isn't it heavenly.

Both
This could be the one
Glory be, when you kissed me
Turtle doves sang two for tea.

Ivor
Yes it's true,
When I kissed you,
Wedding bells rang tea for two.

Natasha
Want to jump the gun?
This could be heavenly
This could be . . .

Turai Now you kiss her! . . .

They kiss demurely. Somewhere round here, Dvornichek enters with a cognac on a tray, heading for Turai.

Turai You call that a kiss? Again!

They kiss again, a little less demurely.

No, no, as if you meant it!

Ivor and Natasha kiss more convincingly, and Adam bangs all the piano keys and leaps up . . . just as Dvornichek is carrying the cognac past him. Adam sweeps the cognac off the tray and downs it in one. Dvornichek, his attention distracted, innocently offers the empty tray to Turai.

Turai Don't worry, Adam, I quite understand – it must be agony for you. (*to Dvornichek*) Cognac.

Dvornichek (*leaving*) No problem.

Natasha (*nervously*) Sandor . . . darling, what can you mean?

Turai It's perfectly obvious what I mean. It is agony for an artist to discover that the fruits of his genius have been delivered into the hands of a couple of wholesale greengrocers. You are supposed to be in love with Justin Deverell, the international jewel thief who came on board at Monte Carlo. He kindled a little flame in your heart the moment you caught sight of him coming up the gangplank. The boat has now travelled south to warmer parts and so has the little flame, and you're kissing him as though he were about to turn into a frog.

251

Ivor Did you call me a greengrocer?

Turai I did. Why do you ask?

Gal I've known some very decent greengrocers. Of course I haven't heard them sing. Anybody care for a little chicken, ham, duck . . .?

Turai Are you still eating?

Gal Barely. My system rejects food, as you know. I have to employ subterfuge to get anything past my lips.

Turai You seem to be employing a firm of caterers. What is the meaning of this picnic? Are you expecting guests?

Natasha Darling Alex . . . I feel like a little duck . . .

Turai You sing like a little duck and (*to Ivor*) you act like an enormous ham.

Ivor I have never met anyone so rude.

Turai You have evidently never met an international jewel thief either. I see him as the sort of chap who travels and steals jewels. A bit of a Raffles if you like, and if you can manage it. Not, shall we say, the sort of chap who cuts a swathe through the lock-up garages of Canning Town.

Ivor Who the hell do you think you are to talk to me like that?

Turai (*surprised and cold*) I think I am your author, a simple teller of tales and setter of scenes . . . on whom your future hangs like a dead fish from a telegraph wire.

Natasha (*warningly*) Ivor . . .

Turai (*smiling at Ivor*) Shall we get on?

Ivor Yes . . . yes . . . let's get on, for heaven's sake.
I mean we're not getting into the part which . . . which
needs the work. (*to Natasha*) Are we?

Natasha He's quite right Sandor we really ought to
work on the Casablanca bit.

Turai Where would you like to go from?

Natasha and Ivor Mother is coming up for sale this
afternoon.

Turai Excellent choice. The cruise ship Dodo has arrived
at Casablanca –

Gal *Dido* for God's sake? You're not going to name a
boat after a typist's error.

Turai I certainly am. That woman was inspired.

Gal She wasn't inspired. She was Polish.

Turai The Dodo has reached –

Natasha You don't have to tell us the plot – we're in it,
aren't we, Ivor?

Ivor Absolutely.

Gal I can't follow it at all.

Ivor But you wrote it.

Gal That's what worries me.

Turai It's perfectly simple. Sir Reginald Sackville-Stew
who has joined the cruise under the name of Reggie
Robinsod –

Gal Are you going to call him Robinsod?

Turai Look, is there anything else which doesn't meet
with your approval?

Gal The mayonnaise isn't really up to snuff.

Turai I'm sorry about that.

Gal Worst things happen at sea.

Turai I'm trying to fix our bearings with a résumé of the plot.

Gal Do, do. I wish I could help.

Turai (*resuming*) Sir Reginald Sackville-Stew, for all his wealth and his famous jewel collection, has been denied happiness since his baby daughter was kidnapped from her pram some . . . (*He glances speculatively at Natasha.*) twenty-nine years ago.

Natasha Who is fighting me in this show? The police?

Turai There won't be any show if you don't keep quiet.

Natasha And where's my real mother, Lady Sackville-Stew?

Turai (*losing patience*) She died giving you a very wide birth! Leaving behind not only you and Sir Reginald but also the famous Sackville-Stew emerald ear-rings, the world's largest pair of matching emeralds, which Sir Reginald has made up into ear-clips as a parturition gift for his lovely wife.

Natasha Parturition gift. (*emotionally*) All my mother wanted was a decent obstetrician and you despatch her with a couple of clips on the ear!

Ivor I see! So in fact the old dragon who's got the other ear-ring isn't Ilona's mother at all . . . because Ilona is, of course, Sir Reginald's missing daughter!

Gal So that's it!

Ivor It's the way we keep calling mother mother. It's confusing.

Gal Turai – I think I see it. It will be like the Chorus in *Henry V.*

Natasha (*stunned*) There's a chorus in *Henry V?*

Gal (*ignoring her*) The curtain rises. The Dodo at sea. Sunny day, gentle swell. Passengers disport themselves on deck. Beach ball here, cocktails there. Half-a-dozen débutantes. A girl – shy, an unspoilt beauty, simply dressed, smiling at an elegant grey-haired man, immaculate white suit. Close by, her amusingly garish mother has paused to speak to a debonair young man in a rakish yachting cap with something mocking about his eyes . . . an Irish policeman appears on the poop . . .

Dvornichek appears at the top of the steps with another cognac.

Gal With one speech he puts us in the picture! It's Murphy.

Dvornichek Me?

Gal No, not you –

Dvornichek No problem. It's like this. Ilona has won the big prize in the raffle at the charity ball, i.e. two tickets for a round-the-world cruise, donated by the Sackville-Stew Line which owns the sister ships Dodo and Aeneas.

Gal (*to Turai*) Excuse me.

Turai There'll be a small change there, Murphy – the sister ships Dodo and Emu.

Dvornichek Much better. Well, then. Sir Reginald Sackville-Stew, spotting the lucky winner across the crowded ballroom, is immediately smitten with Ilona who reminds him a little of his late wife, for very good reason though he doesn't know that yet because Ilona already has a mother as far as she's aware, and being unmarried and a bit of a wallflower until Justin Deverell takes the pins out of her hair but that's getting ahead of the story, she naturally brings mother along on the second ticket, and Sir Reginald decides to join the cruise incognito . . . calling himself Reggie Robinsod, because he wants to be sure that if Ilona returns his feelings on some moonlit deck it won't be because he owns the *deck*, all clear so far? Of course, it's all going to come out with the ear-rings which Sir Reginald gave his wife – one of which went missing soon afterwards, about the same time as the Sackville-Stew baby was kidnapped, say no more for the moment, and the other of which was stolen quite recently by guess who, and given to Ilona during a duet on the poop deck; because when Reggie Robinsod recognizes the ear-ring, Justin realizes that Reggie must be Sackville-Stew, since that's who he's stolen it from, though in fact Reggie has recognized the matching one which has been in Mother's possession for all those years – which is why Mother realizes suddenly whose baby she'd stolen, everybody happy? Mind you, all this is just the sauce for the meat of the matter, which is that owing to the slump, Reg has leased out one of the sister ships to what he doesn't realize is a gang of white slave traders supplying girls to the North African market. Unfortunately, there has been a mix up in the paper work and the Emu is at this moment full of French tarts on a round-the-world cruise while the Dodo is tied up in Casablanca.

Gal Murphy . . . have a cognac.

Dvornichek Thank you sir. (*He drinks the cognac.*)

Turai Would it be all right if I had one too?

Dvornichek Certainly, sir.

Ivor (*stopping Dvornichek*) How did you know all that?

Dvornichek It's in the script.

Dvornichek leaves. Rather suddenly, the Italian Castle appears to have hit rough water. Dvornichek, who has been braced against the non-apparent swell, starts to find his feet as the others begin to lose theirs . . . this happens between the end of his long speech and his exit. The onset of the storm may be indicated by whatever means possible including the movement of furniture, and of the visible horizon if there is one.

Ivor It is?

Gal Of course it is . . . scattered about . . . most of it . . .

Natasha Adam, I know how you feel darling but don't lose heart, it will be all right on the night or even sooner. (*to Turai*) That's what rehearsals are for, aren't they, if we can just get on.

Turai Very well let's get on.

Gal Isn't it a little rough?

Turai Rough? It's simply under-rehearsed. Where were we?

Natasha Was it something about Mother being for sale?

Turai I believe it was. Naples has fallen below the horizon. Mother has eluded the Italian police only to come to grief in Casablanca where she is in the hands of the white slavers. Ilona finds Justin on deck.

Natasha Justin.

Ivor Oh Ilona.

Natasha Mother is coming up for sale.

But almost at once loud electric bells ring out. The rehearsal falters and simultaneously Dvornichek appears upstage and addresses everybody through a megaphone.

Dvornichek Everybody on deck! Go to your panic stations! No lifeboats! Sorry! – Go to your lifeboat stations – no panic!

Turai Stay where you are!

Dvornichek A to K, the starboard davits! – L to Z port beam amidships! – and don't crowd the fences!

Ivor Are we sinking?

Dvornichek I knew there was something! – get your life jackets! (*He rushes out.*)

Turai Did I tell you to dismiss! (*to Ivor*) Where do you think you're going?

Ivor I can't swim! (*He runs up the stairs and disappears.*)

Turai The utter selfishness of it! – The ingratitude! –

Natasha (*who has remained calm*) But Sandor, for all you know we *are* sinking.

Turai What if we are? – A boat this big can take hours to go down! Are you afraid of getting your feet wet?

Turai encounters Gal, who has gathered up a few necessary provisions from the buffet and is taking his leave.

Turai Et tu, Brute?

Gal Excuse me Turai, the life rafts may be overcrowded. I thought I'd book a table.

Adam has not moved from the piano.

Turai Like rats leaving a sinking ship. I shall complain to the captain. Where do I find him?

Gal Try the lifeboat.

This takes Turai and Gal out of sight.

Natasha Adam . . .? If you're staying I'm going to stay with you. You can't get along without me.

Adam plays his reply, 'I Get Along Without You Very Well'.

No, you don't.

Adam plays, 'I Want To Be Happy'.

And I can't be happy either till I've made you happy.

Adam plays, 'Goodbye'.

All right, I'll go.

Adam plays, 'Abide With Me'.

All right, I'll stay. I'll go down singing accompanied by Adam on the piano.

Natasha (*sings*)
    I'll never see eighteen again
    Or twenty-eight or nine
    I'll never be so green again
    To think that love's a valentine.

Adam
    Let's not talk if you don't mind
    I'm not surprised you look surprised
    It's not that I want to be unkind
    But love is harder than I realized.

Natasha
    Who said it would be easy?
    Not me – you never heard it from me.
    Whoever told you that love was just a breeze,
    She was eager to please – not me
    You'll never hear it from me
    Who said it would be cosy?

Adam
Not me – you never heard it from me.
Whoever told you that love was like a rose
He was keen to propose – not me
You'll never hear it from me.

Natasha
Who said it would be easy? – Not me.

Adam
Not me – you never heard it from me.

Natasha
Whoever told you that love was just a breeze.

Adam
He was off his trapeze –

Natasha
Not me –

Both
You'll never hear it from me.

Dvornichek enters, makes immediately for the telephone.

Dvornichek He's coming. He's furious. He wants to talk to the captain.

Natasha Why's that, Dvornie?

Dvornichek We're not sinking. (*into the telephone*) Connect me with the captain – he's in the wardrobe.

Natasha Sandor is furious because we're not sinking?

Dvornichek (*to telephone*) Have it your own way, wardroom. (*to Natasha*) It was just a practice. Like a fire drill when it's not a boat. (*to telephone*) Well, on the *Mauretania* we always called the wardroom the wardrobe. I don't know why – just get on with it – Mr Turai wants him. (*to Natasha*) Good thing it was, too – turned out my job was to make sure there was no one left on board.

Natasha Why you?

Dvornichek It's one of their traditions, apparently. Last on, last off.

Turai enters and is fuming.

Turai Damn cheek!

Dvornichek (*correcting him mildly*) Dvornichek.

Turai Have you got him?

Dvornichek Nearly.

Turai Where's Gal? Where's Fish?

Natasha Sandor, stop pouting. The sea is too rough for rehearsal anyway.

Turai I am about to do something about that.

Natasha (*alarmed*) Sandor, don't you think you ought to lie down?

Dvornichek (*into phone*) Ah! Is that you, Skip?

Turai snatches the receiver out of his hand.

Turai Turai! – Now look here, I haven't got time to rehearse your disasters as well as my own! Turai, Sandor Turai! Oh really, how kind of you to say so. My secret is uninterrupted rehearsal, since you ask. Oh, have you . . .? Yes, I'd adore to read it. Set on an ocean liner, eh? – What a good idea. I'll send the steward to pick it up. Actually, there is something you can do for me. As we are having such a rough crossing – Really? How interesting. Nevertheless, it is a bit rough by the standards of crossing

Piccadilly, and it occurred to me that the boat may not be pointing in the best direction – we seem to be banging against the storm . . . Against the swell, yes . . . so if you could possibly give us an hour or two of pointing the other way . . . What? – Oh, I think you'd enjoy it – I think it's very much your sort of thing . . . It would be my pleasure, they'll be at the box office in your name . . . Absolutely – and about the other matter . . . That's very decent of you. Yes, I'll hold on –

Ivor has entered in a bright yellow jacket which hides most of him.

Natasha You look ridiculous.

Ivor I'm not taking it off.

Natasha (*to Ivor*) I am not singing 'This Could Be The One' to a man in a life jacket.

Ivor I thought we should just read one or two scenes – (*a meaningful glance towards Adam*) The sea is too rough for anything else.

Natasha Sandor is doing something about that.

Turai (*into phone*) Fine, fine – I'm most grateful, go ahead . . .

Ivor (*labouredly amused*) Oh yes? – Who's he talking to? God?

And indeed the dangerously swaying room now rapidly calms down.

Turai (*into phone*) Better . . . bit more . . . that's about it . . . that'll do nicely . . . thank you, I look forward to meeting you too – but not just yet if you don't mind!

Turai replaces the telephone, Ivor approaches it with amazement.

He can only give us an hour. Murphy, get me a cognac.

Dvornichek Aye, aye, sir.

Turai And you'd better pick up the Captain's manuscript.

Dvornichek Aye aye.

Turai By the way, when do you sleep?

Dvornichek In the winter, sir. (*He leaves.*)

Turai I'm not leaving this boat without that man in my retinue.

Ivor (*examining the telephone*) It's a trick, is it?

No one takes any notice of him.

Turai Where's Gal?

Gal enters with a tiny snack, removing a lifejacket.

Gal (*feelingly*) The women and children on this boat don't give an inch.

Turai (*to Ivor*) Take off that absurd article. If we hit an iceberg, I will arrange for you to be informed.

Ivor with ill grace removes himself from the lifejacket. Meanwhile Natasha has carried a tray of delicate sandwiches to Adam.

Natasha Adam, darling, why don't you eat something – you mustn't be so minor key.

Turai Leave him alone. I want to save his voice. (*to Adam*) Me fortissimo, you piano.

Natasha (*losing her temper*) Shut up! I've had quite enough of you!

Ivor So have I. And if we hit an iceberg I would consider it an improvement on the present situation, especially if you go down with the ship.

Turai (*calmly*) So. It seems that my legendary good nature towards petulant children, rabid dogs and actors as a class, coupled with my detestation of sarcasm and mockery in all its forms, especially when directed at the mentally disabled, has lulled you into impudence and given you a misplaced air of indispensibility, what I like to call a sine-qua-nonchalance. I am to blame for this. I have mollycoddled you. I have made obeisance to your exiguous talent. I have forborne to point out the distance that separates your performance from an adequate realization of the character I have created for you. That there is such a distance you may have no doubt. I myself have just sent out for a pair of bifocals, and I'm thinking of borrowing the captain's telescope.

Natasha (*with dignity*) I'm sorry if I do not seem to suit your little play. It requires a large adjustment for someone connected, as I am, with the Shakespearean theatre.

Turai If you are referring to your Juliet, you might as well claim a connection with the Orient Express by virtue of having once been derailed at East Finchley.

Natasha (*leaving*) Rrright. If you require to speak to me you will find me in my cabin.

Turai (*pointedly*) If I require to speak to you I can make myself heard quite easily from my own.

Ivor (*hurriedly*) No, no – let's not quarrel, eh, – I'm sorry, Turai – Natasha is sorry too – We really would like to get on (*to Natasha*) Wouldn't we?

Natasha (*collecting herself*) Yes, let's get on.

Turai (*cheerfully*) That's the spirit. Darling. Dearest
Natasha. Let me see a smile. No, a smile. That's better.
Now I forgive you. Are we friends?

Natasha (*grimly*) Darling, Sandor . . . dearest . . . we are
in your hands.

Turai (*gallantly*) It's a privilege. And for me too. My
angel. Forgive me also. I spoke in anger. I didn't mean it
about your Juliet. It was right up there with your Pauline.
Now where were we?

Ivor Mother is coming up for sale this afternoon.

> *Dvornichek enters smartly with Captain's manuscript
> and cognac on a tray.*

Dvornichek Here we are, sir. One cognac and one copy
of *All In The Same Boat* with the captain's compliments.

Turai About time! Over here and take that rubbish
away. I'd like your opinion of it.

Dvornichek Right. (*He hands Turai the manuscript and
drinks the cognac.*) I've had better. Will there be anything else sir?

Turai A cognac.

Dvornichek Certainly sir.

Natasha (*shouts*) Mother is coming up for sale this
afternoon.

Ivor (*in character*) I know all about it. Reggie is with the
radio officer trying to contact the Emu.

Natasha The Emir?

Ivor No, no, there's been a mix up with the sister ships.
The Emu has reached Athens and the girls who were

supposed to be delivered to the Casbah cash in advance
are running around taking pictures of the Acropolis.

Natasha Oh Justin.

Ivor I can't see any problem. Your mother is for sale.
I will buy her. There's only one thing I need from you,
Ilona.

Natasha Of course! (*She mimes removing an ear-ring
and giving it to Ivor.*)

Ivor So it's farewell to the Sackville-Stew emeralds.

*This, of course, for Adam's benefit . . . but,
unfortunately, Adam has now eaten his way towards
a revelation of the engraving upon the silver tray,
underneath the sandwiches. The engraving, naturally,
is familiar to him. He starts to catch on . . . and
begins to investigate the other silver salvers, emptying
them of their contents one by one, until he has a
collection of perhaps half a dozen trays identical to
the one Turai had presented to him. He has approached
Turai with these trays and now reproachfully hands
them to him – after which Adam leaves the stage.
Gal has noticed all this, and with an anxious glance
at Turai, Gal hurriedly follows Adam off the stage.
Natasha and Ivor have remained unaware of their
departure.*

Turai All right, there's no point in going on with that.

Ivor (*seizing his opportunity*) I'm afraid you're right,
Turai – but don't worry. While you were in Deauville
I thought I'd pen to paper, don't you know, and – erm –
Natasha and I have something to show you.

Turai (*gravely*) I am inexpressively touched.

Ivor Thank you. It's probably no good.

Turai Come, come, I'd be privileged to be given a glimpse.

Ivor Well, it's the bit which starts off with mother coming up for sale – we've rehearsed and rehearsed . . .

Meanwhile Natasha, after a couple of sidelong glances, has missed Adam . . .

Natasha Ivor . . .

Ivor (*heedlessly*) You know, getting it right for you, almost to the last minute – I think you will find it quite moving –

Turai Indeed. What a shame Adam isn't here to see it.

Ivor Yes, isn't it – What? (*He looks around.*) Damn and blast it!

Gal hurries back into the room.

Gal He's not in his room. He seemed upset about something. (*drily*) I see you have recovered some of the family silver. These shipping lines are completely unscrupulous.

Dvornichek enters with a cognac on the usual silver tray.

Dvornichek Here we are sir! One cognac.

Turai, who is already carrying several silver trays, furiously grabs Dvornichek's while Dvornichek deftly saves the glass of cognac.

Turai Will you stop filling this room with these damned trays!

Dvornichek What am I supposed to do with the drink?

Turai Surely you can manage a glass of cognac?!

Dvornichek downs the cognac, remarking . . .

Dvornichek Oh – thank you very much. Good health. Will there be anything else?

Turai (*with great self-control*) Have you seen Mr Adam?

Dvornichek Yes, sir – don't worry, it's all taken care of, no problem.

Turai What isn't?

Dvornichek I gave him the telegram.

Turai What are you talking about?

Dvornichek The telegram from his mother.

Turai I know you did. I was there.

Dvornichek I mean the second telegram.

Turai Second telegram?

Dvornichek Now you're getting it.

Turai What did it say?

Dvornichek She just missed him in Cherbourg and is taking the next boat to New York.

Turai I'm going to faint.

Dvornichek I'll get some brandy.

Turai Don't bother, I'll throw myself overboard.

Turai hands the Captain's manuscript back to Dvornichek. Turai and Dvornichek leave in opposite directions.

Gal Well, shall we get on?

Ivor What for?

Gal What for? I thought we were rehearsing.

Ivor Oh yes.

Gal Where were we? . . . Mother is coming up for . . .

Ivor and Natasha No – no.

Gal What's the matter?

Ivor and Natasha Nothing, nothing.

Gal Perhaps we'd better go from the beginning, I'll set the scene, the curtain rises, the Dodo at sea.

Natasha Oh my God.

Gal Sunny day gentle swell passengers disport themselves on deck. A girl, shy, unspoilt beauty simply dressed . . . A debonair young man in a rakish yachting cap . . . An Irish policeman appears on the poop.

Turai staggers back on, half carrying Adam who is wrapped in a blanket.

Ivor (*baffled*) Is this right?

Natasha My God!

Gal Stand back . . . put him in the chair.

Natasha What happened?

Gal Get some soup!

Turai He's all right – he jumped into the sea.

Natasha Adam darling, you're all wet – I'm sorry – I can explain it to you.

Gal He must know why he's wet.

Turai Stop making such a fuss. He's come to no harm at all.

Natasha But who saved him?

Dvornichek enters wearing a bathing suit. His hair is wet, he carries a cognac on a tray, and Adam's dripping hat, a boater.

Dvornichek Here we are sir! One cognac.

Turai At last.

Natasha Dvornie!

Dvornichek No problem.

Turai reaches for the cognac but Natasha intercepts it and starts feeding it to Adam.

Natasha Darling . . .

Gal Shouldn't we take him to his cabin?

Turai We can't rehearse in his cabin, we'd never get the piano in there for a start.

Natasha For God's sake, Sandor –

Turai For his and for mine and not least for yours, stop pouting and pick up your cue.

Gal Are you serious?

Turai It has been a day of constant and frivolous interruptions. I am not prepared to indulge any of you any more. It's the January sale at the slave market and Mother is lot one. Ilona tells Justin the bad news but Justin has a plan, carry on . . .

Natasha He's right! (*to Ivor, shouts*) Mother is coming up for sale this afternoon, and you can't see any problem!

Ivor (*taking the hint*) I can't see any problem! Your mother is for sale! I will buy her.

Natasha Justin! . . .

Dvornichek Gerald.

Natasha Gerald.

Ivor There's only one thing I need from you, Ilona.

Natasha Of course!

Ivor So it's farewell to the Sackville-Stew emeralds. It's funny how little they mean to me now. It is I who have been robbed, for you have stolen my heart . . . (*sings*) 'You stole my heart and made an honest man of me.'

Turai I can't bear it. Murphy, get me a cognac.

Dvornichek Yes, sir.

Turai Bring the bottle, have one yourself.

Dvornichek (*leaving*) Thank you, sir. Two bottles of cognac.

Turai Stock characters, stock situations, stock economy of expression. What seemed to be delightful and ingenious like a chiming pocket watch, turns out to be a clanking medieval town hall clock where nothing happens for fifteen minutes and then a couple of stiff figures trundle into view and hit a cracked bell with a hammer – bonk! – Justin is a jewel thief! Bonk! Reggie is Sir Reginald! Bonk! Predictable from top to bottom.

Ivor I think it's just the last part, really.

Turai Bonk! Jewel thief reformed by love of good woman! Bonk! They win the mixed doubles at ping-pong!

This is Ivor's big moment.

Ivor Excuse me, Turai. I think I might be able to help you on this one.

Turai Oh really?

Ivor Yes. The fact is that while you three were in Deauville, Natasha and I were talking about the ending and we thought it was a bit bonk bonk, don't you know?

Turai (*coldly*) I beg your pardon?

Ivor Well, we did. A bit predictable, we thought. (*to Natasha*) Didn't we?

Natasha Yes. Sort of bonk . . . bonk.

Turai Bonk bonk?

Ivor Yes. Well, as you know, I have a certain gift for, well, words, really.

Turai How would I know that since you have always gone to such trouble to conceal it?

Natasha Not so much words as construction.

Ivor That's it – I tell wonderful stories.

Turai (*incredulously*) To whom?

Natasha (*snaps*) Let him finish, Sandor!

Ivor Well, the long and the short of it is that I thought I'd put pen to paper and Natasha and I have worked up a little scene if you'd like us to do it for you. All right?

Turai In all my born days I have never encountered such brass. I have had actors who won't take their trousers off, I have had actors who won't work with cats or in the provinces, in short I have had from actors every kind of interference with the artistic process but I have never had an actor with the effrontery to write.

Ivor I say, look here Turai –

Turai The nerve of it!

Natasha (*finally*) Sandor!

Turai What, pray, is the burden of your little scene?

Ivor I suppose you could say it was less bonk bonk . . . and more hiccup.

Turai Hiccup?

Ivor Yes. One more boy-loses-girl before boy-gets-girl.

Gal (*interested*) How do you achieve that?

Natasha Ilona agrees to marry Reggie, then when they announce their engagement, Mother has hysterics because she can't marry her own father and the truth comes out so Ilona is free to marry Justin after all. I thought it was rather clever, actually. Well done, Ivor.

Turai Gal, have you ever heard anything like it?

Gal Yes, but let's not dismiss it on that account. (*to Natasha*) Where do we go from?

Ivor and Natasha 'Mother is coming up for sale this afternoon.'

Natasha and Ivor resume their characters.

Ivor I know, it's rotten luck. At least no one is likely to buy her.

Natasha That's just where you're wrong. Reggie is going to buy her.

Ivor Reggie! That's disgusting! To think that an Englishman –

Natasha No, no he's buying her for me!

Ivor Oh I see.

Natasha You know what this means, Justin?

Ivor We'll have your mother around again.

Natasha Apart from that. I have told Reggie that I will marry him.

Ivor What?

Natasha I must. It's a matter of honour.

Ivor I will outbid him!

Natasha With what?

Ivor You're right, Ilona. I have never put anything aside for the future, not a single cufflink. Wait! – It's not too late! I have stolen the ear-ring twice, I can steal it again!

Natasha It is too late. Look – (*She sweeps back her lovely hair, both sides.*) – my engagement present from Reggie!

Ivor The Sackville-Stew pearls!

Gal Emeralds.

Ivor I've made it pearls.

Gal Why?

Ivor Well –

Natasha A pearl is much better – babies are always swallowing them.

Gal But it was in your little fist.

Natasha No, it was in my little potty.

Gal You said it was obscene.

Natasha An emerald would be obscene. A pearl is perfectly sweet. (*resuming*) Goodbye, Justin.

Ivor Let me kiss you one last time, my darling.

*Adam has been slowly coming to life and taking an
interest. But, having done so, he has lost interest.
He has decided to leave. He begins to depart in an
exhausted kind of way, and it seems that he might
go out of earshot before the critical part of the scene
arrives . . . but noticing him going, Ivor and Natasha
forge ahead resolutely, and as Adam begins to
recognize the words he halts.*

Natasha Just this once. Don't get carried away.

Ivor My angel!

Natasha Now, you promised not to get carried away.

Ivor I can't help it!

Natasha You're not going to begin again!

Ivor Yes, again! And again! I love you, I adore you,
I worship you! I worship you as the moth worships the
candle flame! I love you as the Eiffel Tower loves the
little fleecy cloud that dances around it in the summer
breeze . . .

*Gal and Adam have turned to look at each other in
amazement.*

Natasha You'll soon forget me!

Gal Excuse me . . . What was that he said?

Natasha Please don't interrupt. (*resuming*) You'll soon
forget me.

Ivor No, no I'm mad about you! But you've plucked out
my heart like the olive out of a dry martini and dashed
me from your lips!

Natasha Don't spoil everything we've had together.

Gal (*to Turai*) Excuse me, Turai.

Turai What is it?

Natasha Come, give me your hands.

Gal We've heard this before.

Natasha I will remember your hands –

Turai I thought it seemed familiar.

Natasha Such clever wicked hands too when I think of what they have done.

Turai Who's he got it from? Sardou?

Gal No, we heard it last night!

Turai Of course!

Ivor What's going on? This isn't fair to my work.

Natasha Please be a good boy. Remember this afternoon. Here, let me kiss you.

Ivor That's not a kiss, that's a tip. Let the whole world know I'm a dashed martini!

Natasha That's not true. You will always be the first. If I had ten husbands, no one can take your place, but I'm engaged to be married so please be kind and leave me now.

Ivor All right, I will. Only let me see you as I want to remember you. Lift your hair. Let me move your collar just a little –

Natasha Oh, you're impossible – what are you doing?

Ivor One last look – one touch – I beg you! Oh that pink round perfection! Let me put my lips to its rose smoothness.

Gal Her ear-ring!

Ivor And the other one!

Gal Her other ear-ring.

Ivor How beautiful they hang there!

Turai Enough.

Adam Natasha!

Turai This is revolting.

Ivor What did you think in general?

Turai It won't do.

Adam (*without pause*) Yes, it will. It will do wonderfully!

Turai You thought it good?

Adam (*without pause*) I thought it the best play I've ever seen.

Natasha (*realizing*) Adam –

Adam (*to Natasha*) You were wonderful. I've never liked you better or loved you more.

Gal (*realizing*) I say, Adam, my boy –

Adam (*gaily*) Don't Adam-my-boy me – in my opinion Ivor knocks Gal and Turai and Shakespeare into a cocked heap.

Turai (*realizing*) How extraordinary!

Adam Ivor, let me shake you by the hand.

Ivor How do you do? We've never really said hello.

Adam Hello, hello, hello.

Natasha Adam! You're speaking!

Adam Of course I am!

Natasha You're cured!

Adam hesitates, realizing.

Adam Good heavens. (*Pause.*) So I am.

Natasha Don't stop! I love you. (*Pause.*) Adam?

Adam pauses but he is teasing.

Adam (*rapidly*) I love you, I love you, I love you. Ask me a question – quick – any question.

Natasha Will you marry me?

Adam (*instantly*) Without hesitation, because I love you, I love you, I love you.

Dvornichek with a cognac glass and a bottle on a tray has walked in on this. He approaches Turai.

Dvornichek Here we are, sir – one cognac.

Adam snatches the bottle and glass.

Adam Thank you, Dvornichek. I love you too! I love everybody!

He fills the glass and unexpectedly hands it to Turai. Turai takes it gravely.

Your cognac.

Turai At last.

And drinks it. The telephone rings – Adam picks it up.

Adam (*into telephone*) Yes? Adam here, the conversationalist . . . Hello, captain! Art thou sleeping there below? . . . Hang on, I'll ask him. (*to Turai*) Have you had a chance to look through *All In The Same Boat*?

Turai I will have to ask my literary consultant.

Dvornichek Hopeless.

Turai Hopeless.

Adam (*into the telephone*) Hopeless. (*He hangs up.*) He seemed upset.

> *The ship's hooter sounds. A moment later the boat shudders and everything starts to sway again as the boat moves back into the wrong direction.*

Turai Some people can't take constructive criticism.

Dvornichek Early praise isn't good for them. Let them struggle, otherwise they'll never strive for perfection – writing, rewriting, up to the last minute.

Turai Quite – get me a cognac.

Dvornichek You've got one in your hand. Burning the midnight oil.

Turai I want two cognacs.

Dvornichek The bottle's there. Writing through the night.

Adam (*to Dvornichek*) What was that?

Dvornichek What was what?

Adam Mr Turai was up writing through the night?

Dvornichek (*pause*) Problem!

Adam What a fool I've been. (*to Ivor*) Ivor, did you write that scene while we were in Deauville? I asked you a question. Did you write that scene?

Natasha Of course he did! Answer him, Ivor!

Gal He can't speak. He's got Adam's disease. (*He has.*)

Adam (*to Turai*) I owe you everything, you and Mr Gal. You are my benefactors, my friends. I know that you won't lie to me.

Turai And you are quite right. I am incapable of lying to you. You are like a son to me. You are more. You are youth, idealism. You are the future. To lie to you would be a crime.

Adam Did Ivor write that scene?

Turai Every word.

Gal Thank God.

Natasha You see!

Adam (*not celebrating yet*) Then I have one more question.

Turai You wish to know, in that case, what was I working on last night?

Adam Yes.

Turai I will tell you exactly. Last night I realized we were on the wrong boat.

Gal To New York?

Turai To Casablanca. You are right about the ending, you are right about the beginning, and the middle is unspeakable. I have spent the day in an agony of indecision but now my mind is made up. The Dodo is a dud and we have to scuttle her here and now.

Gal But we're contracted to arrive in New York with –

Turai A much better story is staring us in the face.

Gal What's that?

Turai *The Cruise of the Emu.*

Dvornichek Much better.

Adam Oh, thank God!

Turai I thought you'd like it.

Adam No, no I mean – oh, forgive me!

Dvornichek Adam, what is all this about?

Adam Nothing, a storm in a teapot! I love you all over again! He was writing the cruise of the other thing!

Gal Well, we've got four days. Where do we start?

Turai Well . . .

Gal I know – with Murphy!

Dvornichek Me, sir?

Gal No, actually, I meant . . .

Dvornichek No problem. It's like this. The Emu under the command of a handsome young captain, who is unaware that on board there is a beautiful stowaway who, unbeknownst to him and to her, is a missing heiress, is circumnavigating the globe with a full complement of French tarts, who are ignorant of the fact that the white slavers, little knowing that there has been a mix up with the sister ships, intend to take over the boat with Pepe the Silent.

Turai Who the hell is Pepe the Silent?

Dvornichek (*indicating Ivor*) The white slavers' ugly henchman who's had his tongue cut out and is silently in love with the missing heiress, so saves her life and remains silent while she goes off with the man she loves; very moving, usually.

Turai Fish, you're a lucky man. How did you know all that?

Dvornichek It's the captain's manuscript, sir.

Turai It is?

Dvornichek He can't write but he has a certain gift for construction and absolutely no original ideas of any kind.

Turai He sounds like a natural. Adam, you've got the part.

Adam Who'll play the piano?

Turai Murphy?

Dvornichek I'm a bit rusty.

Turai Serves you right for getting wet. Can you read music?

Dvornichek No problem.

Turai Murphy, have a cognac.

Dvornichek Thank you, sir, and may I say what a pleasure it is to serve you, sir – you are, if I may say so, sir, quite a swell.

> *Dvornichek takes command of the piano. Natasha and Adam go into the song.*

Natasha
When I saw you . . .

Adam
My knees went weak, my throat went dry,
I could hardly speak.

Both
Isn't is heavenly!
– This could be the one.
Glory be when you kissed me,
Wedding bells rang two for tea.
When all's said and done.
This could be the one.

Turai Now you kiss her.

They kiss.
   *Which is the end . . . but, perhaps by way of a
curtain call, Dvornichek at the piano leads the
Company into . . .*

'Where Do We Go From Here?'

We just said hello and now it's goodbye
So mind how you go, we hope it keeps dry,
And please excuse my tear
But where do we go from here?

We'll just catch the tide,
It's anchors aweigh,
So thanks for the ride,
And have a nice day
We have to disappear –
But where do we go from here?

This way, that way, up or down,
We could go both ways.
Forwards, backwards, round and round,
What do I care
So long as when we get together,
And we're sat by the fire
Canoodling and then
You feel the desire
To go round again.
You have a volunteer
So where do we go from here?

So where do we go –
When do we go –
Darling I'm so ready to go –
So why don't we go from here?

ON THE RAZZLE

adapted from
Einen Jux er sich machen
by Johann Nestroy

Characters

Weinberl
Christopher
Sonders
Marie
Zangler
Gertrud
Belgian Foreigner
Melchior
Hupfer
Philippine
Madame Knorr
Mrs Fischer
Coachman
Waiter One
Waiter Two
German Man
German Woman
Scots Man
Scots Woman
Constable
Lisette
Miss Blumenblatt
Ragamuffin

Piper, Citizens, Waiters,
Customers, etc.

On the Razzle was first performed on 1 September 1981 at the Royal Lyceum Theatre, Edinburgh, as part of the 1981 Edinburgh International Festival, and opened to the press on 22 September 1981 at the Lyttelton Theatre. The cast included:

Weinberl Ray Brooks
Christopher Felicity Kendal
Sonders Barry McGinn
Marie Mary Chilton
Zangler Dinsdale Landen
Gertrud Hilda Braid
A Foreigner Paul Gregory
Melchior Michael Kitchen
Hupfer John Challis
Lightning Thomas Henty and Timothy Hick
Philippine Allyson Rees
Madame Knorr Rosemary McHale
Frau Fischer Deborah Norton
Coachman Harold Innocent
Italian Waiter John Challis
German Couple Teresa Codling, Clyde Gatell
Scottish Couple Greta Watson, Andrew Cuthbert
Second Waiter Philip Talbot
Constable Alan Haywood
Fraulein Blumenblatt Joan Hickson
Lisette Marianne Motley

Directed by Peter Wood
Designed by Carl Toms

Author's Note

Although this text, like the first edition, is in two acts, the original production was done with two intermissions, the middle act beginning with 'The Journey to Vienna' and ending with the Restaurant Scene.

Act One

Zangler's shop.

In which customers are served with great panache by Weinberl and Christopher. Marie is the cashier in a gilded cage. Old-fashioned spring-loaded canisters travel on wires between the cage and the counters. A chute delivers a large sack of flour from up above to a position behind Weinberl's counter. There is a trap door to a cellar. Sonders, incognito, is among the customers. A town clock chimes the hour. Customers are being ushered out by Christopher. Sonders remains. Shop closing for lunch.

Zangler's room can occupy the stage with the shop, the action moving between the two.

Zangler and Gertrud. Zangler is usually worked up, as now. Gertrud never is.

Zangler My tailor has let me down again.

Gertrud Yes, I can see.

Zangler No, you damned well can't. I'm referring to my new uniform which hasn't arrived yet, and today is the grand annual parade with the massed bands of the Sporting and Benevolent Societies of the Grocers' Company. It's enough to make one burst a bratwurst. I'll feel such a fool . . . There I'll be, president-elect and honorary whipper-in of the Friends of the Opera Fur and Feather Club, three times winner of the Johann Strauss Memorial Shield for duck-shooting, and I'll have to appear before the public in my old uniform. Perhaps I'd better not go out at all. That fortune-hunter Sonders is after my ward.

293

Gertrud My word.

Zangler My ward! I won't rest easy until Marie is safely out of his reach. Now, don't forget, Marie's luggage is to be sent ahead to my sister-in-law's, Miss Blumenblatt at twenty-three Carlstrasse.

Gertrud Miss Blumenblatt's.

Zangler What is the address?

Gertrud Twenty-three Carlstrasse.

Zangler What is it?

Gertrud Twenty-three Carlstrasse.

Zangler Very well. Marie can stay with her until Sonders finds some other innocent girl to pursue, and furthermore it will stop the little slut from chasing after *him*. I'm damned sure they're sending messages to each other but I can't work out how they're doing it.

> *Zing! In the shop – now closed – a cash-canister zings along the wire to Marie in her gilded cage.*

Zangler's shop.
The shop is closed. Weinberl and Christopher are absent. Sonders, half hidden, has sent the canister. Zangler is on to him.

Zangler Sonders!

Marie Uncle!

Sonders Herr Zangler!

Zangler Unhand my foot, sir!

Sonders I love your niece!

Zangler (*outraged*) My knees, sir? (*mollified*) Oh, my *niece.* (*outraged*) Well, my niece and I are not to be prised apart so easily, and nor are hers, I hope I make my meaning clear?

Sonders Marie must be mine!

Zangler Never! She is a star out of thy firmament, Sonders! I am a Zangler, provision merchant to the beau-monde, top board for the Cheesemongers and number three in the Small Bore Club.

Sonders Only three?

Zangler Do you suppose I'd let my airedale be hounded up hill and – my heiress be mounted up hill and bank by a truffle-hound – be trifled with and hounded by a mountebank?! Not for all the tea in China! Well, I might for all the tea in China, or the rice – no, that's ridiculous – the preserved ginger then – no, let's say half the tea, the ginger, a shipment of shark-fin soup double-discounted just to take it off your hands –

Sonders All you think about is money!

Zangler All I think about *is* money! As far as I'm concerned any man who interferes with my Marie might as well have his hand in my till!

Sonders I make no secret of the fact that I am not the *éminence grise* of Oriental trade, but I have expectations, and no outstanding debts.

A man, a foreigner, visible in the street, starts knocking on the shop door. Marie has emerged from her cage and goes to deal with it.

Foreigner Grus Grott! (*He enters and shakes hands all round.*)

Zangler We're closed for lunch. What expectations?

Foreigner Enshuldigen!

Zangler Closed!

Foreigner Mein heren! Ich nicht ein customer . . .

Zangler What did he say?

Marie I don't know, Uncle, I think he's a foreigner.

Foreigner Gut morgen – geshstattensie – bitte shorn – danke shorn . . .

Zangler We're closed! Open two o'clock!

Foreigner Ich comen looken finden Herr Sonders.

Zangler Here! Sonders!

Foreigner Herr Sonders?

Zangler No, *there* Sonders.

Foreigner Herr Sonders? Ich haben ein document.

Zangler He's a creditor!

Foreigner Herr Sonders!

Zangler No debts, eh?

Foreigner Ja – dett! –

Sonders Nein, nein – I'm busy. Comen backen in the morgen.

> *Sonders ushers the foreigner out of the shop. The foreigner is in fact a legal messenger who has come from Belgium to announce the death of Sonders's rich aunt. He succeeds in this endeavour at the end of the play.*

Zangler I thought you said you had no debts!

Sonders No outstanding debts – run-of-the-mill debts I may have. I probably overlooked my hatter, who is a bit short. But as for my expectations, Herr Zangler, I have the honour to inform you that I have a rich aunt in Brussels.

Zangler A rich aunt in Brussels! I reel, I totter, I am routed from the field! A rich aunt in Brussels – I'm standing here with my buttons undone and he has a rich aunt in Brussels.

Sonders She's going to leave me all her money.

Zangler When is that?

Sonders When she's dead, of course.

Zangler Listen, I know Brussels. Your auntie will be sitting up in bed in a lace cap when Belgium produces a composer.

Sonders I hope so because while she lives I know she'll make me a liberal allowance.

Zangler A liberal allowance!? How much is that in Brussels? I'm afraid I never do business on the basis of grandiloquent coinage, and in the lexicon of the false prospectus 'a liberal allowance' is the alpha and oh my God, how many times do I have to tell you? – I will not allow my ward to go off and marry abroad.

Sonders Then I'll stay here and marry her, if that's your wont.

Zangler And meanwhile in Brussels your inheritance will be eaten to the bone by codicils letting my wont wait upon her will like the poor cat with the haddock.

Sonders The what?

Zangler Look to the aunt! Don't waste your time mooning and skulking around my emporium – I'm sending Marie away to a secret address where you will never find her, search how you will. (*to Gertrud who has entered with Zangler's old uniform*) What is it?!

Gertrud Twenty-three Carlstrasse, Miss Blumenblatt's.

Sonders Twenty-three Carlstrasse . . .! Miss Blumenblatt's!

Zangler (*spluttering*) You old – you stupid –

Gertrud Should I let Marie have the new travelling case?

Zangler – old baggage!

Gertrud *Not* the new travelling case . . .

Sonders (*leaving*) My humble respects . . .

Gertrud Here is your old uniform. And the new servant has arrived.

Sonders Your servant, ma'am!

Gertrud His.

  Sonders goes.

Zangler You prattling old fool, who asked you to open your big mouth?

Gertrud You're upset. I can tell.

Zangler Where is Marie?

Gertrud She's upstairs trying on her Scottish travelling outfit you got her cheap from your fancy.

Zangler My fancy? My fiancée! A respectable widow and the Madame of 'Madame Knorr's Fashion House'.

Gertrud I thought as much – so it's a betrothal.

Zangler No it isn't, damn your nerve, it's a hat and coat shop! Now get out and send in the new servant. And don't let Marie out of your sight. If she and Sonders exchange so much as a glance while I'm gone I'll put you on cabbage-water till you can pass it back into the soup-pot without knowing the difference.

Exit Gertrud.

This place is beginning to lose its chic for me. I bestride the mercantile trade of this parish like a colossus, and run a bachelor establishment second to none as far as the eye can see, and I'm surrounded by village idiots and nincompetent poops of every stripe. It's an uphill struggle trying to instil a little tone into this place.

There is a knock on the door.

Entrez!

There is a knock on the door.

(*Furiously*) Come in!

Enter Melchior.

Melchior Excuse me, are you the shopkeeper, my lord?

Zangler You do me too much honour and not enough. I am Herr Zangler, purveyor of high-class provisions.

Melchior I understand you are in desperate need of a servant.

Zangler You understand wrong. There's no shortage of rogues like you, only of masters like me to give them gainful employment.

Melchior That's classic. And very true. A good servant will keep for years, while masters like you are being ruined every day. How's business by the way? – highly provisional, I trust?

Zangler You strike me as rather impertinent.

Melchior I was just talking shop. Please disregard it as the inexperience of blushful youth, as the poet said.

Zangler Do you have a reference?

Melchior No, I just read it somewhere.

Zangler Have you got a testimonial?

Melchior (*producing a tattered paper*) I have, sir. And it's a classic, if I say so myself.

Zangler Do you have any experience in the field of mixed merchandise?

Melchior Definitely, I'm always mixing it.

Zangler Well, I must say, I have never seen a testimonial like it.

Melchior It's just a bit creased, that's all.

Zangler 'Honest, industrious, enterprising, intelligent, responsible, cheerful, imaginative, witty, well-spoken, modest, in a word classic . . .'

Melchior When do you want me to start?

Zangler Just a moment, aren't you forgetting the interview?

Melchior So I am – how much are you paying?

Zangler Six guilders a week, including laundry.

Melchior I don't do laundry.

Zangler I mean the housekeeper will wash your shirts.

Melchior That's classic. I like to be clean.

Zangler And board, of course.

Melchior Clean and bored.

Zangler And lodging.

Melchior Clean and bored and lodging –

Zangler All included.

Melchior Ah, board and lodging. How about sharing a bed?

Zangler I won't countenance immorality.

Melchior Own bed. As for the board, at my last place it was groaning fit to bust, the neighbours used to bang on the walls.

Zangler I assure you, no one goes hungry here: soup, beef, pudding, all the trimmings.

Melchior Classic. I always have coffee with my breakfast.

Zangler It has never been the custom here for the servant to have coffee.

Melchior You wouldn't like me to drink liquor from the stock.

Zangler Certainly not.

Melchior I should prefer to avoid the temptation.

Zangler I'm glad to hear it.

Melchior Agreed, then.

Zangler What? Well, if you do a good job . . . coffee then.

Melchior From the pot?

Zangler Ad liberandum.

Melchior Is that yes or no?

Zangler Yes.

Melchior Sounds classic. Was there anything else you wanted to ask me?

Zangler No . . . I don't think so.

Melchior Well, that seems satisfactory. You won't regret this, sir – I have always parted with my employers on the best of terms.

Zangler You have never been sacked?

Melchior Technically, yes, but only after I have let it be known by subtle neglect of my duties that the job has run its course.

Zangler That's very considerate.

Melchior I don't like to cause offence by giving notice – in a servant it looks presumptuous.

Zangler That shows modesty.

Melchior Your humble servant, sir.

Zangler Yes, all right.

Melchior Classic!

Zangler Only you'll have to stop using that word. It's stupid.

Melchior There's nothing stupid about the word. It's just the way some people use it without discrimination.

Zangler Do they?

Melchior Oh yes. It's absolutely classic. What are my duties?

Zangler Your duties are the duties of a servant. To begin with you can make my old uniform look like new – and if that tailor shows his face tell him to go to hell.

Enter tailor, Hupfer. Hupfer brings with him Zangler's
new uniform on a tailor's dummy. The complete
rig-out includes a ridiculous hat with feathers etc.,
polished riding boots with monstrous shining
and very audible spurs, and the uniform itself which
is top heavy with gold buttons and braid etc. Leather
strapping supports holsters for knife, gun, sword . . .
The general effect is sporting and musical. The new
uniform is brighter than the old, which is bright.
The tailor is only responsible for the clothes. The rest
of the stuff is already in the room.

Hupfer Here we are – the masterpiece is ready.

Zangler You managed it, my dear Hupfer! In the nick
of time.

Melchior Go to hell.

Zangler Shut up!

Melchior (*to the dummy*) Shut up!

Hupfer Well, with the help of two journeyman tailors
I have done the impossible – let me help you into it.

Melchior Too small.

Hupfer (*reacts to Melchior*) I see you have a new
servant, Herr Zangler.

Zangler (*cheerfully*) Oh yes. I woke up this morning
feeling like a new man. So I got one.

Hupfer Trousers.

Melchior Too tight.

Hupfer (*wary distaste*) He's a personal servant, is he?

Zangler Yes, he is a bit, but I like to give youth a chance
and then I like to kick it down the stairs if it doesn't
watch its lip.

Melchior I worked for a tailor once. I cooked his goose for him.

Hupfer There we are.

Melchior Everything went well until I got confused and goosed his cook.

Zangler Pay attention. You may learn something.

Melchior After that he got a valet stand.

Zangler You'll see how a trouser should fit . . . except it's a bit tight isn't it?

It is more than a bit tight.

Hupfer Snug.

Zangler Snug? I'd be in trouble if I knelt down. I'm thinking of my nuptials.

Hupfer It's the pressing.

Zangler Exactly. I don't *want* them pressed.

Hupfer Try the tunic.

Zangler I like the frogging.

Hupfer Can we please keep our minds on the tunic. Now let me help you.

Zangler It's somewhat constricted, surely.

Hupfer That's the style.

Zangler But it's cutting me under the arms, the buttons will fly off when I sit down, and I can't breathe.

Hupfer It's a uniform, it is not supposed to be a night-shirt.

Zangler I don't understand it. You took my measurements.

304

Melchior Well that explains it. If God had been a tailor there'd be two and a half feet to the yard and the world would look like a three-cornered hat . . .

Zangler And it's a day late.

Melchior And it would have been a day late. We'd all be on an eight-day week.

Zangler Shut up.

Melchior (*to the dummy*) Shut up.

Zangler I suppose it will have to do, at a pinch. How do I look?

Melchior I'd rather not say.

Zangler I order you – how do I look?

Melchior Classic.

Zangler Shut up!

Melchior (*to Hupfer*) Shut up!

Hupfer You dare to let your servant speak to me like that?

Melchior In the livery of the Zanglers I am no man's minion.

Zangler That's well said. What's your name?

Melchior Melchior.

Zangler Melchior, throw this man out.

Hupfer Don't touch me! You, sir, received your measurements from nature. The tailor's art is to interpret them to your best advantage, and move the buttons later. My humble respects. I will leave my bill.

Melchior (*thrusting the dummy at Hupfer*) Oh no you won't – you'll take him with you!

Exit Hupfer with dummy.

What should I do next?

Zangler There's a coach leaving for town in five minutes. I want you to be on it.

Melchior It's been a pleasure. I usually get a week's money.

Zangler No, no, my dear fellow, I want you to go to Vienna and engage a private room at the Black and White Chop House. Order a good dinner for two and wait for me there.

Melchior Dinner for two, wait for you there.

Zangler Tell them it's a celebration – foaming tankards – cold meats – pickles – potato salad – plum dumplings . . .

Melchior You'll spoil me,

Zangler It's not for you. I'm entertaining my fiancée to a birthday dinner.

Melchior A previous engagement? My congratulations, Herr Zangler.

Zangler Thank you. She's the Madame of Madame Knorr's Fashion House. You may know it.

Melchior No, but I think I know the piano player.

Zangler It's a hat shop in Annagasse. Of course she's a millineress in her own right.

Melchior Enough said. And the shop on top.

Zangler No, she's on top of the shop. What are you talking about?

Melchior I don't know.

Zangler I'm going to take her to dinner and name the day. You can expect me after the parade.

Melchior Are we travelling together?

Zangler No, I can't be in a hurry, I'm having trouble with my niece.

Melchior It's the uniform.

Zangler No, it's the Casanova incarnate. Marie is very vulnerable. If she so much as sets foot outside the door she's going to catch it from me.

Melchior How long have you had it?

Zangler No. I mean the Don Juan.

Melchior Has he had it?

Zangler I don't think so. She's in her room trying on her Scottish get-up.

Melchior I'll work it out later.

Zangler After all I am her uncle.

Melchior I've worked it out.

Zangler I sent him packing with a flea in his ointment.

Melchior I think I saw him leave.

Zangler Now here's some money to catch the coach.

Melchior Can't I meet the rest of your staff?

Zangler There isn't time. Do you understand my requirements?

Melchior Perfectly.

Zangler Repeat them.

Melchior Catch the coach – go straight to the Imperial Gardens Café – private dinner for two, champagne on ice . . .

Zangler No – no – no – the Black and White Chop House!

Melchior Sir, I beg you to consider. Madame Knorr is a woman of the world, sophisticated, dressed to the nines with a hat to knock your eye out and an eye to knock your hat off. You want to wine her, dine her and name the day. Now does that suggest to you a foaming tankard and a plate of cold cuts in the old Black and White?

Zangler (*slightly puzzled*) Yes it does. What are you getting at?

Melchior Madame Knorr is not just another hausfrau. Fashion is her middle name.

Zangler More or less. Knorr Fashion House. I think I see what you mean . . . The Imperial Gardens Café is a fashionable place, is it?

Melchior It's the only place for the quality at the moment.

Zangler The quality . . . Are you sure it is quite refined?

Melchior Refined?! The ploughman's lunch is six oysters and a crème de menthe frappé.

Zangler I see . . . well, perhaps just this once.

Melchior Leave it to me, sir – champagne – lobster – roast fowl – birthday cake –

Zangler Pickles – dumplings –

Melchior And to finish off, to get her in the mood –

Zangler Perhaps we should have –

Melchior and Zangler (*together*) A nice bottle of the hard stuff.

Melchior (*leaving*) Schnapps!

Coach horn. Zangler now puts on the rest of his outfit, boots, hat, etc.

Zangler Well, that seems all right. Just the ticket. First class. Why do I have a sense of impending disaster? (*He reflects.*) Sonders is after my niece and has discovered the secret address where I am sending her to the safe keeping of my sister-in-law Miss Blumenblatt, who has never laid eyes on him, or, for that matter, on Marie either since she was a baby – while I have to leave my business in the charge of my assistant and an apprentice, and follow my new servant, whom I haven't had time to introduce to anyone, to town to join the parade and take my flancée to dinner in a fashionable restaurant in a uniform I can't sit down in.

One false move and we could have a farce on our hands.

He exits.

Zangler's shop.
The shop is closed for lunch. Weinberl occupies it like a gentleman of leisure. He is writing a letter at the counter. He has a cigar and a glass of wine. Christopher is at the door leading to the rest of the house. He is holding a broom, the Cinderella-type of broom, not a yard broom.

Christopher He's gone.

He joins Weinberl and is offered a glass. There is also a jar of rollmops to hand.

309

Ah, thank you, Mr Weinberl.

> *Weinberl continues to write. At Christopher's position on the counter there is a stack of torn pages from newspapers used here for wrapping purposes. Christopher leans on the stack, reading the top page.*

Aha, I thought so . . . cocoa is up six points.

Weinberl (*without looking up*) When was that?

Christopher (*examining the top of the page*) Week before last.

> *Weinberl signs his letter and blots it.*

Weinberl Does it ever occur to you, Christopher, that we're the backbone of this country?

Christopher You and me, Mr Weinberl?

Weinberl The merchant class.

Christopher Ah yes.

Weinberl The backbone of the country. The very vertebrae of continental stability. From coccyx to clavicle – from the Carpathians to . . . where you will . . .

Christopher The toe-nails . . .

Weinberl . . . the Tyrol, from Austro to breakfast, and Hungaria to lights out, the merchant class is the backbone of the empire on which the sun shines out of our doings; do you ever say that to yourself?

Christopher Not in so many words, Mr Weinberl.

Weinberl (*pulling Christopher's forelock*) Well you should. What is it after all that distinguishes man from beast?

Christopher Not a lot, Mr Weinberl.

Weinberl Trade.

Christopher I was thinking that.

Weinberl What would we be without trade?

Christopher Closed, Mr Weinberl.

Weinberl That's it. The shutters would go up on civilization as we know it. It's the merchant class that holds everything together. Uniting the deep-sea fisherman and the village maiden over a pickled herring on a mahogany counter . .

Christopher You've put me right off me rollmop. (*He has been eating one.*)

Weinberl . . . uniting the hovels of Havana and the House of Hanover over a box of hand-rolled cigars, and the matchgirl and the church warden in the fall of a lucifer. The pearl fisher and the courtesan are joined at the neck by the merchant class. We are the brokers between invention and necessity, balancing supply and demand on the knife edge of profit and loss. I give you – the merchant class!

Christopher The merchant class!

They toast.

Weinberl We know good times and we know bad. Sometimes trade stumbles on its march. The great machine seems to hesitate, the whirling cogwheels and reciprocating pistons disengage, an unearthly silence descends upon the mercantile world . . . We sit here idly twisting paper into cones, flicking a duster over piles of preserved figs and pyramids of uncertain dates, swatting flies like wanton gods off the north face of the Emmental, and gazing into the street.

And then suddenly with a great roar the engine bursts into life, and the teeming world of commerce is upon us! Someone wants a pound of coffee, someone else an ounce of capers, *he* wants smoked eel, *she* wants lemons, a skivvy wants rosewater, a fat lady wants butter, but a skinny one wants whalebones, the curate comes for a candy stick, the bailiff roars for a bottle of brandy, and there's a Gadarene rush on the pigs' trotters. At such times the merchant class stands alone, ordering the tumult of desire into the ledgerly rhythm of exchange with a composure as implacable as a cottage loaf. Tongue.

During the speech Weinberl has folded his letter and put it in an envelope. Christopher sticks out his tongue and Weinberl dabs a postage stamp on the tongue and slaps it on the envelope. He seals the envelope with satisfaction.

Christopher How is your romance, Herr Weinberl?

Weinberl As well as can be expected of a relationship based on pseudonymous correspondence between two post office boxes. One has to proceed cautiously with lonely hearts advertisements. There is a great deal of self-delusion among these women – although I must admit I am becoming very taken with the one who signs herself Elegant And Under Forty. I am thinking of coming out from behind my own nom de plume of Scaramouche. The trouble is, I rather think I have given her the impression that I am more or less the owner of this place, not to mention others like it . . .

Christopher At least you're not a dogsbody like me.

Weinberl Dogsbody? You're an apprentice. You've had a valuable training during your five years under me.

Christopher You see things differently from the dizzy heights of chief sales assistant.

Weinberl Christopher, Christopher, have a pretzel . . . The dignity of labour embraces servant and master, for every master is a servant too, answerable to the voice of a higher authority.

Zangler (*outside*) Weinberl!

Without seeming to hurry Weinberl instantly puts things to order.

Weinberl I thought you said he'd gone.

Christopher He must have changed his mind.

Zangler enters from the house.

Zangler Ah, there you are. Is it time to open the shop?

Weinberl Not quite, Chief. I was just getting everything straight.

Zangler What about this pretzel?

Weinberl The pretzel defeated me completely. (*to Christopher*) Put it back. Are you going to the parade, Herr Zangler?

Zangler No, I'm going beagling. What do you think?

Weinberl I think you're making fun of me, Chief.

Zangler How does it look?

Weinberl (*tactfully*) Snug.

Zangler Do you think it should be let out?

Weinberl Not till after dark.

Zangler What?

Weinberl No.

Zangler Are you sure?

Weinberl I like it, Chief.

Christopher I like it.

Zangler I can't deny it's smart. Did you notice the spurs?

The spurs announce themselves every time Zangler moves.

Weinberl The spurs? Oh yes . . .

Christopher I noticed them.

Zangler I'm rather pleased with the effect. I feel like the cake of the week.

Weinberl That's very well put, Chief.

Zangler I don't mean the cake of the week –

Weinberl Not the cake of the week – the Sheikh of Kuwait –

Zangler No –

Christopher The clerk of the works –

Zangler No!

Weinberl The cock of the walk?

Zangler That's the boy. I feel like the cock of the walk.

Weinberl You'll be the pride of the Sporting and Benevolent Musical Fusiliers of the Grocers' Company, and what wonderful work they do for the widows and orphans.

Zangler I was just setting off when I suddenly had doubts.

Weinberl I assure you, without people like the grocers there'd be no widows and orphans at all.

Zangler No, I mean I had doubts about leaving.

Weinberl I don't understand you, Chief.

Zangler My niece and ward is preying on my mind. There's something not quite right there.

Christopher My niece and ward *are* preying on my mind –?

Zangler (*ignoring him*) Something not quite the ticket. Sonders is a dyed-in-the-wool Don Juan. He's turned Marie's head and for all I know she's already lost it.

Weinberl Well, she didn't lose it in shop-hours.

Zangler I'm going to frustrate him.

Weinberl Frustration is too good for him, Chief.

Zangler I'm sending Marie away for a few days. You'll have to manage the while the till . . . No –

Weinberl To while the time . . .

Zangler No!

Weinberl The till the while?

Zangler That's the boy. You'll have to manage the till the while, and do the books at the close of business. I suppose you're prepared to do that?

Weinberl Very well prepared if I may say so, Herr Zangler.

Zangler There will be other changes. Prepare yourself for a surprise. I have always prided myself on being a good master who has made every reasonable provision for his staff.

Weinberl You have, Chief.

Zangler Well, what would you say to having a mistress?

Christopher One each or sharing?

Weinberl Congratulations, Chief! We wish you and your bride every happiness.

Zangler Thank you, thank you.

Weinberl May one ask who is the fortunate young lady?

Zangler Actually she's a widow, in business like me. Well not actually like me, far from it, it's a haute couture house catering exclusively to the beau monde with three girls working upstairs. What do you say to that?

Weinberl Well, there's not a lot you can say, Chief.

Zangler What the devil is the matter with everybody! That's another thing that was worrying me – leaving the place in charge of you two. I need someone with a proper sense of responsibility, not a log-rolling counter-clerk and a cackhanded apprentice.

Weinberl I'm mortified.

Christopher I'm articled.

Weinberl Who have you got in mind, Chief?

Zangler Well, you two of course!

Weinberl I mean to put in charge with a sense of responsibility?

Zangler What would you do in my shoes?

Weinberl Jingle.

Zangler What?

Weinberl Jingle make any difference just for one afternoon, Chief?

Zangler It may be longer. The duration of my absence will depend on how things go at a certain engagement

I have this evening. Meanwhile desperate situations call
for desperate measures. Master Christopher! Approach!

Christopher He called me Master. Is it the sack?

Zangler I've been paying for your clothes all these years,
as you know.

Christopher No, I thought you bought them outright
when you took me on.

Weinberl Shut up.

Zangler By rights you owe me another six months'
apprenticeship, but to celebrate my nuptials I have
decided to forgo those months. I am appointing you
chief sales assistant.

Weinberl Such an honour is granted to such a few. Show
your gratitude, then. He's stunned, Chief.

Christopher Chief sales assistant! Oh, Herr Zangler,
your bountifulness!

Zangler You may call me Chief. Stop snivelling –
where's your –

Christopher Thank you, Chief!

Zangler Thank-you-Chief – no –

Weinberl (*worried*) Hang on, Chief –

Zangler Hang-on-Chief – no! –

Christopher Will I have my ceremony, Chief? I've got to
have my –

Zangler What?

Christopher Initiation, Chief!

Zangler Bless you. And we must have the ceremony.
Raise your right trouser and repeat after me . . . I swear.

Christopher I swear . . .

Zangler Weinberl, do you remember how it goes?

Weinberl To strive and to abide.

Christopher To strive and to abide.

Weinberl No – I swear by the sacred apron of the Grand Victualler – no – it's been a long time . . .

Christopher (*rapidly*) I swear by the sacred apron of the Imperial Grand Grocer and by the grocery chain of his office, to strive for his victualler in freehold, to abide by his argument which flows from his premises, to honour his custom, keep up his stock, give credit to few, be credit to all, and not be found wanting when weighed in the scales, so help me God!

Zangler You may jump the counter.

Christopher jumps.

That's that. I will inform you of changes in your duties should any occur to me – except of course that you have to buy your own clothes.

Christopher Thank you, Chief!

Zangler And remember, always give people their change between finger and thumb. Nothing lets down the tone of a place so much as change from the fist.

Christopher Right, Chief.

Weinberl Excuse me, Chief. Am I your chief sales assistant or am I not?

Zangler You are not. I have decided to make you my partner. To take effect from the day of my marriage.

Weinberl (*stunned*) Me? Your partner?

Zangler Yes. As a married man who has come into possession of a couture establishment I will be spending more time away from here. It's only right that you should have an interest in the prosperity of the business, and probably cheaper.

Weinberl Partner . . .

Zangler Yes, yes, as soon as my bride has consummated my expansion into her turnover you will be my partner. If you strive and abide you may find yourself in my old uniform. Now – what shall I do? Shall I go or what?

Weinberl What . . .?

Zangler No, I'll go.

Christopher Good luck, Chief!

Zangler I'm going to join the parade and call on my fiancée – It's her birthday. I'm hoping to have a little sextet outside her hat shop before I take her to dinner.

Christopher Outside? In the street?

Zangler Yes. I can't help it. I'm a fool to myself when I'm in love. If I'm not back by morning you'll know where I'll be.

Christopher In jail?

Zangler In the milliner's arms.

Christopher Have one for me, Chief!

Zangler What? – No. I will go and plait my truss – no –

Christopher Plight your –

Zangler That's the boy! (*He goes.*)

Weinberl (*in a daze*) Partner . . . partner . . . I'm a partner. One moment a put-upon counter-clerk, the next a pillar of the continental trading community.

Christopher Chief sales assistant . . . I've always been at the bottom of the ladder and now . . . (*A thought strikes him.*) Who's going to be under me, then?

Weinberl Book-keeper – that was the Himalaya of my aspirations, but from the vantage point of partnership I look tolerantly down upon the book-keeper's place as if from a throne of clouds.

Christopher He's a partner and I'm the entire staff. I'll have two masters instead of one, three counting the widow, and the weight of my authority will be felt by the housekeeper's cat.

Weinberl And yet – strangely enough – now, now of all times, when fortune has smiled upon me like a lunatic upon a worm in an apple, I feel a sense of . . . (*Pause.*) grief.

Christopher That cat is going to wish it had never been born.

Weinberl What is happening to me? I feel a loosening of obscure restraints . . . Desires stir in my breast like shifting crates on a badly loaded barrow.

Christopher (*breaks out*) Oh, Mother, what is the wherefore of it all?! – Whither the striving and how the abiding for a poor boy in the grocery trade? I'm glad she's dead and doesn't see me chained to this counter like a dog to a kennel, knowing nothing of the world except what happens to get wrapped around the next pound of groceries. Seeing the sunrise only from an attic window, and the sunset reflected in a row of spice jars, agog at travellers' tales of paved streets! Oh, Mr Weinberl, I have come into my kingdom and I see that it is the locked room from which you celebrate your escape! And if I have to wait until I am as old as you, *that's longer than I've been alive!*

Weinberl (*soberly*) Beyond the door is another room.
The servant is the slave of his master and the master is
the slave of his business.

Christopher (*regarding Zangler's old uniform left in the
room*) Try it on.

Weinberl What?

Christopher Try it on.

Weinberl No –

Christopher Go on!

Weinberl Gertrud might come in – I mustn't!

Christopher All right.

Weinberl I daren't!

Christopher All right.

Weinberl Dare I? (*He starts to don the uniform.*) If only
I could look back on a day when I was fancy free, a real
razzle of a day packed with adventure and high jinks,
a day to remember when I am a grand-grocer jingling
through Vienna in my boots and spurs and the livery of
the Grocers' Company or passing the grog and spinning
the yarn with the merchant princes of the retail trade,
when I could say, 'Oh, I was a gay dog in my day, a real
rapscallion – why, I remember once . . .' but I have
nothing to remember. (*desperately*) I've got to acquire a
past before it's too late!

Christopher Can I come with you, Mr Weinberl?

Weinberl Come with me where?

Christopher I want it now!

Weinberl Now?

Christopher This very minute!

Weinberl (*appalled*) What? Lock up the shop?

Christopher It's already locked.

Weinberl While he's at the parade . . .?

Christopher And dinner in town. It's only us two. Marie is confined to quarters. He'll never know.

Weinberl Wait . . . (*He paces about feverishly and then embraces Christopher.*) What about the books?

Christopher We'll cook the books!

Weinberl Yes! – what about the cook?

Christopher We'll fix the cook. We'll tell her he told us to tell her he told us he doesn't want to open the shop.

Weinberl What happens when she tells him we told her he told us to tell her he told us –

Christopher The cook . . .

Gertrud (*offstage*) Isn't it time you opened the shop – it's gone two o'clock.

Weinberl She'll do for us . . . Get me out of this!

Christopher pulls the uniform tunic over Weinberl's head. Gertrud appears.

Gertrud So you're still in two minds, Herr Zangler?

Christopher He is, and he's half out of both of them. (*to Weinberl loudly*) It's Gertrud, Herr Zangler . . . Get it?

All Weinberl's lines are muffled and unintelligible and furious. Weinberl speaks.

Weinberl Got it!

Gertrud Twenty-three Carlstrasse, Miss Blumenblatt's.

This is the wrong answer and Weinberl speaks even more furiously.

Christopher Master says find Mr Weinberl and tell him not to open the shop this afternoon.

Gertrud Don't open the shop. Tell Mr Weinberl.

Weinberl again.

Christopher Strict orders, he says, and now he would be obliged if you would be so kind as to leave him.

Gertrud That doesn't sound like him.

Weinberl dances about and roars. Christopher goes as though to help him into the tunic. Gertrud speaks as she leaves.

That does.

Christopher (*pulling the tunic over Weinberl's head*) She's gone.

Weinberl And now, best foot forward.

Christopher I'll get my worsted stocking.

Weinberl Is that necessary?

Christopher It's got my savings in it.

Weinberl I'll get mine and we'll be off.

Door slam and jingle of spurs.

Zangler (*offstage*) Gertrud!

Weinberl God in heaven he's back again!

Christopher picks up Weinberl's discarded clothes and runs off towards the shop. Spurs however still approach.

I can't let him see me like this!

*Before Weinberl can follow Christopher, Gertrud
enters from the kitchen and Weinberl dives behind the
furniture. Zangler enters at the same time.*

Zangler (*shouts*) Marie! Damn and blast it, that
swinehound Sonders is nowhere to be seen in the village,
and he didn't leave on the coach and Marie's window is
open! God in Himalayas! – If I keep having to come
back I'll miss the parade. I told you not to let Marie out
of your sight.

Gertrud You told me to find Weinberl and tell him –

Zangler Don't tell me what I told you – search her
room. If she's got out of her Scottish get-up, ten to one
he's up there trying it on. I'll keep watch in the garden
if I can find a place to hide.

Gertrud Stand in the herbaceous border.

*They leave in different directions. Weinberl comes out
from behind the furniture and runs into the shop,
looking for his clothes.*

Zangler's shop.
    *Weinberl enters, calling for Christopher. But he has
only just entered when the trap door in the floor starts
coming up and he dives into a cupboard, or perhaps
under the counter. Sonders and Marie, dressed in a volu-
minous, tartan, hooded cape, emerge from the cellar.*

Sonders It's all right – it's deserted – courage mon
amour –

Marie Oh, August – we mustn't – it's not proper.

Sonders Now's our chance – we can escape by the shop
door while they're searching round the back.

Marie Oh, but it's not proper.

Sonders Don't you love me?

Marie You know I love you but I don't want to run away –

Sonders Elopement isn't running away, it's running towards.

Marie It's not proper.

Sonders Is it proper for your guardian to behave as if he owns you?

Marie Yes. That's why they call it property. I think. Oh, August, you're a terrible man, kiss me again. You made me feel all funny down there.

He embraces her, more inside her cape than out.

Sonders Oh, Marie!

Marie I mean in the cellar – Oh, somebody's coming!

Sonders Hide in here!

Marie No, it isn't prop –!

He dives into Weinberl's cupboard, pulling her after him. Christopher enters from a second door with Weinberl's clothes, calling for him and running out of the shop. The cupboard door bursts open. Marie comes out, Sonders comes out and Weinberl's legs come out. Weinberl is lying on his front.

Sonders Someone has been eavesdropping on us –

Marie I thought it was a squash in there.

Sonders drags Weinberl out by his heels, or spurs. He and Marie are aghast to find that Zangler seems to be lying on the floor with his face still in the cupboard.

Sonders and Marie kneel down and bow their heads as Weinberl gets unsteadily to his feet. Weinberl gazes down on to the crowns of their heads.

Marie Oh, my uncle!

Sonders Oh, my God – Herr Zangler!

Marie Don't be angry, dear Uncle, I meant no harm.

Sonders She's blameless, sir, intact I swear, I mean in fact I swear she did it against her will.

Marie I *didn't* do it!

Sonders No she didn't – I haven't – Oh, sir, it was love that drove us to deceive you!

They are kissing Weinberl's hands.

Marie Won't you speak to me, Uncle? Your harshest words are easier to bear than the silence of your anger.

Weinberl, deeply embarrassed, disengages his hands and pats the two heads.

Sonders What do you . . .?

Marie Do you mean . . .?

They try to raise their heads but Weinberl firmly keeps their heads down and presses them together.

Sonders He's blessing our union.

Weinberl guides their faces into a lingering kiss during which he is able to retire, silently, from the room.

Sonders Marie!

Marie Oh, August! Oh, Uncle, you've made me so . . . Where has he gone?

Sonders What a surprising man he is! Beneath his rough manners he is the very soul of tact.

Marie (*getting up*) I always knew he was shy underneath.

Sonders Let me kiss you again.

Marie You can kiss me properly now!

> *They go into another lingering kiss, during which Zangler enters. He has a silent apoplexy. At length Sonders notices him.*

Sonders (*suavely*) Ah, there you are, my dear sir, we were wondering where you'd got to.

Zangler (*strangled*) Sonders! (*A couple of buttons fly off his uniform.*)

Marie Oh, you must call him August now – you're going to be such friends – isn't he handsome?

Zangler I'll kill him.

Marie Uncle, but you just –

Zangler Slut!

Sonders My dear sir, what can have happened?

Zangler You blackguard! You barefaced dastardly –

Sonders He's mad.

> *Gertrud enters.*

Gertrud (*placidly*) Oh, you've found them.

Marie Oh, Uncle, you're not yourself . . .

Zangler I'll make you eat your words, you ungrateful little Messalina!

Gertrud Make you eat your semolina you ungrateful little –

Zangler (*screams*) Shut up!

Marie Oh . . . (*She runs weeping from the room.*)

Sonders Marie!

Gertrud She's upset, I can tell.

Gertrud exits, following Marie.

Sonders This is absurd – I'll come back when you're feeling calmer.

Zangler chases Sonders out.

Zangler You dare to show your nose in here again and I'll cut off your coquette to spite your face! And furthermore I'll disinherit her!

This takes Zangler out of the room. Weinberl, in his own clothes, and Christopher reappear. They are gleeful.

Weinberl Christopher . . . Did you hear that?

Christopher (*looking down the street*) He's still running. I don't think he'll ever come back.

Weinberl Oh my! I feel like a real rapscallion. We're on the razzle at last!

They embrace.

Enter Weinberl riding horse, Christopher leading them.

Weinberl We've done it! We're on the razzle! We're going to get a past at last!

Christopher (*disappointed*) Is this what a razzle is like, Mr Weinberl?

Weinberl No – not yet – wait till we really get into our stride. (*to horse*) Come on Lightning . . .

Christopher How far is Vienna, Mr Weinberl?

Weinberl It's a long way, Christopher.

Christopher How large is Vienna, Mr Weinberl?

Weinberl It is very large, Christopher . . . Whoa, Lightning . . .

Weinberl gets off, and Christopher gets on the horse.

Giddy up, Lightning.

Christopher Will there be women, Mr Weinberl?

Weinberl Beautiful women, Christopher.

Christopher How old are the women in Vienna, Mr Weinberl?

Weinberl Twenty-two, Christopher.

Christopher How does one meet them, Mr Weinberl?

Weinberl They promenade in packs, with parasols, and gloves up to here. They consort with cosmopolitan men-of-the-world in the fashionable cafés.

Christopher I have read that they are often kept, Mr Weinberl.

Weinberl Kept for what, Christopher?

Christopher That's what always puzzled *me*.

Weinberl Whoa, Lightning. Vienna, Christopher, is the place to find out . . . Look!

They are looking out over Vienna.

Christopher (*impressed*) It's just like you said . . .

Weinberl (*enchanted*) It is, isn't it?

Arriving in Vienna . . . gaiety and music . . . Christopher takes it all in wide-eyed. The dialogue is part of the set change.

Christopher Is the city always like this, Mr Weinberl? All this gay panoply . . .

Weinberl (*slightly puzzled*) Well . . . more or less . . .

Christopher (*enthusiastically*) Bands playing – streets full of colourful costumes – it's like a great parade . . .

Weinberl (*thoughtfully*) Yes . . .

Christopher What would old Zangler think if he saw us now?

Weinberl Oh yes . . . (*The penny drops.*) Parade?!

Christopher Parade!

The parade is going right by them.

Weinberl My God, suppose Zangler happens to – There he is! – get down . . .

Weinberl and Christopher obviously see Zangler approaching. The parade music suddenly incorporates the massed spurs of the Grocers' Company. Christopher dismounts and he and Weinberl exit under cover of Lightning.

Annagasse exterior – Madame Knorr's Fashion House. Distant parade. Christopher and Weinberl enter running. They come to a breathless halt outside the windows which flank the entrance door of the fashion house. Windows above.

Christopher Well, we *nearly* had an adventure.

Weinberl Yes that *would* have been our final fling if Zangler had caught sight of us.

Christopher On the other hand we don't want to end up flingless . . .

Weinberl Dishonoured and unflung . . .

Christopher You're not downhearted, are you?

Weinberl I don't know. I've been getting a sharp stabbing pain just here.

Christopher You've got the stitch.

Weinberl I don't think so. It only happens when I see an open grocer's shop. It'll be just my luck if I've got Weinberl's Disease.

Christopher It would certainly be a coincidence. Still, it sounds like the sort of thing people come to Vienna for from all over the world, so to get it while you're here on a rare visit smacks of outrageous good fortune. I'm trying to make you look on the bright side.

Weinberl Christopher.

Christopher Yes, Mr Weinberl?

Weinberl Embrace me. What happened to Lightning?

Christopher She always turns up.

Weinberl What will we do if she's gone?

Christopher We'll bolt the stable door.

Weinberl And keep mum.

Christopher If only she could see me now . . . Well, where's the razzle?

Weinberl There's plenty of time. There's probably an adventure laying in wait for us at this very spot.

Philippine seen moving about inside, putting the lights on. The light illuminates, for the first time, the words 'Knorr's Fashion House'.

Weinberl For all we know we have made an appointment with destiny.

Christopher Nothing is going to happen to us in a pokey little cul-de-sac like this.

Weinberl The parade must be over. Let's go.

Christopher We might run into the boss.

Weinberl No, no – he's got the whole of Vienna to choose from, there's absolutely no reason why . . .

Distant footfalls and jingle of spurs approach. The little street echoes with the sound.

Weinberl It's Nemesis!

Christopher Well, he's got Zangler with him!

They run in opposite directions, then change their minds, then rush through the doorway into the shop. Their faces appear in the windows, one in each, watching the street cautiously as Zangler comes into view. (In the original production Zangler was accompanied by the 'little sextet' which serenaded the windows until summarily dismissed by Zangler after Melchior's arrival.) To their consternation Zangler walks straight to the shop. The faces disappear. As Zangler turns the door handle, two voluminously swathed tartan mannequins leap into the windows, one in each. At the same moment Melchior runs in from the side while Zangler is in the doorway.

Melchior Sir! – Oh what luck! The Classinova person – the whosit incarnate – the Don Juan is at the Imperial

Gardens Café with a nice young lady like a ladylike young niece!

Zangler (*emerging confused*) Eh, what? What? Who's this?

Melchior Herr Zangler!

Zangler Your servant, sir – no, by God it's mine. What are you doing here?

Melchior I came to find you, your eminence.

Zangler I told you to go straight to the restaurant.

Melchior I did but the Cassata incarnate has arrived and the tart!

Zangler But that's just desserts. What about my dinner?

Melchior The dinner is all arranged, but I'm on the trail of the Casserola and you must come immediately before it gets cold.

Zangler Tell them to put it in the oven. You seem to lack a sense of proportion. I am about to present myself to my fiancée in no uncertain terms, and I'm damned if I'm going to be harried and put off my stroke by the ridiculous self-importance of a jumped-up pastry-cook. Honestly, these fashionable eating houses, they think they're doing you a favour by taking your money. I told you to wait for me.

Melchior I was waiting for you, sir, and who should arrive by horsecab but the very same seducer I saw leave your home.

Zangler There you are, you see! – I should have remained true to the Black and White Chop House.

Melchior He had a young woman with him.

Zangler Of course he did – it must be three or four hours since he found himself with a vacancy.

Melchior She was in a Scottish get-up.

Zangler Vienna has been overrun with Scottish get-ups, kilts, tam-o'-shanters, Royal Stuart pencil cases and highland flingery of every stripe since the town lost its head over the Verdi *Macbeth*. In my opinion it's a disgrace. Even the chocolate cake . . . Sachertartan! No, no, a Scottish get-up means nothing – there's even two in the window here . . .

> *Weinberl and Christopher hastily resume rigidity. They mustn't have a proper view of Melchior, by the way.*

Damn it, are you deliberately trying to prick my bubble while I stand knocking at my fiancée's main entrance?

Melchior He called her Marie.

Zangler A very common name. I told Gertrud to put Marie into a locked cab and give the coachman an extra fiver if he delivered her personally into the hands of my sister-in-law, Miss Blumenblatt. What could be surer than that?

Melchior A fiver? Yes, I would say that we must be talking of two different Maries.

Zangler Exactly. And what yours does is no concern of mine.

Melchior I don't think she'll do much. I had a listen and all she said was 'It's not proper.'

Zangler It's them!

Melchior No, no, a tart and ward of an entirely different clan.

Zangler It's them!! Quick, fetch me a half-witted cab you hansom fool!

Melchior We're off!

Zangler (*leaving*) What a situation!

Melchior (*following him*) Classic!

Madame Knorr's Fashion House.
　Weinberl and Christopher come out of the windows into the shop. Christopher disrobes. Weinberl is late and Philippine enters. Weinberl starts sashaying round the shop in his tartan cloak, for Christopher's benefit.

Weinberl What do you think?

Christopher It has a certain Scottish audacity.

Weinberl Ah, there you are at last. Am I addressing the arbiter of this fashion house?

Philippine I'm sure I don't know, sir. I will fetch Madame at once. But excuse me, sir, that is a lady's cape.

Weinberl I know. I was trying it on for a lady of my size and acquaintance.

Philippine That cape is reserved. It has a ticket on it.

Weinberl Yes. I know. (*Reads the ticket.*) Frau Fischer. I have come to collect it and pay for it.

Christopher Not exactly to pay for it.

Weinberl No, not exactly to pay for it, but to confirm payment.

　Christopher has been looking out cautiously through the windows.

Christopher I think it is all clear now, Herr Fischer.

Weinberl Is that clear?

Philippine I'm not sure. I'd better go and fetch Madame.

Weinberl Excellent idea.

Christopher Meanwhile we'll be off.

Weinberl -ally grateful if you would take care of this. (*He hands her the cape grandly.*)

Philippine Yes, sir. Did you say Herr Fischer?

Weinberl Certainly. Would I pay –

Christopher Confirm payment.

Weinberl Confirm payment for somebody else's wife? (*to Christopher*) Why don't you see if our friend is anywhere in sight?

Christopher Good idea. I'll be back in a moment.

Weinberl Is anything the matter?

Philippine Frau Fischer has been a widow for three years.

Weinberl She thinks she has, yes.

Philippine She thinks she has? What about the funeral?

Weinberl It was the funeral that put the idea into her head. That she'd always be a widow. However, three days ago she did me the honour of becoming my wife. (*to Christopher who has paused in admiration on his way out*) You will come back, won't you?

   Christopher goes.

Philippine I'll fetch Madame immediately. She's upstairs in the workroom.

Weinberl Tell her there's no hurry – she's probably busy hemming and hawing.

Philippine goes but instantly returns.

Philippine But, Herr Fischer, why didn't Frau Fischer change her name to yours instead of you changing your name to hers?

Weinberl She did. I didn't. My name, as it happens, is also Fischer. That's how we met. We were placed in alphabetical order in a fire drill at the riding academy.

Philippine Oh, I see.

Philippine goes. Weinberl looks cautiously into the street. While he is so engaged, Mrs Fischer enters the shop. Weinberl bows to her and continues to look out of the window for Christopher's return. After a few moments Madame Knorr enters, gushing.

Mme Knorr There they are! – They're both here! And what a couple of naughty children you are! – Oh, my dear friend, why didn't you tell me?

Mrs Fischer Are you feeling all right, my dear?

Mme Knorr No, I am not feeling all right. I am feeling distinctly put out. Fancy being married for three whole days without saying a word to your oldest friend and leaving your husband to break the news.

Mrs Fischer follows Madame Knorr's gaze towards Weinberl.

However, I forgive you . . .

She walks round Weinberl.

And now that I see your husband I can quite understand why you kept him hidden away.

Mrs Fischer My husband?

She examines Weinberl with interest.

And he announced our marriage himself did he?

Weinberl flinches from her gaze, particularly when she gets out her lorgnettes to scrutinize him all the better. Madame Knorr keeps gushing.

Mme Knorr And none too soon. It is such an honour to meet you. I think it is so romantic – you must have swept her off her feet. Tell me, how long have you known each other?

Mrs Fischer Not long at all.

Weinberl No, not long.

Mme Knorr You must have been married with your head in a whirl!

Mrs Fischer You couldn't say I went into it with my eyes open.

Mme Knorr Of course you did, and I am sure you have not been disappointed.

Mrs Fischer Surprised more than disappointed. My husband has a very individual way of dealing with the banalities of ordinary time – I expect we'll be engaged next week and exchange cards the week after.

Mme Knorr Isn't she priceless?

Weinberl I expect you think I'm rather presumptuous.

Mrs Fischer No, I wouldn't say you were presumptuous. Presumption one has encountered before.

Weinberl Well, a little forward.

Mrs Fischer A little forward? You will meet yourself coming back.

Mme Knorr But why so sudden and secret?

Mrs Fischer There was a reason. My dear husband will tell you.

Mme Knorr Oh do tell.

Weinberl My dear wife can tell you just as well as I.

Mrs Fischer But I would like you to tell her.

Weinberl And I would like you to tell her – after all she's your friend.

Mme Knorr Oh dear, not quarrelling already!

Mrs Fischer It was a whim of my dear husband's.

Weinberl And at the same time a whim of my dear wife's.

Mme Knorr But it is extraordinary.

Weinberl There is nothing extraordinary about it. When two attractive people . . .

Mme Knorr A marriage of true minds.

Mrs Fischer Entirely.

Weinberl Yes, indeed. Well, I must be going.

Mrs Fischer Going? What do you mean?

Weinberl I have some business to attend to.

Mrs Fischer Aren't you going to see me try on my new Scottish cape? After all it wouldn't be fair if you didn't like it.

Weinberl Why?

Mrs Fischer (to *Madame Knorr, joshingly*) Why?! – isn't he the soul of generosity? If I like something, that's enough for him.

Weinberl Actually, I think this tartan fad has had its fling, you know.

Mrs Fischer Had its fling! – such a sense of humour. We'll take it.

Mme Knorr (*to Weinberl*) Will it be cash or account?

Weinberl Account, I think. Well, if that's all you wanted . . . Delighted to have met you at last – my wife has told me so much about you.

Mrs Fischer Don't be so impatient, my dear – I've had such a wonderful idea.

Weinberl One needs a lot of patience in a marriage, I find.

Mrs Fischer I hope I've never given you cause for complaint.

Weinberl Oh no.

Mrs Fischer Have I ever contradicted you on matters large or small?

Weinberl No never – much appreciated.

Mrs Fischer Don't I do my best to enter into your ideas against all reason?

Weinberl You do, you do. And since you make a point of doing so I am sure you won't mind if I now leave you with your friend and your Scottish cape and go about my business.

Mrs Fischer I would mind very much. Out of courtesy to Madame Knorr I cannot let you forget that your only business today is to take us out to a celebration supper.

Mme Knorr A celebration supper! Isn't fate extraordinary! I was hoping my fiancée would pin me down at the Black and White Chop House tonight, but, not for the first time, he preferred to stand me up.

Weinberl Did he?

Mme Knorr He did.

The next seven speeches apply only if Zangler's sextet has put in its appearance in the street scene.

I thought I would be getting a little gold band.

Weinberl And you didn't?

Mme Knorr I did not. It turned out to be a little brass band.

Weinberl Did it?

Mme Knorr It did.

Weinberl Did your finger turn green?

Mme Knorr *I* turned green. But now the evening promises to turn out just as memorable.

Mrs Fischer So you will oblige us, won't you?

Weinberl I would adore to but alas –

Mrs Fischer Very well! – Eugenia, my dear, I'm afraid I have to tell you – that this man –

Weinberl Why don't we all walk around to the Black and White Chop House and raise a foaming tankard to our happiness. And after that I really must dash.

Mrs Fischer The Black and White Chop House? I'm sure it will cause no surprise to anyone here that you would prefer to treat us to somewhere a little better than that. I can change into my new Scottish ensemble. We'll need a cab.

Mme Knorr That's a wonderful idea! I do think your wife deserves a kiss for that.

Weinberl Do you think so?

Mme Knorr Oh, I do!

Weinberl Well, I'm not going to deny anyone their due. Permit me.

Weinberl kisses Mrs Fischer, to her embarrassment.

Mme Knorr Do you call that a kiss? You don't have to stand on ceremony in front of me.

Weinberl Oh very well. (*He gives her a lingering kiss on the mouth.*) And in case my bride has any more good ideas I'll give her one on account.

He kisses her again. Christopher enters the shop.

Christopher All clear.

Weinberl Ah, there you are. I don't think you've met my wife. This is my cousin from the country. I'm the kissing cousin, he's the country cousin. My wife – my wife's friend, Madame Knorr – my cousin – the four of us are going to have supper together at . . . (*He looks enquiringly at Mrs Fischer.*)

Mrs Fischer The Imperial Gardens Café

Weinberl The Imperial Gardens Café. Where else? Go and fetch a cab . . . (*He ushers Christopher out.*) He'll be back in a few moments.

Mrs Fischer We'll keep the cab and go on somewhere else.

Weinberl Another good idea!

He takes her into a passionate embrace. Christopher comes out of his daze. He gives a cry of delight, throws his hat in the air and runs off down the street.

Act Two

The Imperial Gardens Café.

This is a conservatory ante-room. The main restaurant is offstage. Large window in back wall, through which are visible some of the garden, terrace, etc., and a partial view of a hansom cab, possibly with horse attached. There is a door into this garden. There are in-and-out swing doors to the kitchen. Stairs from the main area lead up to a gallery at the back, from which a window looks out over the garden where the cab is.

The place is fashionable, even pretentious; the clientele likewise. At curtain-up we find a traffic of customers, waiters, etc. passing through while music plays. The women's dresses suggest that the town has gone mad for tartan. There is also a disconcerting Scottish influence in the Vienna waltzes; bagpipes have been imported.

There are two dining tables, some chairs, a coatstand. There is a folding screen of Chinese design.

The fashionable scene disperses and the music comes to an end.

After a pause the disembodied voices of Zangler and Melchior, who are hidden on the stage, are heard.

Zangler Melchior.

Melchior Herr Zangler.

Zangler What's happened to the music?

Melchior Yes, I know. It's partly the influence of German Pessimism, partly the decadence of an Empire that has outlived its purpose, and partly Scottish fortnight. I don't hold with it myself. Give me the evergreens every time, that's what I say, those golden oldies of yesteryear, the Blue Danube, and that other one –

Zangler Melchior.

Melchior Yes, Herr Zangler.

Zangler Shut up or I'll kill you.

Melchior Very good, Herr Zangler.

A jingle of spurs announces Zangler's appearance. He is wittily revealed on the stage. Melchior remains invisible. Zangler evidently doesn't know where Melchior is hiding.

Zangler (*looking round*) Melchior.

Melchior Herr Zangler.

Zangler (*looking round*) Have you seen them yet?

Melchior Not yet, Herr Zangler.

Zangler Remember – absolute discretion.

Melchior Yes, Herr Zangler.

Zangler (*looking round*) Don't draw attention to yourself – blend into the background.

Melchior Very good, Herr Zangler.

Zangler Where the devil are you?

Melchior Here, Herr Zangler.

Zangler Ah.

Melchior is evidently located behind the Chinese screen. He remains invisible. Zangler addresses himself to the screen.

Now listen. I don't want any scandal. Just keep them under observation. We may have to assume a false identity.

Melchior Classic! I'll do a waiter – they're imported here, you know.

Zangler What a pretentious place. Trust my niece.

Melchior Yes, I'll do one of my Italian waiters.

Zangler (*glancing round with disgust*) La dolce vita – pah! Cognoscenti! – pooh! (*furiously*) Prima donna!!

Melchior Quite good – put more of a shrug into it – cognos*centi* – prima *don*na –!

    Waiter One enters to move the screen to one side of the room.

Waiter One Permettetemi signori di spostare questo paravento . . . [*Excuse me, gentlemen, may I just move this screen for you . . .*]

    As Waiter One smartly folds the screen shut, Melchior's voice is cut off.

Melchior Now that's a completely different –

    Waiter One moves the screen over to the door and leaves. Zangler follows anxiously and addresses the screen.

Zangler Are you all right?

    Zangler opens up the screen and Melchior now makes his first appearance, limping into view, severely kinked. Zangler is relieved and at once drops the uncharacteristic solicitude.

Honestly, I've never known such a buffoon! I'm going to have to straighten you out when I get you home!

Melchior Thank you very much, Herr Zangler.

Zangler Now go outside and have a look round.

Three Waiters enter, one at a time, a few paces apart, from the door leading to the restaurant. They cross the stage briskly and exit through the swing door into the kitchen.

For all we know Sonders and Marie may have finished their hors d'oeuvres and slipped away for the entrée.

Melchior No, sir, that's their coach outside.

Zangler Is it? Where's the coachman?

Melchior In the kitchen having a quick one.

Zangler Fetch him in here, I want to speak to him.

Melchior At once, Herr Zangler.

The first Waiter re-enters from the kitchen carrying a veritable pagoda of crockery. He crosses briskly in the direction of the restaurant.

Zangler And remember what I said – no scandal – complete discretion

The second Waiter follows the first Waiter in a similar manner.

Melchior Very good, Herr Zangler –

Melchior turns and departs efficiently through the kitchen's exit door. There is an impressive crash of falling crockery beyond the door. Melchior re-enters through the kitchen's entrance door.

He's not there. (*He approaches the garden door.*) Hey you! Coachman! You're wanted in here!

Coachman (*outside, shouts*) What do you want?

Melchior In here!

Zangler (*shouting discreetly*) Discretion, damn you!

346

Melchior (*whispers to Zangler*) Sorry.

The Coachman enters from the garden. He is a large man, immensely cloaked, wearing a tall hat; he carries a whip.

(*Discreetly*) Ah, coachman – my employer wishes to see you – in private – it's a matter of some delicacy – we rely on your discretion – you know what I mean?

Coachman (*roars*) Say no more, lead me to her. Where is she? (*He cracks his whip.*) If she's a goer, and has an arse a man can get a decent purchase on –

Melchior No, no!

Coachman (*relatively quietly*) You're right! – discretion! – Tell her to meet me behind the stables.

Melchior No . . .

Zangler You there!

Coachman Who's that?

Melchior My employer.

Zangler comes forward importantly and halts.

Zangler Zangler. Import and merchandising.

Coachman (*comes forward and clicks his heels*) Bodelheimer. Transport and waiting around.

Zangler Purveyor of high-class provisions, supplier of cooked meats and delicacies to the gentry.

Coachman Horse manure.

Zangler How dare you!

Coachman I supply horse manure.

Zangler Oh, I see. Well, look here, Bodelheimer, I am a man of some consequence in the Grocers' Company.

You'll do what I tell you if you know what's good for your business.

Coachman Horse manure. (*astutely*) And transport.

Zangler Quite. Now. You have been engaged for the evening by a man who is escorting a certain young lady in a Scottish get-up.

The Coachman evidently has two personalities, one for sexual interests and the other for everything else. He drops the other.

Coachman And what a corker! A pippin! She has a poise – a freshness –

Zangler Quite –

Coachman – an arse any man would give his eye teeth to sink into –

Zangler That's quite enough.

Coachman Happy the man who enjoys the freedom of her lacy bodice!

Zangler (*angrily*) You are addressing her guardian, sir!

Coachman What are they like then?

Zangler Will you be quiet!

Coachman (*quietly*) Sorry, what are they like?

Zangler Now listen –

Coachman Round like apples, or slightly pointy like pears?

Zangler How dare you!

The Coachman lifts Zangler off his feet by his lapels.

Coachman Answer me!

Zangler (*gasps*) Slightly pointy!

The Coachman throws him aside triumphantly.

Coachman I knew it, by God!

Zangler reels over to Melchior.

Zangler Are you sure this is him?

Coachman Conference or Williams?

Zangler For God's sake, the man's obsessed!

But the Coachman pulls himself together suddenly and resumes his dignified personality.

Coachman I'm sorry, your honour! – my apologies! – please disregard it. I'll be all right now.

Zangler Are you quite sure?

Coachman Oh yes. These attacks never last long.

Zangler What sets you off?

Coachman Thinking about buttocks, sir.

Zangler Well, can't you keep your mind off them?

Coachman I'm a coachman.

Zangler Thank God we're back on the point. Now, when your passengers re-enter your coach, I want you to take them on a roundabout route to Twenty-three Carlstrasse.

Coachman Where's that?

Zangler Twenty-three Carlstrasse.

Coachman I can't do that, they'll report me.

Zangler The man is abducting my niece.

Coachman Well, I don't know about that.

Zangler I do. I'll go and fetch the constable and explain to him . . . (*He jingles his purse to make the point.*) He can jump up behind and persuade them to enter the house if they give you any trouble.

Coachman It's out of the question.

Zangler Here's one half your compensation. When you deliver the fugitives, Miss Blumenblatt will give you the other.

Coachman Say no more! Is she a goer then?

Zangler I will follow and have the man put on a charge, and thus avoid a public scandal. You go back to your place. As soon as they climb aboard, whip up your arse . . . No!

Melchior Stick up –

Zangler No!

Melchior Horse –

Zangler That's the boy. Whip up your horse and hand the fugitives personally to Miss Blumenblatt.

Coachman Sporty type is she? Likes a good time?

Zangler (*incredulously*) She's fifty-seven!

Coachman (*losing interest*) Oh, well, look . . .

Melchior Or to her French maid.

Coachman French maid? Will she let me in?

Melchior She's known for it.

Coachman turns to leave.

Zangler (*to Melchior*) I've heard remarks.

Coachman What are they like?

Zangler Slightly pointed.

Coachman exits.

How did you know about the French maid?

Melchior You mean there is one?

Zangler I'll go and fetch a constable.

Melchior What about your celebration supper with your fiancée?

Zangler Sonders has ruined my plans. I'll just have some cooked goose while I'm waiting to pickle his cucumber – no – some pickled cucumber while I'm waiting to cook his –

Melchior Got it.

Zangler leaves in the direction of the restaurant.
Waiter Two enters with a trolley bearing Zangler's celebration supper.

Waiter Two Here we are! One birthday supper for two as ordered. Lobster Thermidor, roast fowl, champagne and how many candles will she want on the cake?

Melchior Take that away. Snuff the candles and cancel the cake. Bring me some beer and pickles. I want the table over there, my master wants a clear view of the window.

Waiter Two What am I going to do with all this?

Melchior I am not a clairvoyant. Have you seen a young couple, the woman in a Scottish get-up?

Waiter Two What clan?

Melchior Machiavelli!

Waiter Two leaves. Sonders and Marie enter.

Melchior It's them!

Marie Oh August, it's not proper.

Sonders Here is a paper proving you are of an age to be married without your guardian's consent.

Marie But it's not proper.

Sonders I assure you it is indistinguishable from the real thing. Keep it with you at all times.

Melchior takes a napkin and menu from a table and confronts them boldly.

Melchior Buona sera! – you wisha da carta?

Sonders (*fluently*) No, grazie tante; un bel cioccolato caldo ci aspetta alla nostra tavola in giardino, per me e per la mia amica. [*No thank you very much. My companion and I have some hot chocolate waiting for us at our table in the garden.*]

Melchior Right, squire . . . Sorry . . . I thought you were someone else.

Sonders and Marie exit. German couple enter.

It's them!

The German couple look at him with alarm and incomprehension. Melchior addresses them with hearty innocence.

Nothing! All clear! Take no notice! Carry on!

The German couple ignore him.

What weather we're having, eh! Turning out a bit dank. Is it cold outside?

German Man Bitte?

Melchior Is it? Last night was definitely dank. Would you say tonight was as dank or not as dank?

German Woman (*leaving*) Danke.

Melchior (*amazed*) Danker?

German Man Bitte.

Melchior Please yourselves. Sparkling couple. I don't think it's them – all they can talk about is the weather.

Scottish couple enter.

Scottish Man Flora!

Scottish Woman Ye bluidy great loon, Hamish McGregor –

Melchior It's them!

Scottish Woman And to think we're missing Viennese Week in Fort William!

Scottish couple exeunt. Christopher and Madame Knorr enter, followed by Weinberl and Mrs Fischer. Melchior steps to one side.

Mme Knorr Ah, le beau monde!

Melchior It's them!

Weinberl Look, about us being married –

Mrs Fischer I won't feel married until we've had the consommé.

Melchior Pretzels!

Melchior exits through kitchen. Glass crash. He re-enters.

(*To Weinberl*) I don't care if you're married or not. You can do what you like! (*He exits.*)

353

Mme Knorr What a strange fellow.

Mrs Fischer That's never happened to me before at the Imperial Gardens Café.

Weinberl Yes, it's the first time for me, too.

Christopher It happens to me every time I come.

Mrs Fischer We'll stay here, Eugenia, do you mind?

Christopher Well, I've reached the heights.

Mrs Fischer The restaurant is so crowded and frankly I had no idea these Scottish patterns had become quite so common.

Weinberl I've got four guilders left after paying the coachman.

Mme Knorr It's the penalty of success, Hildegarde.

Christopher If only my mother could see me now!

Mrs Fischer Unfortunately the success is yours, while the penalty is mine.

Christopher She never dreamed that one day I'd be rubbing shoulders with the crème caramel!

Weinberl Have you got any cash?

Christopher People of my class don't carry cash.

Weinberl I only had ten guilders when I set out.

Christopher Ten guilders! You hoped to acquire a past for ten guilders?

Weinberl Well I was single then – how was I to know I'd be married for dinner?

Mme Knorr (*approaching*) Here we are. I'm hungry.

Weinberl (*to Christopher*) You're not.

Christopher Sit down here, my Empress. – (*to Weinberl*) Not what?

Mme Knorr (*to Weinberl*) Your cousin takes great liberties considering I'm engaged to be married.

Christopher Be mine tonight and I will reveal my true identity and give you half my kingdom.

Weinberl (*to Christopher*) Not hungry.

Christopher (*snaps at him*) Not even Herzegovina, but if you don't make the best of yourself you'll end up serving in a shop.

Mrs Fischer (*approaching*) Has the champagne arrived yet?

Weinberl I don't think we should eat here. It's all together too spartan for my taste.

Mme Knorr Don't blame me – it's the penalty of –

Mrs Fischer Spartan! – I know it's not what you're used to but Madame Knorr and I don't know any better. Where's the Mumms? – I'm dying.

Christopher It's probably out the back.

Weinberl The service here is terrible. Waiter! You see? Let's move on.

Mrs Fischer Don't be ridiculous. Anyway you let the coachman go – I don't know why you didn't ask him to wait.

Weinberl I didn't care for him. He seemed a very disagreeable fellow.

Mrs Fischer That was because of your tip.

Weinberl I gave him a very good tip.

Christopher So did I.

Weinberl Ne'er cast a clout till May is out.

Christopher Get into cocoa at five per cent.

Weinberl Two very good tips.

Mrs Fischer My husband likes to pretend he's parsimonious.

Mme Knorr You mean there's another one like him?

Weinberl Anyway I thought it would be nice to walk back across the park.

Mrs Fischer Walk? Not b –

Mme Knorr There's a waiter – call him over.

Weinberl (*feebly*) Waiter . . . waiter . . .

Christopher Waiter!

Waiter Two Coming, sir!

Weinberl (*to Christopher*) Four guilders!

Christopher What?

Weinberl (*bowing his head*) *Four guilders* our sins as we *four guilden* that trespass against us. (*He catches Mrs Fischer's eye.*) Grace.

Mrs Fischer Hildegarde.

Waiter Two Are you ready to order, sir?

Weinberl Ah, waiter! – sit down, my dear fellow. You strike me as being a splendid chap. What will you have?

Waiter Two Sir?

Weinberl Why should we accept the places allotted to us by an economic order that sets one man above another?

I've been giving this matter a great deal of thought lately, and it seems to me that, in a nutshell, the value of labour capital –

Mrs Fischer What are you babbling about?

Weinberl You may call it babble but one day, given its chance, Weinberlism will give birth to a new order. History is waiting.

Mrs Fischer We are *all* waiting.

Waiter Two I wouldn't have the special – it's herring in oatmeal.

Weinberl Society's accounts will be settled once and for all, and when the bill comes, waiter, I want you to think of me as a comrade.

Waiter Two Yes, sir. And I wouldn't have the neeps either, if I were you.

Weinberl What are the neeps?

Waiter Two I wouldn't know, sir. That's why I wouldn't have them.

Mrs Fischer Well, we'd like a drink to begin with.

Weinberl All right – bring us three beers and an extra glass.

Mrs Fischer Such a sense of humour. He knows I never drink beer.

Weinberl Two beers and a glass of water.

Mrs Fischer I must have something hot.

Weinberl Hot water.

Mrs Fischer I mean something hot to eat.

Weinberl Two beers and a radish.

Mme Knorr You're right – he's hilarious.

Mrs Fischer This has gone quite far enough.

Weinberl All right! Bring us two beers, two glasses of the house red and two sausages for the ladies.

Mrs Fischer The house red?

Weinberl The wurst is yet to come. (*smartly to Christopher*) Get it?

Christopher Got it.

Weinberl Good – that's all we got. (*He hands the menu to Waiter Two.*) My compliments to the official receiver.

Mrs Fischer You obviously have no idea how to entertain a lady.

Christopher Watch this! (*He addresses Waiter Two imperiously.*) You there – what's your name – we want the best dinner in the house, and we want it now!

Waiter Two Yes, sir! (*He clearly prefers Christopher's type of customer. A thought strikes him.*) I happen to have a lobster just ready to serve.

Christopher Excellent.

Waiter Two Thermidor.

Christopher Excellent, thermidor!

Waiter And a roast fowl with all the trimmings, and for dessert . . . It's not anybody's birthday, by any chance?

Mme Knorr (*amazed and pleased*) Yes! It's mine!

Waiter Two Gateau l'anniversaire – you get a bagpiper with that.

Christopher A bagpiper – good. We'll drink champagne to start, champagne with the main course and with the dessert we'll have some –

Weinberl (*alarmed*) Champagne?

Christopher Trockenbeerenauslese. You think I know nothing?

Waiter Two An excellent choice, sir. And if I may say so, it is a pleasure to serve a gentleman. (*He glances meaningfully at Weinberl and departs.*)

Weinberl It's people like him who are going to put a spoke into Weinberlist Theory. (*to Christopher*) Nevertheless the bill will come.

Christopher People of my class don't pay the bill.

Weinberl I mean –

Christopher (*very deliberately*) I know what you mean. I am not entirely stupid. Society will pay. *Our* society. Do you follow me?

Weinberl Not exactly . . .

Christopher (*expansively*) It's a damnable thing Weinberl, but when the reckoning comes the clever people are nowhere to be found. They've gorn . . . you see . . . disappeared . . . leaving the bill to be paid by the bourgeoisie . . . the shopkeepers . . . the widows . . . and such like, get me?

Weinberl (*at last*) Got you!

Mrs Fischer Oh, do stop talking politics, we came here for a celebration dinner.

Weinberl's manner has changed dramatically.

Weinberl My dear wife, why didn't you say you were hungry! We'll have a lobster *each*.

Mme Knorr Oh, it's true love.

Weinberl My Empress!

Mrs Fischer (*drily to Madame Knorr*) Another one.

Weinberl I will give you half my kingdom, too!

Mrs Fischer Hungary?

Weinberl Starving! (*to Waiter Two who has reappeared with the Zangler dinner trolley*) Ah, there you are at last – capital! – look sharp if you value your job, there's plenty of others'll do it for the money.

> *Melchior enters from the garden with the other 'Italian' Waiter One. The situation is that the Weinberl party have sat themselves down at the table stage left. The Zangler table is stage right, but both tables are quite near the centre.*

Melchior What's all this? – I've arranged for my employer to eat here . . . and now these people have pushed in.

Christopher It's a free country.

Melchior Oh, classic!

Christopher It wasn't meant to be original.

Waiter One (*Italian accent*) There's room for everybody. (*He pours champagne.*)

Melchior My employer wishes to eat alone.

Weinberl Your employer seems to be confused about the nature of this establishment. It's what we call a restaurant.

Melchior Why don't you have your dinner somewhere else?

Weinberl Why don't you take yourself off before you get a lobster down your britches.

Waiter Two is serving up dinner for four.

Melchior Please! My master wishes to have a clear view of that hansom cabman while he's eating.

Weinberl Your master's taste in cabmen is something we prefer not to discuss.

Melchior If only this stupid place had a dividing wall.

Christopher Perhaps your master should arrange to be preceded everywhere by a couple of rather fetching bricklayers.

Waiter One (*Italian accent*) Signor, there is a Chinese screen which we use sometimes when a customer feels the drought – droot – draught.

Melchior That will have to do. Come here and help me with it.

Mme Knorr What a nuisance!

Mrs Fischer (*shudders*) Chinoiserie . . . and tartan . . .

Christopher Wait a minute! We can't be shown up like this in front of your wife and her friend.

Weinberl and Christopher get up and accost Melchior and Waiter One who are bringing forward the screen.

Weinberl We don't intend to eat our dinner screened off from public view like a lot of –

Christopher Journalists –

Weinberl – So unless you want your Chinese screen folded round your ears –

Melchior I warn you, my master will not be put out for the likes of you.

Weinberl You may tell your master that if he has a bone to pick with me I don't wish to see his dog.

Melchior You can tell him yourself. I can hear him coming.

The sound of spurs approaching. Weinberl and Christopher speak together.

Weinberl and Christopher (*levelly*) Screen.

Weinberl and Christopher change tack with great smoothness and take the screen in hand, moving it so that it separates the two tables.

Melchior Classic . . .

Zangler enters. Weinberl and Christopher sit down at their table visibly cowering.

Zangler Melchior.

Melchior Your honour.

Zangler Everything's arranged. The constable is poised to pursue Sonders. He's emptied my seal but his lips are pursed. No – he pursed to suppose – no –

Melchior Supper is served –

Zangler No! – Oh, supper is served!

Melchior That's the boy.

Zangler sits down at his table. Waiter One sets out the beer and pickles and leaves. Waiter Two wheels away the empty trolley.

Zangler What is this screen doing here?

Melchior There's a very rough crowd at the next table – a couple of tarts and their night's work. I didn't want you to be disturbed.

Zangler Good.

At the other table Weinberl has poured the champagne. Supper commences.

Mme Knorr Well, life is full of surprises! I wish you all the luck in the world!

Christopher (*quietly*) Thank you. We're going to need it.

Mme Knorr I mean the newly-weds.

Christopher (*quietly*) Oh yes. (*to Weinberl*) All the luck in the world.

Weinberl (*squeakily*) Thank you.

Zangler (*to Melchior*) Fetch me the paper and meanwhile go and keep an eye on Sonders and Marie.

Melchior procures, at the side of the room, a newspaper on a pole which he hands to Zangler.

They're at a table in the garden. Let me know if he gets up.

Melchior I'll throw a bucket of water over them.

Zangler No – no scandal!

Mrs Fischer . . . And not forgetting *your* wedding plans, Eugenia . . . all the luck in the world! (*She toasts Madame Knorr.*)

Mme Knorr Thank you.

Mrs Fischer Chink glasses.

They chink glasses.

Christopher (*quietly*) All the luck in the world. (*He chinks glasses with Madame Knorr.*)

Mme Knorr Thank you. Chink glasses. (*to Weinberl*) Thank you.

Weinberl is staring into space. Christopher speaks quietly to Weinberl.

Christopher Chink glasses.

Weinberl (*squeakily*) Are they? They must go with the screen.

Mrs Fischer Why are you speaking like that?

Weinberl (*squeaks*) Like what?

Mrs Fischer You're speaking in a peculiar way.

Weinberl (*to Christopher*) Am I?

Christopher (*quietly*) Not that I noticed.

Mme Knorr (*to Christopher*) What's happened to your voice?

Christopher (*quietly*) Nothing – there's no need to shout.

Mme Knorr I'm not shouting, I'm speaking normally.

Weinberl (*squeaks*) Not so loud.

Mrs Fischer And why aren't you eating? – lost your appetite?

Christopher (*quietly to Weinberl*) Chicken?

Weinberl (*squeaks*) Wouldn't you be?

Mme Knorr I'd like some chicken. And some more champagne. I can feel it working already.

Christopher (*quietly*) Breast or leg?

Mme Knorr All over.

Christopher (*quietly to Weinberl*) Breast or leg?

Weinberl (*squeaks*) I'll take wing – have you got it?

Christopher (*quietly*) Got it. (*to Madame Knorr*) The bottle's empty. I'll get a waiter.

> *Christopher gets up and moves to the coatstand where, unnoticed by the women, he puts on Mrs Fischer's full-length tartan coat and puts the hood over his head.*

Weinberl (*squeaks*) I'll get one too.

Mrs Fischer We don't need two waiters.

Weinberl (*squeaks*) All right, I'll help him get the first one.

Mrs Fischer Don't be silly –

Mme Knorr Oh, look – I've got the wish-bone!

Weinberl Have you?

Mme Knorr Come on, Hildegarde –

> *Madame Knorr and Mrs Fischer pull the wish-bone.*

Ah, well done! You've got the main part.

Weinberl (*squeaks to Madame Knorr*) That means it's your wish.

Mme Knorr No – it's your wife's wish.

Weinberl (*squeaks*) That's not how we play it.

Mrs Fischer I'm beginning to regret that I ever married you.

Weinberl You'd better both have a wish.

Mme Knorr Oh – all right –

Weinberl Close your eyes, count to twenty and don't tell me what you wish.

Mme Knorr and Mrs Fischer (*together*) One – two – three – four – (*fade out*).

> *Madame Knorr and Mrs Fischer close their eyes. Christopher has crept along the back wall into Zangler's area and leaves through the garden door. Zangler is distracted by his newspaper.*

Zangler (*shakes his head sadly*) Viennese champion cabertosser fails to qualify at Braemar – (*then puzzled*) What paper is this?

> *Meanwhile Weinberl has crept away up the stairs and is leaving by the gallery window in order to drop into the cab.*

Mme Knorr and Mrs Fischer (*together*) seventeen – eighteen – nineteen – twenty.

Mrs Fischer Good heavens! It works!

> *Constable enters from garden.*

Constable Sir – a young couple have leapt into your coach.

Zangler Did one of them look Scottish?

Constable I don't know but the other one had a tartan cloak.

Zangler It's them! Jump up behind and take them to Miss Blumenblatt's, Twenty-three Carlstrasse.

> *Constable exits. Two waiters enter and move the screen.*

Waiter One Off with the lights.

Enter Busboy with birthday cake, followed by Piper.

All (*singing*)
'Happy birthday to you,
Happy birthday to you,
Happy birthday dear Madame Knorr,
Happy birthday to you.'

Mme Knorr Thank you.

Waiter One Turn on the lights.

Zangler My cake!

Mme Knorr Zangler!

Zangler My fiancée!

Sonders and Marie enter.

Sonders My cab!

Zangler Sonders!

Sonders My God!

Marie My uncle!

Zangler My ward!

Busboy (*to Zangler*) Your bill!

Zangler faints at the sight of it.

Living room, Miss Blumenblatt's flat.
Double entrance doors, interior door, window to dark exterior, the bottom of a staircase, and another exit route which could be a chimney. Geraniums in pots. Candlesticks.

Miss Blumenblatt is sitting reading the newspaper aloud to Lisette, the French maid. She is twice interrupted by a parrot in a cage; the parrot says, 'Anything in the paper?' receives a glare of reproof from Miss Blumenblatt, and then the parrot says, 'Sorry', and Miss Blumenblatt reads from the paper:

Miss Blumenblatt '. . . In deploring these scenes of un-Austrian excess, we do not make the error of confusing café society with society in general. Yet the example of the Roman Empire lies ever before us. When those who presume to set standards are seen to have abandoned decent Aryan values for the degenerate postures of an alien culture, we say enough is enough. We have nothing against the Celtic race as such. We are assured that the Celts have a long and obscure history, and have made their contribution to science and the arts, such as it is. But their ways are not our ways, and we cannot but condemn this infatuation with the barbarian baroque universe of Sir Walter Scotch and his ilk. It is a moral issue . . .'
That's all very well, but it doesn't stop them advertising Hunting-Stuart underdrawers in the same paper. Hardly comme il faut.

Lisette Oui, Madame, 'ardly like he must. But 'ow late it is for our guest not arriving.

Miss Blumenblatt I can't think what has happened. My brother-in-law's letter definitely said that he was sending Marie to my safe keeping today. I was looking forward to seeing the dear child again after these ten years. She will find me more sympathique than Zangler has bargained for. Her fate is just like my own. I too know what it is to have loved and to have been separated from the man who stole my heart . . .

Lisette Oh, Madame, 'ow I long for a man to steal mine! 'Ow will I know when it 'appens?

Miss Blumenblatt You will know, never fear. With me it was on a horse-tram in the Bahnhofstrasse . . . The chestnut trees were in bloom . . . He sat down opposite me. Our eyes met. I smiled.

Lisette What 'appened to 'im, Madame?

Miss Blumenblatt He jumped off between stops and got knocked down by a tram coming the other way. But it was still love, and it was still separation. I'll never forget the pain as he passed out of my view for ever!

Approaching sound of bawling.

Is that those people next door playing the bagpipes again?

Lisette I think it is a commotion outside. I will go to see.

She goes and immediately the Constable enters, driving Weinberl and Christopher before him. Christopher is still dressed as a girl in the stolen Scottish cloak from the restaurant. The cloak is very similar to the one worn by Marie.

Constable In you go and no arguments.

Weinberl Someone is going to pay for this.

Constable What makes you think they haven't?

Christopher I'm not the woman you think I am. I'm not even the woman you *think* is the woman you think I am.

Miss Blumenblatt (*rising to her feet*) To what am I owed this scene of un-Austrian excess?

Screams offstage. Coachman enters with Lisette over his shoulder showing her Scottish bloomers.

Lisette! – déshabillé!

Constable Hold your horses!

Coachman (*putting Lisette down*) A thousand apologies
. . . please disregard . . . I'll be all right now. It's these
cold nights – the steam rising off their sleek rippling
haunches.

Lisette Wait! (*She kisses him firmly on the mouth.*) At
last!

Coachman (*highly gratified*) Are you a goer?

Lisette I am a goer! You have horses?

Coachman I have the finest pair of chestnuts of any
coachman in the city!

    Lisette swoons in his arms.

(*Bewildered*) What did I say?

Lisette (*reviving*) Tonight, my window will be open!

Miss Blumenblatt Who are all these people? What are
they doing here?

Constable My instructions are that this couple are to
remain here until the arrival of your brother-in-law.

Miss Blumenblatt What? Surely this can't be the young
woman?

Weinberl Of course she isn't –

Christopher And I can prove it.

Weinberl – if she has to. (*to Christopher*) At the same
time we don't want to be taken for someone who leaves
society to pay his bills.

Constable I have a letter here from your brother-in-law
which explains.

Miss Blumenblatt Let me have it.

    Constable hands her Zangler's letter.

Constable I'll station myself on the front steps, and wait for your brother-in-law. (*He exits.*)

Weinberl Thank heavens! Now you can see that my friend and I are the innocent victims of a police force the like of which would explode the credibility of a comic opera.

Miss Blumenblatt finishes reading letter.

Miss Blumenblatt (*folding up the letter*) Ah – now I understand.

Weinberl Thank goodness –

Miss Blumenblatt Lisette . . . you know where we keep the tin of broken biscuits. Take the coachman into the kitchen and give him one.

Lisette Oui, Madame. Walk zis way.

Lisette exits followed by the Coachman.

Weinberl We must be going – we have a long way to get home.

Christopher Yes, and somebody really ought to give us our fare for our trouble.

Miss Blumenblatt (*barring their way*) Stop! You are not leaving here.

Weinberl What!

Christopher It wasn't our fault. Don't blame us.

Miss Blumenblatt takes him into an embrace.

Miss Blumenblatt My dear pretty child – of course I don't blame you! Your fate is exactly like my own. It happened to me on a horse-tram in the Bahnhofstrasse!

Weinberl You mean, the minute you got on it took off like a rocket –?

Miss Blumenblatt I mean *love*! Oh, you have behaved recklessly but who can gainsay the power of love? And you, sir, you have much to answer for but do not give up hope. I am not the woman you think I am.

Christopher What? You don't mean –

Weinberl Of course she doesn't – Madame, would you mind telling us exactly what is in that letter?

Miss Blumenblatt Only what you would expect a possessive guardian to write when his virgin niece has been abducted by a notorious Don Juan.

Weinberl He's as wrong about me as he is about her.

Christopher Wronger if anything.

Miss Blumenblatt Of course he is. Have no fear. I will see you married in the morning.

Weinberl (*without thinking*) Thank you. No – I think we ought to wait – she's so young, and I'd like to sleep on it, elsewhere –

The doorbell is heard.

Miss Blumenblatt (*shouts*) Lisette!

The kitchen door opens smartly and Lisette appears, breathing heavily, her maid's cap back to front, the tartan ribbons falling over her face. She marches to the door.

By the way did the Coachman take the biscuit?

Lisette He is taking it now, Madame.

She opens the double doors and goes to the unseen front door.

Miss Blumenblatt (*to Christopher*) This may be your uncle.

Christopher None too soon.

Weinberl This'll clear things up.

Lisette appears with Melchior.

. . . on the other hand maybe it won't.

Lisette This man insists on being admitted. (*She continues towards the kitchen and leaves without ceremony.*)

Melchior Fraulein Blumenblatt!

Miss Blumenblatt Well, sir?

Weinberl and Christopher are naturally surprised and dismayed.

Christopher That's –

Weinberl Zangler's servant!

Melchior My employer has sent me ahead to explain to you that this young couple who got into the coach are not actually the young couple . . . (*He notices Weinberl and Christopher.*) It's them!

Miss Blumenblatt Of course it's them!

Melchior Not only is it them, it's him!

Miss Blumenblatt Do you know this man, Herr Sonders?

Weinberl looks around in surprise and then realizes that he is being addressed.

Weinberl Sonders?

Christopher Marie's lover! She must think I'm –

Miss Blumenblatt What's the matter, Marie?

Christopher (*panicking faintly*) Oh, I've got it!

373

Weinberl (*terrified*) I think I gave it to you.

Melchior Shame on you, sir!

Miss Blumenblatt Don't be impertinent.

Melchior But this man is –

Miss Blumenblatt I know all about that –

Melchior My employer was obliged to pay this man's bill.

Miss Blumenblatt What bill?

Melchior To save the ladies from being turned over to the police.

Miss Blumenblatt What ladies?

Melchior And now he's got another one. (*to Christopher*) Don't have dinner with him, miss! – he'll alter you before the dessert – no – he'll desert you before the altar.

Miss Blumenblatt What is all this nonsense? Who sent you?

Melchior Your brother-in-law, Herr Zangler. He mistook this man for Sonders, and this lady for his niece –

Weinberl Exactly! So he wants you to let us go before he gets here –

Miss Blumenblatt But that's the exact opposite of what it says in this letter. (*to Melchior*) You're obviously not to be trusted.

 The doorbell sounds again.

(*Shouts*) Lisette!

 Lisette enters in even more disarray and goes to open the door.

Melchior This must be Herr Zangler.

Lightning whinnies offstage.

Christopher Lightning! . . . (*to Weinberl*) Are you a goer?

Weinberl I am a goer!

Weinberl starts to climb out of window when Lisette re-enters.

Lisette Herr Weinberl is here.

Weinberl has one leg over the windowsill. He pauses.

Weinberl Weinberl? (*He puts his leg back into the room.*)

Miss Blumenblatt Herr Weinberl? Show him in. A thoroughly reliable man, I've heard Zangler speak of him.

Weinberl Have you?

Miss Blumenblatt Don't concern yourself. You haven't a care in the world.

Lisette reappears with Sonders.

Lisette Herr Weinberl.

Lisette makes a dignified but determined exit to the kitchen. Sonders bows.

Sonders Madam, my apologies for calling so late. Weinberl.

Miss Blumenblatt I'm delighted to make your acquaintance. Let me introduce you to Herr Sonders.

Weinberl and Sonders scrutinize each other suspiciously.

Herr Sonders . . . Herr Weinberl. Herr Weinberl . . . Herr Sonders. But perhaps you two already know each other.

Weinberl (*stiffly*) I don't believe I've had the honour.

Sonders No, I don't believe so.

> *Sonders is very aware of Christopher, who is hiding his face in his hood.*
> *Sonders reaches for Christopher's hand and kisses it. Melchior is puzzled and mutters to himself.*

Melchior Madam, it's him!

Sonders Marie and I must leave immediately. Herr Zangler has changed his mind and instructed me to take Marie away. Come on, my dear, your uncle is waiting for us –

Miss Blumenblatt Just one moment, Herr Weinberl. Kindly desist from ordering people in and out of my house as if it were a blazing cuckoo-clock. Marie happens to be in love with Herr Sonders.

Sonders Well, yes and no –

Melchior Excuse me . . .

Miss Blumenblatt (*shouts*) Yes and no! The moment they met she was absolutely bowled over. It is something I can understand because her fate is precisely my own, except that in my case it was a horse-tram in the Bahnhofstrasse.

Sonders You were run over by a tram?

Melchior Madam . . .

Miss Blumenblatt Furthermore one only has to look at Herr Sonders to see that he is no Don Juan. Look into his eyes. I have seen more treachery in a cocker spaniel. (*She takes Weinberl by the arm and turns aside* *to confer with him.*) This is what we must do. I will send Zangler a message with this Weinberl to come here and . . .

Sonders is making sidelong attempts to capture Christopher's attention. Christopher is cowering from the possibility.

Sonders Marie . . . Marie . . . Who is this impostor? How . . .?

Meanwhile Melchior is scrutinizing Sonders from closer range.

Melchior Madam . . . It's him!

Sonders How dare you!

Miss Blumenblatt What?

Melchior He is the real imposter!

Sonders What does this man want? Who are you?

Miss Blumenblatt (*to Sonders*) You mean you don't know him? And he's been putting himself about as Zangler's servant! I knew he wasn't to be trusted! (*shouts*) Lisette!

The kitchen door crashes open, Lisette sways in the doorway, glazed, discreetly disarrayed, utterly changed, and goes to the door.

Fetch the constable in here.

Lisette passes through on the errand like a practised drunk.

(*To Melchior*) I am having you arrested.

Melchior (*aghast*) Me?

Miss Blumenblatt For false impersonation.

377

Melchior This place is teeming with frauds! I am about the only person here who isn't pretending to be somebody else!

The Constable enters. Lisette remains outside.

Constable What can I do for you, Ma'am?

Miss Blumenblatt Apprehend this person.

Melchior Watch yourself, flatfoot.

Constable 'Have a care, Constable.'

Blumenblatt I mean arrest him.

Sonders Get rid of him.

Weinberl Yes, the man's a menace.

Lisette now appears in the doorway.

Lisette Herr Zangler and party!

Miss Blumenblatt Show him in.

In the moment between her announcement and Zangler's entry, Sonders, Weinberl and Christopher leave the room by different routes but with identical timing. Weinberl leaves by the window. Christopher goes up the stairs. Sonders leaves by the chimney, if possible.
Zangler comes in with Madame Knorr and Mrs Fischer on his arm and Marie following.
The Constable pauses but still keeps hold of Melchior. Lisette, without pause, goes straight back to the kitchen.

Zangler Here we are, better late than never!

Parrot Who's a pretty boy, then?

Melchior Oh, thank goodness –

Zangler First things first. Let me introduce my fiancée and my fiancée's friend, Frau Fischer – Fräulein Blumenblatt

Miss Blumenblatt Enchantée.

Zangler And this is my ward, Marie.

Miss Blumenblatt Are you sure?

Zangler The wedding is tomorrow.

Miss Blumenblatt (*looking round and noticing their absence*) What happened to Herr Sonders and . . .?

Zangler Not *her* wedding – my wedding.

Miss Blumenblatt Such haste?

Zangler I'm not letting Madame Knorr out of my sight until we're married. I have my reasons. Why has the constable got my Melchior by the geraniums?

Miss Blumenblatt You mean he's really –?

Melchior Oh, tell her who I am!

Zangler He's my servant, of course.

The Constable releases Melchior.

Melchior And do you have a salesman called Weinberl?

Zangler I have.

Melchior Where is he now?

Zangler At home fast asleep above the shop.

Melchior I rest my case.

Mrs Fischer Weinberl! Wasn't that the name of –?

Mme Knorr It was! The one with the cousin who stole your coat!

Miss Blumenblatt Not a tartan coat with a hood just like Marie's?

Mrs Fischer Yes, I'm afraid it was.

Zangler Surely it can't have been Weinberl.

Miss Blumenblatt They were here!

Melchior I told you it wasn't Sonders.

Mrs Fischer It was my so-called husband.

Zangler Well, was he so-called or wasn't he? Where is he?

Miss Blumenblatt He was here just now. And the window is open.

Zangler rushes to and through the window.

Zangler My God, I was just about to make him my partner! If I find he's been on the razzle –

Melchior is helping Zangler out through the window, and he follows.

Melchior (*disappearing*) Classic!

Sounds of Zangler and Melchior rushing round the garden. Madame Knorr watches from the window.

Mme Knorr (*fondly*) Isn't he masterful? Did you notice the spurs?

Mrs Fischer I think I prefer him to your first husband, Eugenia.

Mme Knorr Oh yes, *he* had two left feet, poor Alfred . . .

Miss Blumenblatt What happened to him?

Mme Knorr He got knocked down by a horse-tram in the Bahnhofstrasse.

Miss Blumenblatt faints.

Miss Blumenblatt's garden.

A high wall running across the stage with a door set into it. The side of Miss Blumenblatt's house. Door into house from garden. Upper bedroom window.

Zangler and Melchior are, as it were, beating the bushes.

Zangler The garden is completely walled in and the gate is locked, but there's no sign of them. What's happened to the coachman?

Melchior He's very thick with the parlourmaid, apparently.

Zangler Well, he's supposed to remain outside.

Melchior He didn't want to frighten the horses.

Zangler Tell him to bring his coach round to the gate. If we set off now we'll be home by first light. Weinberl won't be expecting me back so early, I'll catch him on the hop. If it's the same Weinberl, he's finished in high-class groceries – I'll see to that.

Lisette enters the garden from the house in great excitement. Light spills from the open door.

Lisette Monsieur! One of the persons is fled to my room.

Zangler Lock the door on him!

Lisette The person, he has locked it.

Zangler Break it down!

Lisette I have another key.

Lisette, Zangler and Melchior pile back into the house, closing the door and leaving the garden dark again. Weinberl comes out of hiding. Moonlight.

Weinberl (*whispering loudly*) Christopher!

He looks round vainly. Christopher is at the upstairs window however.

Christopher (*whispering loudly*) Herr Weinberl!

Weinberl Is that you?

Christopher Yes!

Weinberl Where are you?

Christopher Here – and someone's trying to unlock the door!

Weinberl Can you get down?

Christopher No. Can you get over the wall?

Weinberl No. We're done for. I'm sorry, Christopher.

Christopher It wasn't your fault, Mr Weinberl. Thank you for everything. It was a wonderful razzle.

Weinberl Yes. Not bad, really. To hell with them.

Christopher (*urgently*) There's somebody coming behind you!

Weinberl goes back into hiding. Sonders approaches cautiously with a ladder. Sonders, looking around in the dark.

Sonders (*whispers*) Marie . . .

Christopher August! . . .

Sonders looks up and sees him.

Sonders Marie! Courage, mon amour! I have a ladder!

Christopher (*unwisely*) First class!

Sonders Is that really you?

Christopher (*changing tack*) Oh, August, it's not proper!

Sonders It's you! Courage, my little cabbage – (*He puts the ladder up against the window.*) Trust me!

Christopher I will, I will! (*He comes down the ladder.*)

Sonders Have you got the documents?

Christopher What?

Sonders Have you got the documents?

Christopher What documents?

Sonders You can't have forgotten the documents I gave you in the restaurant.

Christopher Oh those documents!

Sonders Well, where are they?

Christopher points dramatically upwards.

I'll have to go and get them.

Sonders climbs up. Lightning whinnies offstage.

Christopher Lightning!

Christopher and Weinberl take ladder to the wall. They hear the coach approaching – they hide again behind the summerhouse.
The Coachman climbs from his coach on to the wall and hears Lisette scream.

Coachman Lisette! Oh, here's a ladder!

Coachman climbs down the ladder, takes it to the window and climbs through, into Lisette's bedroom where he loudly encounters Sonders.
At the same time the door from the house is flung open. It releases, in a high state of excitement, Zangler, Melchior, Madame Knorr, Mrs Fischer, Marie and Miss Blumenblatt.

Zangler There's a ladder! They've got away! Unlock the gate!

Miss Blumenblatt runs forward with a large key and unlocks the gate in the wall.

Where's the coachman?

From the now darkened bedroom, Sonders, wearing the Coachman's hat and cloak, descends by the ladder. Everybody else, except Miss Blumenblatt, who is holding the gate open, is passing through the wall and straight into the interior of the coach outside the gate. Marie is last in the queue. Sonders removes the ladder from the window and places it against the wall.

Sonders (*to Marie*) Courage, my darling!

Marie gasps and passes through into the coach. Sonders goes up the ladder and takes the Coachman's seat. Everybody is now inside the coach, which departs. Lightning whinnies offstage.

Christopher Lightning!

Lightning enters, Christopher mounts up and Weinberl leads them off.

Weinberl Giddy up Lightning!

They exit.

Zangler's shop.
 Weinberl and Christopher arrive on Lightning.
 The coach is now seen through the panes of Zangler's shop window. The occupants are all unpacking themselves from the interior.
 Sonders gets down from the coach.
 Zangler, Madame Knorr, Mrs Fischer, Marie and Melchior disappear noisily from view and enter the

384

Zangler premises offstage. None of this is especially explicit. The stage is mainly occupied, of course, by the empty interior of the shop. It is early morning and the shop is not open yet.

Weinberl and Christopher try the shop door from the outside, unsuccessfully. There is a desperation about them and they disappear from view. Meanwhile, Zangler has been heard from within shouting for Weinberl.

Zangler (*offstage*) They're not upstairs – they're not downstairs – if they're not in the shop we've got them!

The trap door in the floor opens and Christopher emerges. He drops the trap door as Zangler hurries into the shop. Zangler is somewhat taken aback by seeing Christopher.

Ah – it's you.

Christopher Good morning, Herr Zangler. (*He goes to the street door and starts unbolting it.*) Just opening up, Herr Zangler!

Zangler Where's Weinberl?

Christopher He's here, Herr Zangler.

Zangler Where?

Christopher Where?

Zangler Yes, where?

Christopher You mean, where is he now, Herr Zangler?

Zangler (*impatiently*) Yes, yes –

Christopher Herr Weinberl –?

Zangler *Yes!* – Where is Herr Weinberl now, you numskull!

Weinberl plummets out of the chute and arrives behind the counter in a serving position.

Weinberl Good morning, Herr Zangler.

Zangler Shut up! Weinberl . . . My dear fellow . . . I thought . . .

There is a general entry now. Firstly, Sonders enters from the street door which has just been opened by Christopher.
Marie enters from the house, followed by Madame Knorr, Mrs Fischer and Melchior.

(*To Sonders*) What do you want? . . . Ah Marie . . . pay the coachman from the till.

Marie goes to the till and Sonders goes to her. Zangler's attention turns to Madame Knorr and Mrs Fischer. Mrs Fischer reacts to Weinberl's presence behind the counter and she approaches him so that only the counter is between them. Meanwhile Madame Knorr is taking in the presence of Christopher.

May I present my faithful partner, Herr Weinberl. We owe him an apology, I feel . . . and my chief sales assistant, Master Christopher . . . Madame Knorr . . . my fiancée, the future Frau Zangler: the wedding is tomorrow.

Christopher Congratulations. Haven't we met before?

Zangler What?

Mme Knorr No!

Christopher No, I thought not.

Zangler Of course you haven't. This is the first time that Madame Knorr has had the privilege of being swept round the heap of my camp fire.

Christopher That's very well put Chief.

Zangler I don't mean the heap of my camp fire.

Christopher Humped round the scene of your memoirs –

Zangler No.

Christopher Squired round the hub of your empire.

Zangler That's the boy – this is the first time Madame Knorr has had the privilege of being squired round the hub of my empire – What do you think of it all, Eugenia? Rather empirical, eh? – Every modern convenience – a spring-loaded cash flow to knock your eye out and your hat off!

He demonstrates the cash canister machine, which knocks Sonders's hat off.

Sonders!

Sonders Herr Zangler!

Zangler I'll kill him!

Marie Oh, Uncle!

The Belgian Foreigner enters from the street, rather dramatically.

Foreigner Herr Sonders!

Everybody stops and gives him their attention.

Sonders Go away – for God's sake are you still dogging me for a miserable unpaid hat-bill?

Foreigner Herr Sonders! I am coming from Brussels. I am coming from the lawyer of your relatively departed ant.

Sonders What?

Foreigner Alas, your ant is mortified!

Sonders Mortified?

Foreigner As a door nail.

Sonders My aunt! How dreadful! You mean my dear auntie in Brussels has unfortunately passed away?

Foreigner (*pointing to Sonders*) This man is too rich!

Marie Oh, oh darling, does this mean . . .?

Sonders (*to Zangler*) Sir . . .

Zangler Juan, isn't it? –

Sonders August.

Zangler August, of course! . . . my dears . . . (*to foreigner*) How much exactly . . .? Well, never mind for now – I think we all deserve a champagne breakfast. Entrez tout le monde! (*shouts*) Gertrud! Bubbly all round!

Gertrud enters.

Where have you been?

Gertrud Fetching the post.

Zangler Jereboams! Bollinger!

Gertrud You're upset. I can tell.

Zangler Get out and catch the pox – no –

Gertrud Pack my bags –

Zangler No.

Gertrud Pop the corks –

Zangler That's the boy – get out and pop the corks.

Gertrud exits.

We have two happy couples to toast. After all, Marie is of mortgageable age and August – (?) – (*Sonders nods.*) August here is a credit. To his profession. What are you in, by the way?

Sonders Risk capital, mainly, I think, Uncle.

Zangler Have you thought about high-class provisions?

Sonders We'll open an account as soon as we're married.

Zangler Open an account? Tush, man, come in with me and you'll eat wholesale for the rest of your life! And that's another thing, August . . . (*piously*) I haven't got long . . .

Sonders (*briskly*) We ought to be going too.

Zangler One day, August, the Zangler empire will need a new hand in the till – no.

Sonders On the tiller.

Zangler That's my boy!

Gertrud enters with tray.

Ah! – let the first glass be for the one who has entered my life and changed my fortune.

Gives first glass to Foreigner and then to Sonders and Madame Knorr. Gertrud carries tray down the line.

Marie . . . Frau Fischer . . . my faithful partner, Herr Weinberl.

Gertrud (*to Weinberl*) There's a letter for you, Herr Weinberl.

She gives Weinberl a letter which is of interest to Mrs Fischer.

Zangler . . . and my Chief Sales Assistant, Christopher. I give you the Grocers' Company!

All The Grocers' Company!

Zangler You can be a victualler too, Julie.

Sonders August!

Zangler August! . . . You can have my old uniform.

Gertrud (*to Weinberl*) Old uniform – why you crafty old . . .

Zangler What is it?

Gertrud Twenty-three Carlstrasse. Miss Blumenblatt's.

Zangler Where have you been?

   Gertrud exits.

Herr Weinberl . . . would you escort Frau Fischer? You might become better acquainted.

Mrs Fischer I am already well acquainted with Herr Weinberl.

Zangler You are?

Weinberl You're not, are you?

Mrs Fischer How can you say that after writing me all those romantic letters, Scaramouche!

Weinberl Elegant and Under Forty!

Zangler Well! *Three* happy couples to toast, I believe!

   Enter Gertrud.

Gertrud Breakfast is served.

Zangler Thank you Gertrud.

   He starts to load everybody out, Mrs Fischer bringing up the rear.

– Eugenia –

Sonders Marie.

Weinberl May I take you in Hildegarde?

Mrs Fischer You've been taking me in for months, Herr Weinberl.

Mrs Fischer exits. Weinberl and Christopher embrace with (premature) relief.

Zangler (*outside*) Melchior!

Weinberl and Christopher simultaneously realize that they could still be undone.

Weinberl Melchior!

But Melchior approaches with champagne bottle, recharges Weinberl's and Christopher's glasses, produces a third glass from his pocket, fills it, and toasts them.

Melchior Classic!

Melchior goes out. Weinberl and Christopher go to their places behind the counter. They drink a silent toast. They look at each other.

Christopher (*as Weinberl*) 'I don't think you know my wife!'

Weinberl splutters with pleasure.

Weinberl (*as Christopher*) 'We want the best dinner in the house and we want it now!'

They splutter joyfully and pummel each other about the shoulders.

Christopher (*as Miss Blumenblatt*) 'Herr Weinberl – Herr Sonders – Herr Sonders, Herr Weinberl . . .'

Weinberl (*as Sonders*) 'Marie – who is this impostor?'

But their joy evaporates almost immediately. Weinberl sighs and reaches for the broom.

Well . . . my chief sales assistant . . . Would you do me the honour . . .

He bows and offers the broom which Christopher takes. The street door opens to admit a small Ragamuffin.

Ragamuffin Are you the grocer, your eminence?

Weinberl I believe I am, sir.

Ragamuffin I understand you have an opening for an apprenticeship in the grocery trade.

Weinberl I believe I have, sir. The successful applicant will receive a thorough training in grocery, green grocery, charcuterie, weights and measures, stock-taking, window-dressing, debit, credit and personal hygiene. The hours are from dawn to dark and the pay is six guilders per month, less four guilders for board and lodging, one guilder for laundry, and one guilder put aside in your name against clothing and breakages. Would that be satisfactory?

Ragamuffin Yes, sir. I think that would be satisfactory.

Weinberl Have you any commercial experience?

Ragamuffin I have been chiefly holding horses' heads outside the Dog and Duck, sir. But I am my own master and can leave at any time.

Weinberl Christopher! Give him the broom!

Ragamuffin (*joyfully*) Oh – thank you, sir!

Christopher gives him the broom.

Weinberl You will find me a stern master but a fair one. I think I have some reputation in the mercantile world for –

Outside there is a roar of 'Weinberl' from Zangler.

(*Pause, gravely*) Excuse me. I was away in Vienna yesterday and there are matters to discuss with my partner. (*He leaves.*)

Ragamuffin Vienna! Have you ever been to Vienna, sir?

Christopher Me? Oh yes. Good Lord. Of course.

Ragamuffin What is it like, sir?

Christopher (*carelessly*) Vienna? Well it's . . . (*coming clean*) wonderful!

The Ragamuffin sweeps with furious delight. Christopher watches him.

THE SEAGULL

a new version of
the play by
Anton Chekhov

Characters

Irina Arkadina
Konstantin
Sorin
Nina
Shamraev
Polina
Masha
Trigorin
Dorn
Medvedenko
Yakov
Housemaid

Note

*Words bracketed in the dialogue
are unspoken.*

The Seagull was first performed in this version by the Peter Hall Company at The Old Vic, London, England, on 28 April 1997, produced by David and Ed Mirvish in association with Bill Kenwright. The cast was as follows:

Irina Arkadina Felicity Kendal
Konstantin Dominic West
Sorin Peter Blythe
Nina Victoria Hamilton
Shamraev Peter Gordon
Polina Anna Carteret
Masha Janine Duvitski
Trigorin Michael Pennington
Dorn David Yelland
Medvedenko Greg Hicks
Yakov Christopher Bianchi
Housemaid Olga Lowe

Director Peter Hall
Associate Producer Gillian Diamond
Associate Director Cordelia Monsey
Designer John Gunter
Costume Designer Liz Waller
Lighting Designer Mark Henderson
Sound Designer Matt McKenzie

Act One

Part of the park on Sorin's estate.

A stage, hastily knocked together for a private performance, with a curtain which is at present closed, hiding a view of a lake.

A few chairs, a small table.

The sun has just gone down. On the stage behind the curtain are Yakov and other workmen; coughing and hammering can be heard. Masha and Medvedenko enter, returning from a stroll.

Medvedenko Why do you always wear black?

Masha I'm in mourning for my life. I'm unhappy.

Medvedenko Why are you? I don't see why. You've got your health, [and] your father may not be rich but he doesn't go short here. Look at me with my twenty-three roubles a month – I don't go about in mourning. And that's before they take off the pension.

Masha Money isn't everything. A pauper can be happy.

Medvedenko A happy pauper? Yes . . . yes, in theory, but in practice what you've got is me and my mother, my two sisters and little brother, and my salary of twenty-three roubles a month. It isn't as if we don't have to eat and drink – is it? – [or] don't need tea – and sugar – tobacco . . . it's everywhere you turn.

Masha looks at the stage.

Masha [It's] nearly time for the performance, anyway.

Medvedenko Oh, yes: the performance. Nina Zarechnaya: appearing in: a play by: Konstantin Gavrilovich. They're in love and today their two souls will merge into one in an effort to create a single work of art. Your soul and mine, by way of contrast, don't meet at all. I love you and can't stay at home for longing for you, every day I walk four miles here and back again, and you don't care. Well, why should you? I have no money, large family to support . . . Who wants to marry a man who can't even feed himself?

Masha takes snuff.

Masha That's all rot. I'm touched that you love me but I can't return your feelings and that's all there is to it, [so] have a pinch of snuff.

Medvedenko I don't want a pinch of snuff . . . thank you all the same.

Masha It's stifling. There'll be a storm tonight, I shouldn't wonder. You're always either philosophizing or talking about money. You think there's nothing worse than being poor. I'd a thousand times rather go about in rags and beg than – well, I wouldn't expect you to [understand] . . .

Sorin, leaning on a stick, and Konstantin enter.

Sorin With me, what it is is, the country somehow doesn't agree with me and never will, that's what and there you have it. Last night I went to bed at ten – woke up at nine – had the feeling I'd slept so long my brain was stuck to my skull, and the rest of it. (*He laughs.*) Then after dinner I dropped off without knowing it and now I feel a complete wreck, it's like one long nightmare, that's what.

Konstantin You're right, you ought to live in town.

(*Having caught sight of Masha and Medvedenko.*) Look out, you two – members of the public aren't allowed – you'll be called when it starts. Please go away.

Sorin Be a good girl and speak to your father about letting the dog off its chain, otherwise it howls all night – my sister never slept a wink again.

Masha You can speak to him yourself – I'm not [going to], and I'd rather you didn't ask me. (*to Medvedenko*) Come on, then.

Medvedenko You'll let us know when it's starting . . .

They both go off.

Sorin So the dog will be howling all night again. It's a funny thing – I never get my own way in the country, never have. In the old days one used to take a month's leave to come down here and relax, recoup, and the rest of it, and from the moment you got here you'd be so pestered with every kind of nonsense, you couldn't wait to get away. Leaving was always the best part of coming here. But now I'm retired there's nowhere else to go, I have to live here like it or not, and there you have it.

Yakov Konstantin Gavrilovich, sir – we're going for a swim.

Konstantin All right, but [be back in your] places in ten minutes. Not long now.

Yakov Yes, sir.

Konstantin Now there's a theatre for you. Curtain – wings – then nothing but empty space – no scenery, sightlines straight to the lake and the horizon. Curtain up eight-thirty on the dot, as the moon is rising.

Sorin First rate.

Konstantin If Nina's late, of course, the whole effect will be lost. She ought to be here by now. Her father and stepmother watch her like hawks. Getting out of the house is like breaking out of prison. Your hair and beard could do with a comb – actually, a pair of scissors, do you think?

Sorin (*combing his beard*) It's the tragedy of my life. I looked like a down-and-out even as a young man, as if I drank and the rest of it – [it] used to put all the women off [me]. Why is my sister out of sorts?

Konstantin Because she's bored and she's jealous, that's why. She's taken against the performance just because Nina's acting and might catch the fancy of her writer fellow. She doesn't know anything about my play and she already hates it.

Sorin Oh, now really, come now . . .

Konstantin She's cross in advance because here on this pathetic little stage it's Nina who's going to get the applause and not her. She's a case, my mother. Talented all right – not stupid – quite capable of shedding tears over a novel – [she] can reel off Nekrasov by heart – wonderful with the sick . . . But just try praising Eleonora Duse in her presence – oh-ho-ho! – no one's got to be praised but her – she's the one who has to be written up, bravo'd, encore'd, and generally send people into raptures over her amazing performance in *La Dame aux Camelias* or one of those – but here in the country this drug is not available so she gets bored and crotchety – she has to take it out on someone, so it's us, it's all our fault. And then, she's superstitious – terrified of three candles on the table, the thirteenth of the month . . . And mean, too – she's got seventy thousand in the bank, I know that for a fact, but ask her for a loan and she'll start to weep.

Sorin What it is is you've convinced yourself your mother won't like your play, that's what, and you're upsetting yourself before the fact and the rest of it – calm down, your mother adores you.

Konstantin (*plucking the petals from a flower*) She loves me, she loves me not, she loves me, she loves me not, she loves me, she loves me – not: you see? My mother doesn't love me. Of course she doesn't! – she wants to live and love and dress like a girl, and there am I, twenty-five years old, a constant reminder that she's not as young as she thinks. When I'm not there she's thirty-two, when I am she's forty-three, no wonder she hates me. Furthermore, she knows I don't believe in her theatre. She worships the theatre, she thinks she's serving humanity and the sacred flame of art, while I happen to think [that] the modern theatre is a narrow-minded and predictable ragbag of worn-out routines. Up goes the curtain, and there in a room with a wall missing, inexplicably bathed in artificial light, are these great artists, these high priests of the sacred mystery, demonstrating how people eat, drink, make love, walk about and wear their coats; and when they strain to squeeze out from their trite little scenes some trite little moral for us to take home for use about the house – when I'm handed this same old stuff in a thousand variations over and over and over, then I'm afraid I run – like Maupassant ran when he clapped eyes on the Eiffel Tower and took to his heels thinking his brain was about to be crushed by the sheer weight of all that vulgarity.

Sorin But we must have theatre.

Konstantin We need a new kind of theatre. If we can't make it new [it's] better to have none. I love my mother, I love her very much, but what a futile life [she leads] ... forever obsessed with that novelist, her name constantly bandied about in the newspapers – I'm so tired of it; though it's also simple egotism – not wanting a famous actress for a mother, thinking I'd be happier if she were just anybody . . . Honestly, Uncle, can you think of anything more hopeless and stupid than being me in mother's drawing-room when she's got celebrities in . . . writers and artists everywhere you look; and me, the only nobody in the lot, indulged only because I'm her son. Who am I? What am I? Sent down from university without a degree for having opinions which are not necessarily those of the editor as the saying goes – I have no talents, no money, and in my passport I'm down as shopkeeper class, from Kiev – I'm from the Kiev shop-keeping classes! My father actually did keep a shop in Kiev, but he had a name as an actor. So anyway – when all those artists and writers in her drawing-room'd politely turned their glance on me I'd have the feeling they were sizing up my insignificance. I knew what they were thinking, and I felt so humiliated.

Sorin A propos – could you tell me – what sort of fellow is this writer of hers? I can't make him out, he never says anything.

Konstantin Intelligent – unaffected – a melancholy streak, I'd say . . . a decent fellow, famous at still well under forty, and tired of it all. As for his writing – well, how can I put it? – a very pretty talent, but if you've been reading Tolstoy or Zola you don't feel any urge to read Trigorin.

Sorin Still – I'm rather keen on literary men. There was a time when there were two things I passionately wanted – to get married and to be a literary man. Never managed either one. Even to be an unknown literary man must be very nice, that's what.

Konstantin I can hear her coming. (*He embraces his uncle.*) I can't live without her! – even the sound of her footsteps is enchanting – I could go mad, I'm so happy –

Konstantin quickly hurries to meet Nina as she enters.

My angel! – my dream –

Nina (*agitatedly*) I'm not late – tell me I'm not late.

Konstantin (*kissing her hand*) No . . . no . . . no . . .

Nina I've been worried sick all day – oh, I was so terrified my father would stop me coming. But they've gone out – he and my stepmother. The sky was red, the moon was rising, and I was urging on the horse – come on – come on – come on! (*She laughs.*) I feel happy now, though. (*She shakes Sorin firmly by the hand.*)

Sorin Oooh, do I see tears? That won't do!

Nina It's nothing – I'm just out of breath. I've got to go in half an hour, we have to hurry, I can't be late. I simply can't – don't make me late, for God's sake – my father doesn't know I'm here.

Konstantin It's time to start anyway – we must call everyone.

Sorin I'll go, I'll go – all done, that's what and there you have it. (*He goes and sings.*)

> Two grenadiers were riding to France,
> Home from their prison in Russia . . .

He looks round.

I once started to sing like that, and one of the assistant prosecutors said to me, 'You have a powerful voice, Your Excellency,' then he thought for a moment and added, 'powerful, but perfectly horrible.' (*He laughs and goes out.*)

Nina My father and his wife don't let me come here – they say you're all bohemians. They're terrified I'll go on the stage. But I'm drawn here like a seagull drawn to the lake. Oh, my heart's so full of you.

Konstantin [It's all right,] we're alone here.

Nina I think there's someone . . .

Konstantin There isn't anyone.

They kiss.

Nina What kind of tree is that?

Konstantin Elm.

Nina Why does it look so dark?

Konstantin The light's going now – everything starts looking dark. Don't leave too soon, please don't!

Nina I can't stay on.

Konstantin What if I came back with you, Nina? I'll stand the whole night in your garden looking up at your window.

Nina You'd better not! – The watchman would see you! – Tresor isn't used to you, he'll bark.

Konstantin I love you.

Nina Shh . . .

Konstantin Who's that? – is that you, Yakov?

Yakov Yes, sir, it's me.

Konstantin Everyone [get] ready, we'll be starting. Is the moon up?

Yakov Yes, sir.

Konstantin Have you got the methylated spirits? – and the sulphur? We must have the smell of sulphur as soon as the red eyes appear. (*to Nina*) Go on then – everything's ready for you – Are you nervous?

Nina Very. I don't mind your mother, I'm not nervous about her, but to have Trigorin here, I've got stagefright just thinking about acting in front of him, I feel so unworthy – such a famous writer! Is he young?

Konstantin He is, yes.

Nina All those wonderful stories he writes!

Konstantin I wouldn't know, I haven't read them.

Nina Your play's difficult to do. Being as there aren't any real people in it.

Konstantin Real people! The idea is to show life the way we experience it in dreams – not the way it is or [the way] you think it ought to be.

Nina Yes, but there isn't much *action* in your play, it's all – you know – *lines*. I think there ought definitely to be love in a play . . .

They both go behind the stage.
Polina and Dorn enter.

Polina It's getting damp. Do go back and put on your galoshes.

Dorn I'm too hot.

Polina You don't look after yourself. It's plain mulishness. You're a doctor, you know perfectly well dampness in the air is bad for you, [but] you just do it to upset me. Last night you deliberately sat the whole evening out on the verandah . . .

Dorn (*hums*) 'Say not your youth was ruined.'

Polina You were so carried away talking to madam you never noticed the cold. You like her – admit you do.

Dorn I'm fifty-five.

Polina Oh, tarradiddle – that's not old for a man. You've worn well and you're still attractive to women.

Dorn What is it you want me to do about it?

Polina You men would kiss the ground for an actress – not one of you wouldn't.

Dorn (*hums*) 'Again I stand before you . . .'
   If it so happens that artists in our society are treated differently from, say, tradesmen, that's only natural, that's called idealism.

Polina You've always had women throwing themselves at you – that's idealism too, is it?

Dorn Well, in a way . . . What women liked most about me was that I was a damn good doctor. If you remember ten or fifteen years ago, I was the only decent obstetrician in the whole province. And besides – I was always straight with them.

Polina Oh, my dear –!

Dorn Hush – they're coming.

Enter Arkadina on Sorin's arm, with Trigorin, Shamraev, Medvedenko and Masha.

Shamraev In 1873 at the Poltava Fair, she was amazing – gave a superb performance, quite wonderful. Do you happen to know what became of the comedian Chadin? He gave an incomparable Raspliuyev – better than Sadovsky, you have my word, ma'am. What is he doing now?

Arkadina You keep asking me about people from before the Flood! How should I know?

Shamraev Pashka Chadin. They don't make them like that any more. The theatre's not what it was. There used to be mighty oaks! – now we've got nothing but stumps.

Dorn There aren't as many outstanding actors nowadays, that's true, but the average level is much higher.

Shamraev There I have to disagree. But it's all a matter of taste. *De gustibus aut bene aut nihil.*

Konstantin comes out from behind the stage.

Arkadina My darling! – isn't it starting?

Konstantin In a minute – if you could just be patient.

Arkadina
'Oh, Kostya, speak no more!
Thou turn'st mine eyes into my very soul;
And there I see such black and grained spots
As will not leave their tinct.'

Konstantin
'. . . Nay, but to live
In the rank sweat of an enseamed bed
Stew'd in corruption, honeying and making love
Over the nasty sty . . .'

A horn sounds behind the stage.

Ladies and gentlemen, the performance is about to begin. Your attention, please. Here we go, then. (*He taps with a stick and speaks in a loud voice.*) Harken, ye ancient and hallowed shades that haunt the hours of night about this lake – send us asleep, perchance to dream of what will be two hundred thousand years from now!

Sorin Two hundred thousand years from now there'll be nothing.

Konstantin Then let them show us the nothing that will be!

Arkadina Let them, do. We're asleep.

The curtain parts; the view over the lake is revealed, the moon above the horizon, its reflection in the water; Nina, all in white, is sitting on a large rock.

Nina Mankind and monkeys – ostriches and partridges, antlered stags, ganders, spiders – unfathomable fishes that dwell in the deep and all creatures too small to be seen – every living thing and life itself – all has come to the end of its melancholy round and is now extinct. Thousands of centuries have passed since the earth bore any living creature, and this poor moon lights its lantern all for nothing. No more do the cranes wake and cry in the meadows, no more are the may-bugs heard in the lime groves. There is nothing but the cold – the cold, cold emptiness – emptiness and more emptiness – terrible it is – terrible – it is terrible ... (*Pause.*) The bodies of all creatures that ever lived are as dust – their indestructible matter is become stones, water, clouds – and their souls are become one soul, and that soul is – me! – I am the souls of Alexander the Great, of Caesar, of Shakespeare, of Napoleon and of the lowest of the leeches. In me, godlike reason is fused with animal instinct, every memory is in my memory, and every life is lived again in me.

Marsh light appears.

Arkadina (*quietly*) Sounds like one of those Decadents ...

Konstantin Mama!

Nina I am all alone. Once in a hundred years I open my lips to speak and my voice echoes dismally in the void and there is no one to hear me . . . not even you, pale fires – born at the turn of the night, from the rotting swamps, to wander the earth till day is breaking – devoid of thought or will or any pulse of life. The Devil – Lord of Eternal Matter – fearful of life coming to life in you, has caused a ceaseless exchanging of your atoms as in rocks and water, so [that] you are forever altering as you alter, and in the whole universe spirit is the only constant. (*Pause.*) I'm like a prisoner cast into a deep empty well, not knowing where I am or what awaits me. One thing only has been made known to me – [that] in the bitter struggle with the Devil who commands the forces of matter, I am destined to be victorious, and then will follow a wondrous fusion of Matter and Spirit to bring about the rule of the Cosmic Will. Yet first, the Moon and bright Sirius and the Earth, little by little, over millennia after millennia, must come to dust. Until that time, there shall be only the horror – the horror – the horror.

> *Pause: two red spots appear in the background over the lake.*

Look where he comes! – my mighty adversary the Devil approaches – I see his terrible crimson eyes –

Arkadina I can smell sulphur – is that part of it?

Konstantin Yes.

Arkadina (*laughing*) Oh, yes – I see – it's an effect!

Konstantin Mama!

Nina He's so lonely without Man . . .

Polina (*to Dorn*) Now you've taken off your hat – put it on before you catch cold.

Arkadina The doctor's taken his hat off to the Devil, Lord of Eternal Matter.

Konstantin Right! The play's over! Curtain!

Arkadina What are you so cross about?

Konstantin That's enough! Curtain! Can we have the curtain closed please?

The curtain is closed.

I must apologize. I quite forgot that writing and acting in plays is only for the chosen few. I have defied the monopoly! I'm – I – (*He wants to say something more but waves his hand and goes off.*)

Arkadina What's got into him?

Sorin Irina – my dear girl – that's no way to treat a young man's self-respect.

Arkadina Why, what did I say?

Sorin You've hurt him.

Arkadina But he told us himself it was going to be a bit of fun and I took it as a bit of fun.

Sorin Even so . . .

Arkadina Now it turns out he's written a masterpiece. I ask you! So he got up this show and stank out the place with sulphur not to amuse us after all but to teach us the kind of thing we ought to be writing and acting in. Really, it's becoming a bore . . . and his constant digs and pointed little remarks, I don't care what anyone says, it'd bore anybody – he's a petulant, conceited little boy.

Sorin He was trying to please you.

Arkadina Was he? Then why couldn't he choose a proper play instead of making us sit through this oh-so-decadent-my-dear gibberish. I don't mind listening to gibberish once in a while if it's to entertain, but this was apparently supposed to be a new theatrical form, the art of the future. Since when has the exhibition of a morbid personality been a new art form?

Trigorin We write as we must, and as best we can.

Arkadina He's welcome to write as he must but don't drag me into it.

Dorn When Jupiter's angry, Jupiter's wrong.

Arkadina Jupiter wasn't a woman. (*She lights a cigarette.*) Anyway, I'm not angry, I'm just annoyed that a young man should spend his time being such a bore. I hadn't the slightest intention of offending him.

Medvedenko It's quite unsound, you know, to take spirit and matter separately, for the simple reason that, for all we know, spirit itself is nothing else but the totality of material atoms. (*animatedly to Trigorin*) But actually, what someone should do is put on a play showing what life is like for schoolteachers, it's a hard life, you know, very hard.

Arkadina I'm sure you're right but can we not talk about plays or atoms. What a lovely evening! – is that singing? Can you hear? Heaven.

Polina It's coming from across the lake.

Arkadina (*to Trigorin*) Come and sit by me. A dozen years ago you could have heard music and singing across the water almost every evening. There are six properties on this side. There was laughter – noise – gunfire . . . and the love affairs, love affairs going on all the time – and the leading man in all of this, the idol of all six estates, was none other than – your very own – Dr Yevgeny Sergeyevich. He's still attractive but in those days he was irresistible. However, my conscience is beginning to prick me. How could I have hurt my poor little boy's feelings like that? – Now I'm worried about him. (*She calls loudly.*) Kostya! – Darling! – Kostya.

Masha I'll go and look for him.

Arkadina Would you? There's a dear.

Masha Halloo-oo – Halloo-oo . . .

Masha goes off.
Nina enters from behind the stage.

Nina We're obviously not going on, I might as well come out. Hello! (*She kisses Arkadina and Polina.*)

Sorin Bravo! Bravo!

Arkadina Yes, bravo! – We were all enchanted. With those looks, and that lovely voice it's a sin for you to be hidden away in the country. I'm convinced you must have talent. You hear? – you definitely have to go on the stage!

Nina Oh, it's what I dream of! But it won't ever come true.

Arkadina Who can tell? Now – let me introduce – Trigorin, Boris Alexeyevich.

Nina Oh, I'm so pleased to – I've read all your books . . .

Arkadina (*making her sit down beside them*) No need to be shy, my sweet, he's a famous man but a simple soul. Look – he's as bashful as you are.

Dorn I suppose it's all right to open the curtain now – it's rather sinister like that.

Shamraev Yakov, open the curtain, would you.

The curtain goes up.

Nina (*to Trigorin*) It's certainly an unusual play, didn't you think?

Trigorin I didn't understand a word. But I liked watching it. You did it with such sincerity. And the scenery was wonderful. (*Pause.*) There must be plenty of fish in this lake.

Nina Oh, yes.

Trigorin I love fishing. There's nothing nicer than sitting on the bank as the evening comes on, watching the float.

Nina I'd have thought that for someone who has experienced the joy of creation, all other pleasures must be insignificant.

Arkadina Oh, you mustn't talk like that. When people make pretty speeches at him he wants to run away and hide.

Shamraev I remember once in Moscow at the opera, the famous Silva took a bottom C. Well, by no coincidence, it happened that the bass from our church choir was up in the gallery. Imagine our astonishment when suddenly we heard above our heads, 'Bravo, Silva!' a whole octave lower, like this . . . (*in a deep bass*) 'Bravo, Silva!' – The entire audience froze.

Pause.

Dorn An angel flew over.

Nina I've got to go. Goodbye.

Arkadina Go where? Where do you have to go so early? We shan't let you go.

Nina My father's waiting for me.

Arkadina Too dreadful of him – really . . .

They kiss each other.

But if you must, you must. What a shame – it's a shame to lose you.

Nina If you only knew how much I'd like to stay.

Arkadina Somebody should see you home, my precious.

Nina Oh – no! – no –

Sorin Please stay a while –

Nina I really can't.

Sorin Just for an hour, no more – surely –

Nina hesitates a moment.

Nina (*through her tears*) No – I simply can't. (*She shakes hands and goes off quickly.*)

Arkadina Poor girl! – literally. They say her mother left her entire fortune to the husband and the girl's going to get nothing because he's leaving it all to his second wife. Perfectly scandalous.

Dorn Oh yes, her dear papa's a regular swine, to give him his due.

Sorin We should go in, too, good people – it's getting damp. My legs hurt.

Arkadina Your legs are like peg-legs, they barely work – well, off we go then, foolish, fond old man.

Dorn speaks to no one in particular; no one in particular takes note.

Dorn I don't know – perhaps I'm fooling myself, or I've lost my mind, but I liked the play. There is something in it. When that little girl was saying how lonely it was . . .

Shamraev (*offering his arm to his wife*) My dear?

Dorn . . . and then the Devil appeared with his red eyes,

my hands were shaking with excitement. There was
something fresh and artless about it . . .

Meanwhile Arkadina has taken Sorin by the arm.

Sorin There's that dog howling again. (*to Shamraev*)
Would you be good enough to have him let off the
chain?

Shamraev Not possible, Piotr Nikolayevich – I'm afraid
of thieves getting into the barn. I've got the millet in there.
(*to Medvedenko, who is walking beside him*) Yes, a whole
octave lower – 'Bravo, Silva!'. And he wasn't an opera
singer, mind – simply a member of our church choir.

Medvedenko And how much would a member of the
choir get paid?

Dorn That's him coming, I think. I feel one should say
something encouraging . . .

But no one is listening to him. He is left alone.
Konstantin enters.

Konstantin Cleared off already.

Dorn I'm here.

Konstantin Mashenka's been looking for me all over the
park. Unbearable woman.

Dorn Konstantin Gavrilovich, I liked your play very
much indeed. It was a bit strange, and of course we
never heard the end, but all the same it made a powerful
impression. You're a young man with talent. You must
carry on.

Konstantin shakes his hand warmly and embraces him
impetuously.

Oh – go along – what a sensitive creature [he is]! Tears
in his eyes! . . . What is it I'm trying to say? You took

your subject from the realm of abstract ideas: which is right, because a work of art must express a serious idea. Without seriousness there can be no art . . . Now he's gone quite pale!

Konstantin So what you're saying is – I should go on?

Dorn Yes . . . but only write about what's important and permanent. You know, I've lived a pick-and-choose sort of life, plenty of variety, I'm not complaining, but let me tell you, if I'd ever experienced that transcendent feeling artists get in the moment of inspiration, then I believe I would have had nothing but contempt for my physical life and everything that goes with it and I'd have left the earth behind me and soared away into the skies.

Konstantin Excuse me – sorry – where's Nina?

Dorn And there's another thing. When you write something, you must have a clearly defined thought. You have to know why you're writing. Otherwise – if you set off along that enchanted path without a definite goal in mind – you'll lose your way, and your talent will turn on itself and destroy you.

Konstantin Where is Nina?

Dorn What? She went home.

Konstantin What am I going to do? I have to see her! – it's vital that I see her – I'm going after her.

Masha enters.

Dorn Now, you mustn't get so worked up – my dear boy –

Konstantin I'm going anyway – I have to go.

Masha Come indoors, Konstantin – your mother's waiting, she's worried about you.

Konstantin Tell her I've gone away. I wish you'd all leave me alone! Just leave me! Stop following me about!

Dorn No, no, don't talk like that – that's not the right way to . . .

Konstantin (*through tears*) Goodbye, Doctor. Thank you . . . (*He goes.*)

Dorn Oh . . . youth . . . youth . . .

Masha When there's nothing more to be said, people say 'Youth, youth'.

Masha takes snuff. Dorn takes her snuff box and flings it away.

Dorn Disgusting habit! (*Pause.*) They'll be playing cards now. I'd better go.

Masha Stay a minute.

Dorn What is it?

Masha There's something quite apart from all this I want to . . . [tell you]. Can we talk for a bit? I don't love my father . . . but I feel I can open my heart to you . . . I feel somehow [that] you're close to me. You have to help me. Help me or I'll do something stupid and make a shambles of my life, I'll ruin it – I can't go on . . .

Dorn What? Help you how?

Masha I'm so unhappy. No one knows the agony I'm going through. (*She lays her head against Dorn's breast, quietly.*) I love Konstantin.

Dorn Another one! These sensitive creatures! They're all so sensitive! And [there's] all this love about! – It's that lake! – they're all bewitched! (*tenderly*) But what can I do, my child? – what can I do?

Curtain.

Act Two

The lawn near the house. It is midday and it is hot. At the side of the lawn Arkadina, Dorn and Masha are sitting on a garden seat in the shade of an old lime tree. On Dorn's lap is an open book.

Arkadina (*to Masha*) Stand up a minute.

They both get up.

[Stand] next to me. You're twenty-two and I'm nearly twice that. Yevgeny Sergeyevich, which of us looks younger?

Dorn You, naturally.

Arkadina There you are. And why? Because I work – I feel things – I do things! You don't stir from the same place – you're not alive . . . And I have a rule: not to look ahead. I never think about old age or death. What will be will be, if it be not now – and so on.

Masha Yes, well, I feel as if I was born about a century ago, and I'm dragging my life behind me like the train of a dress going back as far as I've come. A lot of the time I don't feel like going on. That's silly, of course. You've got to shake yourself out of it.

Dorn (*hums softly*) 'Tell her, my flowers . . .'

Arkadina Next, I'm always properly dressed on parade, like an Englishman. I keep myself tip-top and up to the mark, with my hair done *comme il faut*. Have you ever seen me go out of the door – even into the garden – in my housecoat and my hair not done? – never! The reason

I'm in this remarkable state of preservation is that I refuse to be a frump or let myself go like some people . . . Look! – you see? Frisky as a fifteen-year-old – I could still play one any day.

Dorn Albeit and regardless, I'm going to go on [reading]. (*He picks up the book.*) We stopped at the cornchandler and the rats . . .

Arkadina And the rats. Read on, Macduff. (*She sits down.*) Or rather, give it to me. It's my turn [to read]. (*She takes the book and searches with her eyes for the place.*) And the rats. Here we are. (*She reads.*) 'The truth is, it's as inadvisable for people in society to fawn over writers and invite them into their houses as for a corn-chandler to raise rats in his granary. And yet writers are considered a catch, and much pursued. So it happens that when a woman has picked out the lion she intends to bag, she stalks him with compliments, favours, little acts of kindness . . .' Well, it may be true with the French but it's not like that here, we don't work to a programme. Here it's madly in love first and then the pursuit. You don't have to look far – take Trigorin and me.

Sorin enters leaning on a stick, with Nina beside him and behind them Medvedenko pushing a wheelchair.

Sorin So we're feeling cheerful today, are we? – we're happy now are we? We're all smiles because Papa and Stepmama have gone away and we are now free as a bird for three whole days.

Nina sits down next to Arkadina and embraces her.

Nina I'm so happy. Now I can be all yours.

Sorin (*sitting down in his wheelchair*) [She's] looking pretty as pretty can be.

Arkadina [She's] turned herself out just so and very fetching – she's a clever little miss. (*She kisses Nina.*) But we mustn't overdo the compliments, it arouses envy in the fates – where is Trigorin?

Nina Fishing by the bathing place.

Arkadina You'd think he'd get tired of it.

Nina What is your book?

Arkadina Maupassant, my sweet. *On the Water* – The next bit is dull, without being true. (*She closes the book.*) There is something in my soul o'er which my melancholy etcetera. Will somebody tell me what is the matter with my son? Why is he so boring and churlish? He spends every day on the lake, I hardly see him.

Masha He's heartsick. (*to Nina, shyly*) Please, would you do a bit from his play?

Nina Do you want me to? It's not very interesting.

Masha When he reads something his eyes burn and he goes quite pale. He has a beautiful sad voice – really, he's just like a poet ought to be.

Sorin is snoring.

Dorn Good night.

Arkadina Petroosha!

Sorin Eh!

Arkadina Are you asleep?

Sorin Certainly not.

Arkadina You're not taking anything for yourself, are you? – you're very silly.

Sorin I'd be happy to take something for myself if only the doctor here would give me something to take.

Dorn What's the point at your age?

Sorin Even at sixty, one would rather stay alive than not.

Dorn Oh, very well – take some valerian drops.

Arkadina I think it would do him good to go to a spa somewhere.

Dorn No harm in going, no harm in not going.

Arkadina Make sense of that if you can.

Dorn Nothing to make sense of – couldn't be plainer.

Medvedenko Piotr Nikolayevich shouldn't smoke.

Sorin Nonsense.

Dorn No, it's not nonsense. Wine and tobacco rob you of your identity. After a cigar or a glass of vodka you're no longer just you, you're you and this other fellow – your first-person-singular-self goes out of focus and before you know where you are you start thinking of yourself in the third person – oh, *him*.

Sorin (*laughs*) Well, that's all very well for you, you've lived a bit in your time but what about me? – twenty-eight years in the Department of Justice, and I haven't lived at all, I haven't experienced anything. You've had your fill and you don't care any more, which is why you're inclined to be philosophical, whereas I still want to have a bit of life, which is why I'm inclined to drink sherry at dinner and smoke cigars, and there you have it. There you have it.

Dorn Life is serious. Taking cures when you're sixty and complaining you didn't have fun when you were young is frivolous. To speak frankly.

Masha stands up.

Masha It must be time for lunch. My leg's gone to sleep. (*She goes out.*)

Dorn [She's] gone to get down a couple of vodkas before lunch.

Sorin Poor girl – she doesn't have much fun either.

Dorn You're talking like a fool, Your Excellency.

Sorin And you're talking like a man who's had his fill.

Arkadina Oh, what could be more weary than the sweet weariness of life in the country . . . The heat and quiet, no one feels like doing anything – it's very pleasant . . . listening to one's friends disputing away . . . and yet . . . there's nothing to compare with sitting in a hotel room somewhere learning one's lines.

Nina Oh – yes! – that's what I think!

Sorin Town is best, that's what. You're sitting in your office, no one gets in without sending their card up with the porter . . . telephone to hand . . . cabs on the streets . . . and the rest of it.

Dorn (*hums*) 'Tell her, my flowers . . .'

Shamraev enters, Polina follows him.

Shamraev So here you are: good morning! (*He kisses Arkadina's hand and then Nina's.*) Delighted to find you in good health. My wife tells me you were intending to go into town together. Is that so?

Arkadina Are intending.

Shamraev Hm. That's all very well but, with great respect, ma'am, how were you thinking of getting there? We're carting rye today, all the hands are busy. Which horses were you thinking of using, may one ask?

Arkadina Which horses? How should I know?

Sorin We have carriage horses.

Shamraev Carriage horses? And where do I get harness from? Where do I get harness? It's incredible! It beggars belief! Madam – forgive me, ma'am – I worship your talent – I am ready to give you ten years of my life, but horses I cannot give you.

Arkadina But what if I *had* to go? How very odd.

Shamraev With the greatest respect, you don't understand about farming.

Arkadina Oh, that one again! – In that case I'm going back to Moscow today. Be so good as to have horses hired for me in the village, otherwise I'll walk to the station!

Shamraev In that case, I resign! You can find yourself another manager! (*He goes.*)

Arkadina It's the same every summer! Every summer I come down here and I'm insulted! I will not set foot in this place again! (*She goes.*)

Sorin This is sheer impudence! This is the devil knows what it is! I've finally had my fill of this, and there you have it! Have all the horses brought round at once!

Nina (to *Polina*) Imagine refusing Irina Nikolayevna the famous actress! – surely her every wish – even her slightest whim – is more important than your farming. It's simply incredible!

Polina What can I do? Put yourself in my place. What can I do?

Sorin (to *Nina*) We'll go to her, that's what. We'll plead with her not to go. Impossible man! Tyrant!

Nina prevents Sorin from getting up. She and Medvedenko begin to push the wheelchair.

427

Nina Sit down – sit down – we'll push you. Oh, what a dreadful thing to happen!

Sorin Yes – yes, it's dreadful – but it won't come to him leaving. I'll have a talk with him.

They go off; only Dorn and Polina remain.

Dorn [God] how tedious people are. The simple truth is your husband should be thrown out on his neck. But it'll finish up with that old woman and his sister asking him to forgive them, you'll see.

Polina He's put even the carriage horses to work in the fields. Some mess-up like this happens every day. You don't know how it upsets me. It's making me ill – look, I'm shaking. I can't bear his rudeness. (*pleading*) Yevgeny – my dearest – my beloved – please let me come to you – our time is running on, we're not young any more, and if only we could end our days no longer having to hide and pretend.

Dorn I'm fifty-five years old. It's a little late to change my life.

Polina I know it's because I'm not the only one . . . and you can't have them all come to you – I know that – I'm sorry – I'm being a nuisance.

Nina is seen near the house; she is picking a posy of small wildflowers.

Dorn No, you're never . . .

Polina I go through agonies of jealousy. I know you can't avoid women, being a doctor – I know that –

Dorn (*to Nina who is approaching*) What's happening up there?

Nina She's in tears and he's got his asthma.

428

Dorn (*standing up*) I'll go and distribute valerian drops.

Nina (*giving him the posy*) For you.

Dorn *Merci bien.*

> *Dorn goes towards the house. Polina goes with him.*

Polina Oh, aren't they pretty, so tiny and delicate . . . (*Near the house she speaks in a muffled voice.*) Give me those [flowers]. Give them to me!

> *On getting the flowers she tears them apart and throws them aside.*

> *Polina and Dorn enter the house. Nina is alone.*

Nina How strange to see somebody famous crying . . . and over something so ordinary like that. But then it's just as strange to think that a famous writer idolized by the public, written about in all the papers, his photograph in shop windows, his books translated into foreign languages – to think he should spend the whole day fishing and be delighted with himself if he catches a couple of chub! I thought famous people were proud and remote and looked down on the common crowd, I thought [that] with their fame and the glamour of their names they were somehow getting their own back on rank and wealth and birth being always put first. But here they are, crying, fishing, playing cards and losing their tempers just like anybody else.

> *Konstantin enters with a gun and a dead seagull.*

Konstantin Are you alone here?

Nina Yes.

> *Konstantin lays the seagull at her feet.*

And what's that supposed to mean?

Konstantin I sank low enough today to kill this seagull.
I lay it at your feet.

Nina What has got into you?

Konstantin Soon I'm going to kill myself in the same
way.

Nina I don't know you like this.

Konstantin That's true. And I don't know you like that.
You aren't like you were. You look at me from so far
away. You find my presence an embarrassment.

Nina Well, you've become so cross lately, and you keep
saying things somehow crosswise, in symbols or
something – I mean, look at this seagull, a symbol if ever
I saw one, but of *what*, I'm sorry, I've no idea. I'm not
clever enough to make it out.

Konstantin It's all since that night when my play was
such a fiasco. Women can forgive anything but failure.
I've burned it, every last shred of it. You can't know how
unhappy I am. Your detachment is literally terrifying,
something inconceivable, as if I were to wake up one
morning and this lake had gone, simply evaporated, or
run away into the ground. Not clever enough? – what's
there to make out? My play was a failure, you despise
my inspiration, now you think I'm just another
insignificant nobody just like they all – oh, I know about
this!, believe me I do know about this! It's like having a
nail hammered into my brain. To hell with it all! – and
my pride, too – that feeds on my blood, sucks it out of
me like leeches!

He sees Trigorin who is reading a book as he walks.

Oh – here comes the genuine article! Walking like
Hamlet. He's even got the book. (*Mimics.*) 'Words.
Words. Words.' The sun's rays have not yet kissed you

but you're already smiling – your glance melted in their warmth – well, let me not stand between you and the . . . [sun] (*He goes off, quickly.*)

Trigorin (*making notes in a small book*) Takes snuff, drinks vodka, wears black, loved by teacher . . .

Nina Good morning, Boris Alexeyevich!

Trigorin Oh, good morning! I gather we're leaving today, [owing to an] unexpected turn of events. I don't suppose we'll meet again. Pity. It's not often I have the occasion to meet young women, young and interesting women. Now that I've forgotten and can't really imagine how it feels to be eighteen or nineteen, the young women in my books and stories don't quite ring true. I wish I could put myself in your place for an hour or so, just to know how you think and generally what kind of little creature this is.

Nina I'd like to put myself in your place, too.

Trigorin Why's that?

Nina Just to know how it feels to be a celebrated writer. What is fame like? What does it feel like to be famous?

Trigorin What does it feel like? Well, it feels like not being famous. Probably. I never think about it. (*having thought*) Well – two possibilities: either I'm not as famous as you think, or it doesn't feel like anything.

Nina What about when you read about yourself in the newspapers?

Trigorin When they're nice about me I like it. When they're nasty I'm depressed for a day or two.

Nina Oh – how wonderful! You don't know how I envy you. How different is different people's lot in life! Some of them can barely drag out their dull, dim lives – all much alike and equally miserable – while others, like you for one, the one in every million, are blessed with an interesting, brilliant life that means something. You're so lucky.

Trigorin Am I? (*shrugging his shoulders*) Hm . . . here you are talking about fame and fortune and some interesting, brilliant life I'm supposed to be having, but I'm afraid these fine-sounding words mean no more to me than a bag of toffees, which I never eat. You're young and you mean well.

Nina But you have such a marvellous life.

Trigorin I don't see what's so specially good about it. (*He looks at his watch.*) I have to go and do some writing now – excuse me – I haven't the time – (*He laughs.*) – You've trodden on my pet corn, you see! – and I start getting upset and irritable – All right, let's talk about my wonderful, brilliant life . . . Well, where should we begin? (*after a little thought*) Well – there are people who develop an obsession with something – say, a man who can think about nothing but the moon, day and night. Well – I have my own moon. Day and night I'm driven by one constant thought: I must be writing – I must be writing – I've scarcely finished one story before – God knows why – I have to write another – then a third, and after the third a fourth – I keep on without a break like the mailcoach changing horses – on and on, and I can't do anything else. What's so wonderful and brilliant about that? It's a ridiculous life. Here I am with you, I've got myself all worked up – and the whole time, I'm thinking [that] there's a story waiting to be finished on my desk. I look up and see there's a cloud shaped like a grand piano. I think – I must get that into a story some time, [that] a cloud floated past like a grand piano. I can smell heliotropes – I make a quick mental note, sickly

sweet scent, colour of widows' weeds, mention when
describing summer evening. I snap up every word and
phrase we utter and hurry off to shut them away in my
bottom drawer. When I finish something, I escape to the
theatre or go fishing. There you'd think I'd be allowed to
relax, lose myself – but no: something is already moving
in my brain like a heavy iron ball, a new idea, a new
story, and it's dragging me back to my desk. I have to rush
back and write – and write – and that's how it is, all the
time. I'm never left in peace, and it's as if I'm devouring
my own life – to make the honey for the readers out
there, I'm gathering up the pollen from my best flowers,
breaking off the flowers themselves, trampling on their
roots. I could be a madman. Are my friends and
acquaintances actually treating me as if I'm sane? 'What
are you working on?' 'When are you going to give us
your next?' – over and over, it never stops – and I sometimes think, all this fascination – this admiration and
congratulation – it's all an act, they're humouring me
like an invalid and getting ready to creep up behind me
and pounce on me and carry me off to the madhouse like
in Gogol. Back in the days when I was starting out – the
years of one's youth, the best years – it was continuous
torture. A young writer, especially if he isn't having much
luck – feels awkward and not *for* anything – he's on edge,
his nerves are a wreck – he can't stop himself hanging
around the literary crowd, unknown and ignored, afraid
to look people in the eye, like a compulsive gambler with
nothing to bet with. I never met my readers, but for
some reason I always imagined them to be sceptical,
hostile. I was afraid of the public – the thought of them
terrified me. When I came to have a play put on I'd look
at the audience and decide that everyone with dark hair
had made up their minds to hate it, and everyone with
fair hair wasn't interested enough to care either way.
Oh – it was a nightmare! Sheer torture!

Nina I'm sorry, but – surely when you're in mid-inspiration – actually in the very act of creation – doesn't that give you, just for that moment, a feeling of being lifted up – of transcendent happiness?

Trigorin (*casually*) Oh yes, I love writing. Writing is very enjoyable. Correcting proofs is very nice too . . . But then it's got to be published. The moment the thing is off the press I can't stand it. It's already no good – a mistake – ought never to have been written in the first place – and I feel tetchy and worthless. And people read it and say, 'Oh yes, a very pretty talent, quite charming, but not a patch on Tolstoy' – or, 'Not bad at all, but *Fathers and Sons* is better.' And it will go on like this till I die. I'll never be anything more than charming and talented. And when I'm dead it'll say on my gravestone, 'Here lies Trigorin. He was good – but not as good as Turgenev.'

Nina Well, I'm sorry but I refuse to sympathize. You've simply become jaded with your success.

Trigorin What success are you referring to? I've never felt I've succeeded, I don't like myself as a writer. The worst of it is, I often write in a kind of fog and don't understand what I'm writing about. I love this stretch of water here – the trees – the sky – I have a feeling for nature, it excites a passion in me – that irresistible desire to write. But when all's said and done I'm not just here to do landscapes, I'm a citizen. I love Russia and its people, and I feel that if I'm a writer it's up to me to speak out about people's troubles, their fate, and to have something to say about science, and the rights of man, and so on and so on – so I speak out about everything! – I rush around, urged on from every side – people getting cross with me – I dash this way and that like a fox with the hounds on its trail. Ahead of me I can see Science and the Rights of Man leaving me behind as I chase after them like some yokel missing a train. And in the end I feel that landscape is the only thing I know how to write and in everything else I'm a fake, a fake to the marrow of my bones.

Nina You've been working so hard you've no time and no curiosity to realize who you are. You may be dissatisfied with yourself but for everyone else you're a great and important writer. If I were great like you I'd dedicate my whole life to my public, but I'd always remember that it's [the] reaching up to me which is what makes them happy – and they'd pull my chariot through the streets.

Trigorin Oh, in a chariot – now you think I'm Agamemnon.

Nina To have that feeling – whether as a writer or an actress – I'd put up with family and friends turning against me. I'd endure poverty and disappointment – I'd live on black bread in a garret – [I'd] suffer self-doubt and knowing I'm not good enough – but!, in return I would demand fame – real resounding fame! – My head's whirling – oof! –

Arkadina calls from the house.

Arkadina Boris Alexeyevich!

Trigorin I'm being summoned. To pack, no doubt. I wish I wasn't leaving. Look how lovely it all is . . . Paradise!

Nina You see that house with a garden on the other side . . .?

Trigorin [Yes.]

Nina That used to belong to my mother. I was born there. I've grown up around this lake. I know every little island.

435

Trigorin Well – you live in a magical place. (*He sees the seagull.*) What's this?

Nina A seagull. Konstantin shot it.

Trigorin Beautiful bird. I really don't want to leave. What if you were to persuade Irina to stay? (*He makes notes in his little book.*)

Nina What are you writing?

Trigorin Idea for story – young girl, like you, brought up on the shores of a lake. She loves the lake like a seagull and is happy and free just like a seagull. Then a man happens to come along, he sees her, and, having nothing much to do, destroys her, like this seagull.

Pause.
Arkadina appears at a window.

Arkadina Boris Alexeyevich – where are you?

Trigorin I'm coming.

He goes, then looks back at Nina; Arkadina is at the window.

Arkadina We're staying!

Trigorin goes into the house.

Nina [Oh, I see – it's] a dream!

Curtain.

Act Three

The dining-room in Sorin's house. A sideboard and a cupboard with medicines. In the middle of the room, a table. A trunk and hat boxes; preparations for a journey are to be seen. Trigorin is having lunch. Masha stands by the table.

Masha I'm telling you this because you're a writer. You can use it. I'm telling you in all honesty, if he'd seriously wounded himself I wouldn't have gone on living another minute. [It's] not for lack of courage, mind you. I've decided – I'm going to tear this love out of my heart, just tear it out by the roots.

Trigorin How are you going to do that?

Masha I'm getting married. To Medvedenko.

Trigorin The schoolteacher?

Masha [Yes.]

Trigorin I think that's rather overdoing it.

Masha Loving without hope – waiting years on end for something, you don't know what . . . Better off married and forget about love, I'll have new troubles to blot out the old ones – and anyway, anything for a change. Shall we have another [drink]?

Trigorin Wouldn't that be rather [overdoing it]?

Masha pours out a glass each.

Masha Oh, come on. You don't have to look [at me] like that. Lots of women drink – more than you think.

437

Not so many openly like me – mostly in secret. Vodka or brandy for preference. (*clinking glasses*) Here's to you! You're all right [I approve of you]. I'm sorry you're leaving.

Trigorin I'm sorry too.

Masha Ask her to stop on.

Trigorin No, she won't stay now. Her son is being awfully difficult. Not content with trying to shoot himself, he now wants to challenge me to a duel, apparently. I've no idea why. He sulks and stamps his foot and preaches his doctrine of new forms. But there's plenty of room for all, there's no need to push and shove.

Masha Yes, but he's jealous. Not that it's any of my affair.

Yakov crosses the stage with a trunk. Nina enters and stands by the window.

My schoolteacher's not very clever but he's kind, and he's got nothing. He's devoted to me. I'm sorry for him. I'm even sorry for his old mother. Well – time to wish you all the best. Spare me a thought now and then. (*She shakes Trigorin warmly by the hand.*) Thank you very much for being nice to me. Send me your books and don't forget to write in them – only, not the usual 'To so-and-so, best wishes' – put 'To Masha, God knows whence and God knows why.' Goodbye!

Masha leaves.
Nina stretches out her hand towards Trigorin, her fist clenched.

Nina Odd or even?

Trigorin Even.

Nina Wrong. That means 'No'. I'm trying to decide whether or not to go on the stage. If only somebody would tell me what to do.

Trigorin It's not the sort of thing anybody can decide for you.

Nina We're parting today and I don't suppose we'll ever meet again. I've got you this little medallion – to remember me by. I've had your initials engraved on it – and on the other side, the title of one of your books, *Days and Nights.*

Trigorin But how sweet of you. (*kissing the medallion*) It's a lovely present.

Nina Will you think of me sometimes?

Trigorin I'll think of you as you were on that sunny day a week ago – do you remember?, wearing your light-coloured dress . . . We talked . . . and there was a seagull lying on the seat.

Nina Yes . . . the seagull.

Trigorin (*reading the medallion*) '*Days and Nights*, page 121, lines 11 and 12.'

Nina We can't talk now, they're coming – please – I beg you – give me two minutes before you go –

She leaves. At the same time, Arkadina enters, with Sorin in a tail coat with a star, and then Yakov, who is preoccupied with the packing.

Arkadina What wilt thou do, old man, driving into town with your rheumatism? Why don't you stay at home? (*to Trigorin*) Who was that who just went out? Nina?

Trigorin Yes.

Arkadina *Milles pardons* for interrupting . . . I think everything's packed. I'm exhausted.

Yakov is clearing the table.

Yakov Are the fishing rods to go?

Trigorin Yes – I'll be wanting them. The books can be handed out.

Yakov Yes, sir.

Trigorin (*to Arkadina*) Have you got any of my books here in the house?

Arkadina In my brother's study – in the corner bookcase.

Trigorin goes out.

I mean it, Petroosha, you'll be better staying at home.

Sorin It's depressing to be here by myself when you're leaving.

Arkadina But what is there to do in the town?

Sorin Nothing in particular, but still . . . They're laying the foundation stone for the municipal buildings, and the rest of it – I want to get myself going if only for an hour or two, I've been lying about the place like an empty cigarette packet far too long. I've ordered the trap round for one o'clock – we'll set off together.

Arkadina Well, your place is here, don't let yourself get bored, and don't catch colds. Keep an eye on my son, look after him and keep him out of trouble. I'm going, and I still don't know why Konstantin tried to shoot himself. I think it was mostly jealousy. So the sooner I take Trigorin away from here the better.

Sorin Well, look now, how do I say this? – there's other things. It's obvious – he's an intelligent young fellow, buried in the country, without a penny or a position or a future – he has nothing to do and he's ashamed of it and frightened by it. I'm very fond of him and he's attached to me but when it comes down to it he feels he has no place here, that he's a sponger, a parasite. It's his pride – only natural.

Arkadina Oh, that boy is a constant trial! Perhaps if he got a job . . .

Sorin whistles to himself for a moment.

Sorin I think the best answer is if you were to give him a bit of money – It would be a good start if he dressed like a human being, and the rest of it. He's been wearing out the same coat for three years and does without an overcoat – It would do him good to have a bit of fun – go abroad perhaps – it wouldn't have to cost very much.

Arkadina Just the same . . . well – I might manage a suit of clothes for him, but as for going abroad . . . No – just at this moment I can't even manage the suit. I haven't any money!

Sorin laughs.

I haven't.

Sorin (*whistles*) I'm sorry, don't get angry, my dear – I believe you – you're a wonderful woman, too generous for your own good.

Arkadina I have no money!

Sorin Of course, if I had any money I'd give it to him, but I haven't, not a five-kopeck piece. My farm manager takes every penny of my pension and spends it on cattle-breeding, bee-keeping and the rest of it, and that's the last I see of it, the bees get lost, the cows die, there's never a horse when I want one . . .

Arkadina I mean, I *have* some money, but I'm an artist! – my costumes alone have simply ruined me.

Sorin You're a dear kind girl . . . I really do sympathize . . . I . . . I'm having another of my . . . (*He staggers.*) . . . the room's going round . . . I've just come over a bit queer, that's what.

Arkadina, frightened, tries to support him.

Arkadina Petroosha! – Oh, Petroosha!, my dear – (*calls*) Someone come and help – Help!

Konstantin, with a bandage round his head, and Medvedenko come in.

He's taken ill!

Sorin It's nothing, nothing . . . (*He drinks some water.*) . . . all gone, that's what.

Konstantin (*to Arkadina*) [It's] nothing to be afraid of, Mama, it's not serious – Uncle has these turns – (*to Sorin*) You should go and lie down.

Sorin I will for a while, all right . . . But I'll be going into town just the same – I'll have a little lie-down, that's what, and then I'll go . . .

Medvedenko leads Sorin by the arm.

Medvedenko There's a riddle – in the morning on four, at midday on two, in the evening on three.

Sorin (*laughs*) Quite so. And at night on your back. Thank you, I don't need help to walk.

Medvedenko Just for form's sake, then –

They go out.

442

Arkadina He gave me such a fright.

Konstantin Living in the country isn't good for him, it doesn't suit him. It gets him down. Now, if you had a fit of generosity and lent him a couple of thousand, he'd be able to live in town all year round.

Arkadina I have no money, I'm an actress, not a banker.

Konstantin Mama, can you change my bandage? – no one does it like you do.

Arkadina takes a box of dressings from the medicine cupboard.

Arkadina The doctor's late.

Konstantin Yes, it's midday – he said he'd be here at ten.

Arkadina Sit down. (*She takes the bandage off his head.*) You look like somebody in a turban. There was someone asking in the kitchen last night what country you were from. There . . . it's practically healed over, just a tiny bit left. Now promise me there'll be no more (*pulling an imaginary trigger*) chk-chk! when I'm gone.

Konstantin [I] promise. I just went mad for a moment, I was in such despair I lost control . . . it won't happen again. (*He kisses Arkadina's hands.*) The hands of a ministering angel. I remember – ages ago – when you were still working at the Imperial – when I was a little boy – there was a fight in the courtyard where we were living, and a washerwoman in our building got badly hurt – do you remember this? – she was out cold when they picked her up . . . You were always going in to see her, you brought her medicine, you used to wash her children in her washtub. Can't you remember that?

Arkadina puts on a fresh bandage.

Arkadina No.

Konstantin There were two dancers living in our building at the time . . . they used to come in and have coffee.

Arkadina That I remember.

Konstantin They had religion. (*Pause.*) These last few days, I've loved you as tenderly and trustfully as I did when I was little. I have nobody but you now. Only – why do you let that man have such a hold over you?

Arkadina You don't know him, Konstantin. He has the noblest nature in the world.

Konstantin Oh, has he? Well, when he heard I wanted to fight him his noble nature didn't get in the way of his prudence. He's running away like a coward.

Arkadina What nonsense. He's leaving because I said we're leaving.

Konstantin Noble nature! Here we are, practically falling out over him, and he's next door or in the garden somewhere laughing up his sleeve and improving Nina's mind in a last-minute attempt to convince her he's a genius.

Arkadina You seem to take pleasure in being horrible to me. I have the greatest respect for that man and I'll thank you not to speak of him like that in my presence.

Konstantin Well, I haven't the slightest respect for him. You'd like me to think he's a genius, too, but – I'm sorry – I can't lie, his books make me sick.

Arkadina That's envy. Talentless people with ideas about themselves can't do anything but run down anybody who's got any real talent – it's their consolation.

Konstantin Real talent! If it comes to that, I've got more talent than the lot of you put together! (*He tears off the* *bandage.*) You hacks and mediocrities have grabbed all the best places for yourselves and you think the kind of art you do is the only kind that counts – anything else, you stifle or stamp out. Well, I'm not taken in by any of you! – not by him and not by you either!

Arkadina My son the Decadent!

Konstantin Go off to your cosy little theatre and act in your pathetic stupid little plays.

Arkadina I have never in my life appeared in a play of that description! Get away from me! You can't even write a wretched little comic sketch! Go back to Kiev and open a shop! Parasite!

Konstantin Skinflint!

Arkadina Rat's nest!

Konstantin sits down and cries quietly.

Little nobody! Crybaby. Stop crying. Don't cry. There's nothing to cry about. Please don't cry . . . Please, there's no need to . . . Oh, darling, I'm sorry – forgive me – forgive your awful mother – your poor miserable mother . . .

Konstantin embraces her.

Konstantin If you only knew! – I've lost everything. She doesn't love me – I can't write any more – I've lost all hope.

Arkadina Don't say that – it'll all turn out all right. Now he's going away she'll love you again. It'll be all right. (*She wipes away his tears.*) There . . . we're friends again, aren't we?

Konstantin (*kisses her hands*) Yes, Mama.

Arkadina (*tenderly*) Make it up with him, too. There's no reason to fight him – there really isn't, is there?

Konstantin Yes, all right – only don't make me see him – I couldn't face it – I'm not up to it . . .

Trigorin enters carrying his book.

[It's] all right, I'm going. (*He quickly puts things away in the medicine cupboard.*) The doctor can do my bandage later.

Trigorin (*to himself, with the book in his hand*) Lines eleven and twelve. 'If you ever have need of my life, come and take it.'

Konstantin picks up the bandage from the floor and goes out.

Arkadina They'll be bringing the horses round soon.

Trigorin (*to himself*) 'If you ever have need of my life, come and take it.'

Arkadina All packed?

Trigorin Yes, yes . . . (*to himself*) [Oh, but] why such a note of sadness in this cry from an innocent heart? – and why is it my heart that is pierced? 'If you ever have need of my life, come and take it.' (*to Arkadina*) Let's stay one more day! Why can't we?

Arkadina Because, my love, I know why you want to. But you mustn't let it make you forget yourself. You're a little intoxicated, that's all. You have to come to your senses.

Trigorin No – you have to come to yours – yes, to be sensible – and wise – I beg you, see this as a true friend – you're capable of the sacrifice – be generous, let me go.

Arkadina Are you so besotted with her?!

Trigorin It's as if I'm being called to her – perhaps this is the one thing that's always been missing in my life.

Arkadina What, the love of a little miss nobody? That's all [how little] you know about yourself.

Trigorin People sometimes walk and talk and they're fast asleep – it's like that, I'm talking to you but it's as if I'm really asleep and she's my dream – I'm possessed by such sweet visions . . . Oh, please, I beg you, let me go!

Arkadina No – no – you can't say those things to me – I'm just a woman like any other – you mustn't torture me like this – Boris, you're frightening me –

Trigorin It's your chance to be a woman *unlike* any other. Young love – an enchanting, lyrical love – is taking me off into the land of my dreams. No one but her can bring me happiness on this earth. I've never known love like this . . . When I was young I spent every minute dogging editors, struggling to survive – there was never the time. But now it's come – the love I never knew, it's calling to me, what's the sense in running away from it?

Arkadina You've gone mad!

Trigorin I don't care.

Arkadina You're all in a plot to torment me today!

Trigorin She doesn't understand! – She refuses to understand!

Arkadina Am I really so old and ugly that you think you can prattle to me about other women without any shame? (*She embraces and kisses Trigorin.*) Oh, you've lost your poor mind! My dear darling wonderful man – my life's last page! – my joy, my pride, my sweet content! If you left me even for an hour, I won't be alive at the end of it, I'll go mad – my magician – my prince – my king in all his glory –!

Trigorin Look, somebody could come in at any moment –

Arkadina Let them! I'm not ashamed of loving you as
I do! My treasure, my reckless darling, what you're doing is lunacy and I don't want you to, I won't let you . . .
You're mine . . . you're mine – this brow is mine . . .
these eyes, this soft hair . . . all of you is mine – You're
so brilliant – so gifted – you're the best writer there is –
you're the only hope for writing in Russia! – you have
such integrity – such simplicity and freshness, and
humour – you bring off the essence of a character or a
landscape with one stroke – your people are alive, it's
impossible to read you without a thrill. Do you think I'm
flattering you, putting you on a pedestal? Look into my
eyes – are these eyes lying to you? There – you see? – I'm
the only one who knows your true worth – the only one.
Nobody else tells you the truth, my darling, my
marvellous boy. You'll come, won't you? Won't you?
You won't abandon me . . .

Trigorin I've no will of my own. I've never had a will of
my own . . . spineless – feeble – submissive to the last –
is that really what women want? – so have me – take me
away – only don't relax your grip for an instant.

Arkadina Got him. Well, stay if you want to. I'll go and
you can come on later in a week or so, there's no hurry.

Trigorin No, no – we'll go together.

Arkadina Whatever you like. Well, all right, together
then – we'll go together.

Trigorin makes a note in his little book.

What are you doing?

Trigorin [I] heard someone use that phrase this morning
– virgin territory . . . might come in handy one day . . . .
So – off on our travels again. Railway carriages, railway
stations, railway cutlets . . . conversations in compart-
ments . . .

Shamraev enters.

Shamraev I have the honour to announce, with infinite regret, that the carriage awaits. It's time to go to the station, ma'am, the train is at five minutes past two. Would you do me the favour, if you can remember, to ask where that actor Suzdaltzev is nowadays? – whether he's alive and well? I used to have a drink with him in the old days. He was simply incomparable in *The Mail Robbery*. I remember at the time there was a tragedian, Izmailov, who worked with him at Elizabetgrad – another remarkable character. No need to hurry yourself, my lady, you still have a few minutes. Once, they were playing conspirators in some melodrama and when they were discovered there was the line, 'We're caught like rats in a trap,' and Izmailov said – 'Caught like traps in a rat!' Traps in a rat!

While he is speaking, Yakov bustles about with suitcases and a Maid brings in Arkadina's hat, coat, umbrella and gloves. Everyone helps Arkadina to dress. The Cook looks in from the door and after a while enters hesitatingly. Polina, carrying a little basket, comes in followed by Sorin, wearing a coat with a cape, carrying a hat and stick, and Medvedenko.

Polina I've got you some plums for the journey, they're lovely and sweet. You might feel like something nice.

Arkadina That's so kind of you, Polina.

Polina Goodbye, my lady. If there was anything not as it should be, please forgive me.

Arkadina Everything was just right, only don't cry –

Polina Our days are passing.

Arkadina But what's to be done?

Sorin Time to go if you're not going to miss it after all. I'm going to get on board. (*He goes out.*)

Medvedenko I want to walk to the station to see you off – I'd better hurry – (*He goes out.*)

Arkadina Goodbye, my dears. If we live we'll meet again next summer.

The Maid, the Cook and Yakov kiss her hand.

Don't forget me. (*She gives a rouble to the Cook.*) Here's a rouble. It's for the three of you.

Cook Thank you kindly, my lady – Have a good journey . . . Most grateful . . .

Yakov May God bless you.

Shamraev If you wrote sometime we'd like that. Goodbye, Boris Alexeyevich!

Arkadina Where is Konstantin? Tell him I'm leaving. We have to say goodbye. Well – remember me fondly. (*to Yakov*) I gave the cook a rouble, it's for the three of you.

They all go out. The stage is empty. Offstage are the sounds of people leaving. The Maid returns to fetch the basket of plums from the table and goes out again. Trigorin returns.

Trigorin Left my stick somewhere . . . On the verandah . . . (*He walks towards the door and meets Nina who is coming in.*) Is that you? We're going.

Nina It's all right, we'll see each other again. Boris Alexeyevich, I've made up my mind once and for all! – the die is cast – I'm going on the stage! Tomorrow I'll be gone from here. I'm leaving my father, leaving everything. I'm starting a new life. I'm going to Moscow, too [like you] – we'll see each other there.

Trigorin Stay at the Slavyansky Bazaar – let me know as soon as you arrive – the Grokholsky House on Molchanovka. I have to hurry.

Nina Only one more minute.

Trigorin You're so beautiful. It makes me so happy knowing we'll soon be seeing each other . . . that I can look into those wonderful eyes – that inexpressibly sweet smile, this lovely face – with its gaze of pure innocence like an angel's – my darling . . .

They kiss.
Curtain.

Act Four

Two years have passed.

One of the reception rooms in Sorin's house, turned into a study by Konstantin. Doors leading to inner rooms, and a glass door leading on to the verandah. Apart from the usual drawing-room furniture there is a writing desk in the corner and an ottoman. There is a bookcase, and books lie on windowsills and on chairs.

It is evening. One lamp lit. Semi-darkness. The sound of the wind shaking trees and howling in the chimneys. The night-watchman is heard on his round, knocking on a plank. Medvedenko and Masha enter.

Masha (*calls*) Konstantin! – Hello! – are you here? No. The old man keeps asking for him, 'Where's Kostya?, where's Kostya?' – every minute. He's lost without him.

Medvedenko He gets frightened being on his own. This awful weather . . . for the second day . . .

Masha turns up the lamp.

Masha There're waves on the lake, really big ones.

Medvedenko It's so dark outside. Somebody should get that stage pulled down . . . It's standing out there naked and ugly as a skeleton, the curtain flapping in the wind . . . Last night when I passed it, it sounded as if someone was crying inside.

Masha Someone crying . . .?

Medvedenko Let's be getting home, Masha.

Masha I'm staying the night.

Medvedenko Come on, Masha – the baby's probably hungry –

Masha Rot. Matryona will feed him anyway.

Medvedenko Poor little mite. This'll be three nights without his mother.

Masha What a bore you've turned out to be. At least one used to get a bit of philosophy with it but now it's all the baby – come on home – the baby – come on home – that's all I hear.

Medvedenko Well, come on home, Masha.

Masha You go.

Medvedenko Your father won't give me a horse.

Masha Yes, he will if you ask him.

Medvedenko Perhaps I will. So you'll come tomorrow, then?

Masha takes snuff.

Masha Yes – yes – tomorrow. Don't you ever let up?

Konstantin and Polina come in. Konstantin carries pillows and a blanket and Polina bed linen; they put them on the ottoman, then Konstantin goes to his desk and sits down.

What's this for, Mama?

Polina Piotr Nikolayevich wants his bed made up in Kostya's room.

Masha [I'll help], let me have that.

Polina Old people are like children. (*She walks up to the desk and looks at a manuscript.*)

Medvedenko Well, I'll be off, then. Goodbye, Masha.

(*He kisses Masha's hand.*) Goodbye, Mother. (*He tries to kiss Polina's hand.*)

Polina Well, get along if you're going.

Medvedenko Well, goodbye, Konstantin Gavrilovich.

Konstantin gives him his hand in silence. Medvedenko goes out.

Polina Who'd have thought, Kostya, [that] there was a proper writer in you? – and now, thank the Lord, you're starting to earn money from the magazines. And you've got so handsome . . . Dear Kostya, be nicer to my little Masha.

Masha is making the bed.

Masha Leave him alone, Mama.

Polina She's a good girl. (*Pause.*) Women only need a kind glance now and then, Kostya. I should know.

Konstantin gets up from the table and goes out in silence.

Masha Now you've annoyed him. What did you have to pester him for?

Polina I feel so sorry for you, Mashenka.

Masha Well, you don't have to be.

Polina My heart aches for you so. I'm not blind.

Masha Oh, it's all foolishness. Hopeless love is just something you read about. It's nonsense. All you have to do is get hold of yourself, not sit waiting for something to change like waiting for the weather. If love worms its way into your heart, dig it out. Semion's been promised a transfer to another district. Once we're there I'll forget it all – tear it out of my heart by the roots.

Two rooms away a melancholy waltz is being played.

Polina That's Kostya [playing]. He does that when he's unhappy.

Masha noiselessly does two or three turns of the waltz.

Masha The main thing is not to have him under my nose all the time, Mama. Believe me, when Semion gets his transfer I'll forget him in a month.

The door opens. Dorn and Medvedenko push Sorin in in his wheelchair.

Medvedenko I've got six mouths to feed now, and flour at two kopecks a pound.

Dorn It's everywhere you turn.

Medvedenko You can laugh. You've got pots of money.

Dorn Money? After thirty years' practice, with all the responsibilities – when I couldn't call my soul my own day or night – I've managed to put away two thousand roubles, and I've just spent the lot on my Grand Tour. I haven't a kopeck.

Masha [Are] you still here?

Medvedenko I'm sorry, but they won't give me a horse.

Masha (*mutters*) Why did I ever have to set eyes on you?

The wheelchair is positioned. Polina, Masha and Dorn sit down near by. Demoralized, Medvedenko stands apart from them.

Dorn Well, there've been some changes here! You've turned this drawing-room into a study.

Masha It suits Konstantin to work in here, he can walk out into the garden whenever he feels like a think.

Sorin Where's my sister?

Dorn She went to the station to meet Trigorin – she'll be back in a minute.

Sorin If you thought you should send for her it must mean I'm seriously ill. (*He is silent for a moment.*) Well, I must say, it's very odd – I'm seriously ill and no one gives me any medicine.

Dorn What would you like? Valerian drops? Soda? Quinine?

Sorin Oh, it's the doctor of philosophy! My life sentence. Has that [bed] been made up for me?

Polina [Yes] just for you.

Sorin I thank you.

Dorn (*hums*) 'The moon glides through the night sky . . .'

Sorin I've got an idea for a story for Kostya. A good title would be *The Man Who Wanted To. L'Homme qui a Voulu.* Long ago when I was young I wanted to become a writer. But I never did. I wanted to be a good speaker – and I was abominable. 'And, er, as I was saying, so to speak, as it were . . .' There were times when I'd be so long getting to the point of my argument I'd break out in a sweat. I wanted to be married and I didn't marry. I wanted to live in town and I'm dying in the country. And there you have it.

Dorn You wanted to become an Actual State Councillor and you did.

Sorin I never set my sights on that. It just happened.

Dorn It hardly shows a magnanimous spirit, does it?, complaining about your life when you're sixty-two.

Sorin He never gives up! Can't you understand? – I want to live!

Dorn Pure frivolity. Everyone dies. Law of nature.

Sorin That's the argument of a man who's had his fill. You're content so you're indifferent. But you'll be afraid, too, when it's your turn.

Dorn Fear of death insults your humanity, and ought to be overcome. The only people who can fear death rationally are those who believe in life hereafter, because they fear retribution for their sins. But you – in the first place you don't believe, and in the second place, what sins? You've never done anything except spend twenty-five years in the Department of Justice.

Sorin Twenty-eight . . .

Konstantin comes in and sits down on a little stool near Sorin's feet. Masha doesn't take her eyes off him the whole time.

Dorn We're stopping Konstantin from working.

Konstantin No, it's all right.

Medvedenko May I ask you, Doctor, which foreign city did you like best?

Dorn Genoa.

Konstantin Why Genoa?

Dorn The crowds in the streets. When you step out of your hotel in the evening, the streets are swarming with people. You drift along with the crowd this way and that, back and forth, it's got a life of its own and you become part of it, body and soul, you start to think there really might be a universal spirit like the one Nina acted in your play. Where is she, by the way? How's she getting on?

457

Konstantin All right, I think.

Dorn One hears that she's been leading a somewhat untidy life. What is she doing now?

Konstantin It's really too long a story.

Dorn Well, make it brief.

Konstantin She left home and went to live with Trigorin . . . [as] I suppose you know.

Dorn [Yes.]

Konstantin She had a baby. The baby died. Trigorin got tired of her and went back to his old ties, as you might expect. Or rather, he never let go of them. Having no backbone he was able to bend both ways. From what I know, Nina's private life hasn't exactly been a triumph.

Dorn And the stage?

Konstantin Even less, I'd say. She started off in summer theatre outside Moscow, then went to the provinces. At that time I never had her out of my sight. Where she went I went, too. She played some big parts but she played them crudely with a lot of declaiming and throwing her arms about. There were moments when she showed some talent, but only moments . . . letting out a cry . . . dying . . .

Dorn But [she did show] talent?

Konstantin Hard to tell. Probably. I saw her but she'd never see me – she'd tell them at the hotel not to let me up. I understood how she felt, and let it go. What more can I tell you? Later, when I got back home, I'd get letters from her, sensible friendly interesting letters. She never complained but I could feel how terribly unhappy she was, every line ached with unhappiness. Her mind kept wandering, too. She'd sign herself 'The Seagull' –

like in Pushkin's play where the miller is so mad with grief he calls himself a raven, so in her letters she'd keep calling herself a seagull. She's back here now.

Dorn How do you mean, back here?

Konstantin She's in town at the hotel, she's been there for several days. I went in to call on her, Masha tried, too, but she won't see anyone. Semion says he saw her yesterday after dinner, crossing the fields, only a mile or two from here.

Medvedenko That's right, I did. She was walking back towards town. I greeted her and asked her why she hadn't come to call, and she said she would.

Konstantin She won't. Her father and his wife won't have anything to do with her. They've posted watchmen all over to stop her getting anywhere near. Life out there is harder than is dreamt of, Doctor, in your philosophy.

Sorin [She was a] delightful girl.

Dorn What?

Sorin I said she was a delightful girl. In actual fact, Actual State Councillor Sorin was just a little in love with her for a while.

Dorn You old seducer!

Shamraev's laugh is heard.

Polina I think they're back from the station.

Konstantin Yes, that's Mama's voice.

Arkadina and Trigorin come in followed by Shamraev.

Shamraev We're all getting older and battered by the elements, but you, ma'am, are forever young, so full of life and grace in your gay colours . . .

Arkadina And you're tempting the fates again, you dreadful man.

Trigorin (*to Sorin*) How are you, Piotr Nikolayevich? – What's all this about you being ill again? – that won't do – And Masha!

They shake hands.

Masha You still recognize me?

Trigorin Married?

Masha Long married.

Trigorin Happily? (*He exchanges greetings with Dorn and Medvedenko and then goes up to Konstantin with some hesitation.*) Your mother tells me . . . [you've let] bygones be bygones . . . and you're not angry with me any more.

Konstantin offers him his hand.

Arkadina Look, Boris Alexeyevich has brought you the magazine with your new story.

Konstantin Thank you. That's very kind of you.

Trigorin I bring greetings from your many admirers. People are interested in you, both in Petersburg and Moscow, they're always asking me about you – what's he like? How old? Dark or fair? For some reason they think you're older than you are – and of course no one knows *who* you are, behind your nom de plume you're a mystery, like the Man in the Iron Mask.

Konstantin Are you staying for a while?

Trigorin No, I think I ought to get back to Moscow tomorrow, I've got a story I'm desperate to finish, and after that I've promised something for a collection – in other words, as ever.

*While they are talking Arkadina and Polina are setting
up a card table in the middle of the room. They open
it out. Shamraev lights candles and puts out chairs.
They get Lotto out of the cupboard.*

Not a very nice welcome from the weather. You couldn't
fish in this wind. If it dies down by morning I'll go to the
lake. Incidentally, I want to take a look at that place in
the garden – remember? – where you had your play. I've
got a new story and I want to refresh my memory of the
scene.

Masha Father, can you let Semion have a horse, he has
to get home.

Shamraev A horse. Get home. See for yourself, they've
only just been to the station. I can't send them out again.

Masha They aren't the only horses – (*Seeing that
Shamraev says nothing she waves her hand.*) Talking to
you is like . . .

Medvedenko I'll walk, Masha, really . . .

Polina Walk, in this weather . . . Come along, then,
everyone who's playing.

Medvedenko It's only a few miles. Goodbye. (*Kisses his
wife's hand.*) Goodbye, Mother.

Polina reluctantly holds out her hand for him to kiss.

I wouldn't have wanted to be a nuisance, but the baby
. . . Well . . . goodbye. (*He bows to everyone and goes
out apologetically.*)

Shamraev He'll make it all right. He's not a general.

Polina Come on, please, let's not waste any time or
they'll be calling us in for supper.

Shamraev, Masha and Dorn sit down at the table.

461

Arkadina (*to Trigorin*) We always play Lotto here when the long autumn evenings set in. Look – it's an old set of my mother's when she used to play with us as children. Why don't you have a turn with us before supper? (*She sits down with Trigorin at the table.*) It's a stupid game but after a while you don't notice.

She gives each person three cards.
Konstantin is leafing through the magazine.

Konstantin He's read his own story, but not even cut the pages on mine. (*He puts the magazine on his table, then goes towards the door. Passing his mother he kisses her on the head.*)

Arkadina Are you in [the game], Kostya?

Konstantin No, if you don't mind, I don't really want to . . . I'm going for a breath of air . . . (*He goes out.*)

Arkadina The stake is ten kopecks. Would you put in for me, Doctor?

Dorn *Bien sur.*

Masha Has everybody put in? Here we go . . . Twenty-two.

Arkadina Here.

Masha Three.

Dorn Yes.

Masha You've covered '3'? Eight! Eighty-one! Ten!

Shamraev Don't go so fast.

Arkadina You should have seen the reception I had in Kharkov, my goodness, my head hasn't stopped spinning.

Masha Thirty-four!

A melancholy waltz is heard.

Arkadina The students gave me such an ovation . . . three baskets of flowers . . . two garlands – and this – (*She takes a brooch from her breast and tosses it on the table.*)

Shamraev That's certainly something.

Masha Fifty!

Dorn Five O?

Arkadina I wore a marvellous ensemble. If I know nothing else, I know how to dress.

Polina Kostya's playing . . . He's unhappy, poor lamb.

Shamraev They've been having a go at him in the newspapers.

Masha Seventy-seven!

Arkadina Who cares about the newspapers?

Trigorin It's rotten luck – he can't seem to be able to find his own voice, there's something oddly unfocused about his writing, like a kind of delirium at times. And not a single living character.

Masha Eleven!

Arkadina (*looking at Sorin*) Petroosha, are you bored? (*Pause.*) He's asleep.

Dorn His Excellency sleeps.

Masha Seven! Ninety!

Trigorin If I'd lived by a lake like this I wonder if I'd ever have started writing. I would have conquered the urge and just gone fishing.

Masha Twenty-eight!

Trigorin To catch a perch or a chub is very heaven.

Dorn Well, I believe in Konstantin. He's got something. He's really got something. He thinks in images. His stories are pictures, vivid and full of colour, I'm strongly affected by them. The only trouble is, they don't go anywhere in particular. He leaves you with a picture but that's all, and you can't get far on that. Are you pleased you've got a writer for a son?

Arkadina Can you imagine, I still haven't read anything of his – there's never the time!

Masha Twenty-six!

Konstantin comes in quietly and goes to his desk.

Shamraev (*to Trigorin*) By the way, Boris Alexeyevich – we've still got something of yours here.

Trigorin What's that?

Shamraev Konstantin shot a gull once and you asked me to have it stuffed.

Trigorin I did? I can't remember that.

Masha Sixty-six! One!

Konstantin flings open the window and listens.

Konstantin It's so dark! I don't know what it is, I can't settle.

Arkadina Kostya, shut the window, there's a draught.

Konstantin closes the window.

Masha Eighty-eight!

Trigorin Full house, ladies and gentlemen!

Arkadina Bravo! Bravo!

Shamraev Bravo!

Arkadina The man's luck is always in, wherever he goes. Time for supper. Our celebrity hasn't eaten all day. We can carry on later. (*to Konstantin*) Kostya, leave off your writing, we're going to supper.

Konstantin I don't want any, I'm not hungry.

Arkadina As you wish. (*She wakes Sorin.*) Petroosha – time to eat. (*She takes Shamraev's arm.*) I must tell you about the reception I got in Kharkov . . .

> *Polina puts out the candles on the table, then she and Trigorin push the wheelchair. Everyone goes out, except Dorn and Konstantin who remains at his desk. Konstantin glances at Dorn.*

Konstantin After all I've said about new forms I think I'm just slipping back bit by bit into the same old conventions myself . . . (*He reads.*) 'The poster on the fence proclaimed . . .' 'A pale face in a frame of dark hair . . .' Proclaimed. A frame of dark hair. Hopeless. (*He crosses out.*) I'll start with my main character being woken up by the sound of rain.

> *Dorn reacts slightly: a living character after all? He waits.*

The rest will have to go. There's a description of the moonlit evening which goes on for ever. Trigorin has worked out a formula for himself, it makes it easy for him . . . He'll have the moon reflected in a broken bottle on the weir, the dark shape of the mill-wheel, and there's your moonlit night done. I've got shimmering dark, twinkling stars, fading pianos, sweet-smelling air . . . excruciating. (*Pause. He glances at Dorn.*) Yes, the more I think of it the more I'm convinced it's nothing to do with old or new – one has to write without thinking of forms at all – just let it flow naturally from the heart.

Dorn nods. He seems about to speak. A burst of laughter from the dining-room: Arkadina calling for Dorn. Konstantin starts writing. Dorn leaves.

Someone taps on the window nearest to the desk.

[What's that?] (*He looks out of the window. Calls out.*) Hello? – who's there? (*He opens the glass door and looks into the garden. Sound of footsteps receding. Calls out.*) Who's out there?! (*He goes out and can be heard walking quickly across the terrace. Half a minute later he comes back with Nina.*) Nina! Nina!

Nina lays her head on his breast, near to tears.

Oh, Nina – Nina . . . It's really you. Oh, I had a feeling . . . my heart's been aching all day – (*He takes her hat and cape from her.*) Oh, my dear darling love, you've come! – don't cry . . . don't cry . . .

Nina There's someone here.

Konstantin No – no one –

Nina Lock the door in case anybody . . .

Konstantin No one will come in.

Nina I know your mother's here. Lock the doors . . .

Konstantin locks the one door and puts an armchair against the other.

Konstantin This one doesn't lock – I'll put a chair against it. Don't be afraid, no one's going to come in.

Nina Let me look at you. It's nice and warm in here . . . This was the drawing-room, before . . . Have I changed?

Konstantin Yes. You've grown thinner . . . your eyes are bigger. I feel so strange, I can't believe I'm looking at you . . . Why wouldn't you let me come and see you? Why haven't you come before? I know you've been here nearly a week. Every day – several times a day – I've gone and stood under your window like a beggar.

Nina I was afraid you'd hate me. I dream of you every night looking at me and not knowing me. If only you knew! Since I got back I've spent hours walking all round here – by the lake. Often I came right up to the house without daring to come in. Can we sit down?

They sit down.

Let's sit and talk and talk. It's nice in here, so cosy and warm. Listen to the wind. Remember Turgenev? – 'Happy the man who on such a night as this has a warm corner under his own roof . . .' I'm the seagull. No, that's not what I mean. What was I talking about? Yes – Turgenev – 'And Lord help all those homeless wanderers.'

Konstantin Nina – you're crying again . . . Nina.

Nina It's all right, it makes me feel better to cry. I haven't cried for ages. Then, yesterday when it was dark, I came to look in the garden to see if our theatre . . . and to think it's been standing there all this time. I began to cry for the first time for two years – it was such a relief to cry, like a weight lifting from my heart. Look, I've stopped now. (*She takes him by the hand.*) So you've become a writer. You're a writer and I'm an actress – we both scrambled on to the merry-go-round. Life used to be so carefree, I was like a child, I'd wake up singing. I loved you and dreamed of being famous . . . And look at me now, first thing tomorrow I'm off to Yeletz, travelling third class with the peasants. And in Yeletz I'll be fending off the local business types who like a bit of culture. It's not a glamorous life.

Konstantin Why Yeletz?

Nina I'm booked for the winter season, I have to be there tomorrow.

Konstantin Oh, Nina . . . I've cursed you, hated you, torn up your letters and photographs – but I knew all the time [that] I'm yours heart and soul and for ever. I can't stop loving you whatever I do. Ever since I lost you – all this time I've been getting my work published – my life's been unbearable – I've felt so wretched, I felt as if my youth had suddenly been snatched away, I felt about ninety. I speak your name – I kiss the ground where you walked – I see your face wherever I go, that sweet face that smiled on me when life would never be so good again.

Nina (*bewildered*) Why are you talking like this? – What are you . . .?

Konstantin I'm alone with no one's love to warm me, I feel cold like in a dungeon – and everything I write is lifeless – stale and dreary – stay here with me, Nina, please, please, please stay – or let me come away with you!

Nina quickly puts on her hat and cloak.

Nina – what're you? – for God's sake –

Pause.

Nina My trap is waiting at the gate. Don't come out, I'm all right. (*in tears*) Can I have some water?

Konstantin gives her water.

Konstantin Where are you going?

Nina Back to town. Is your mother here?

Konstantin (*nods*) My uncle was taken ill on Thursday, we sent her a telegram . . .

Nina What do you mean you kissed the ground I walked on? You should want to kill me. I'm so tired. If only I could rest – I need rest! I'm the seagull – but I'm not really. I'm an actress. Yes. (*She hears Arkadina and Trigorin laughing.*) So he's here, too . . . well, it doesn't matter. He never believed in theatre – [he] always laughed at me for my dreams of being famous . . . and bit by bit I stopped believing, too, and lost heart . . . there were all the other things to worry about – love, jealousy . . . and always the worry about the baby. I became trivial and commonplace. My work lost all meaning. On stage I didn't know what to do with my hands or how to stand, I couldn't control my voice . . . You can't know what it's like when you're up there feeling you're acting so badly. The seagull. No, that's *not* me . . . You remember how you once shot that seagull? A man happened to come along and see her, and having nothing much to do, destroyed her. Idea for a short story . . . Wrong story, though. What was I talking about? Yes, about acting. I'm not like that any more. I've become a real actress. I love acting, when I'm on stage I feel drunk on the sheer joy of it, and I feel beautiful. While I've been back here I've spent a lot of time walking and thinking – and every day I've felt my spirit getting stronger. What I've realized, Kostya, is that, with us, whether we're writers or actors, what really counts is not dreaming about fame and glory . . . but stamina: knowing how to keep going despite everything, and having faith in yourself – I've got faith now and that's helped the pain, and when I think to myself, 'You're on the stage!', then I'm not afraid of anything life can do to me.

Konstantin So you've found yourself, you know where you're going – and I'm still adrift in a chaos of dreams and images, with no faith in myself, and no idea where I'm going, or what I'm for.

Nina (*listening*) Shh . . . It's time. Goodbye. When I'm a great actress, come and see me. Promise? But now . . . It's late. I'm so tired and hungry, I can hardly stand.

Konstantin Stay while I fetch you something to eat.

Nina No – no. Don't see me off – I'll go alone. So she brought him with her. Well, it makes no difference. When you see Trigorin don't tell him you've seen me . . . I love him. I love him more than ever. I love him passionately, I love him to despair. An idea for a short story. Oh, wasn't it good before, Kostya! – when everything was so clear, and life was so simple and happy – the feelings we had . . . feelings as delicate as tiny flowers. Remember that time? – 'Mankind and monkeys, ostriches and partridges . . . antlered stags, ganders and spiders . . .' And the poor moon lighting her lantern all for nothing . . . (*She embraces Konstantin impetuously and runs out through the garden door.*)

Konstantin I hope nobody sees her in the garden and tells Mama. It might upset Mama.

> *The next two minutes he spends silently tearing up all his manuscripts and throwing them under the table, then he unlocks the door and goes out.*
> *Dorn tries to open the other door.*

Dorn (*outside*) That's odd – door's locked. (*He enters and puts the chair back in its place.*) Obstacle course.

> *Arkadina and Polina come in, Yakov behind them, with bottles, and Masha followed by Shamraev and Trigorin.*

Arkadina Bring in the wine and beer for Boris Alexeyevich. We'll have a drink while we're playing. Sit down, everyone.

Polina (*to Yakov*) We'll have the tea in now, too.

Shamraev leads Trigorin to the cupboard.

Shamraev Here's the thing I was telling you about . . . (*He takes the stuffed seagull out of the cupboard.*) Just as you ordered.

Trigorin No memory of it. Not the faintest.

There is a shot offstage. Everyone jumps.

Arkadina What was that?

Dorn Nothing – probably something going pop in my medicine chest. Nothing to worry about. (*He goes out and returns half a minute later.*) Just as I said. [A] bottle of ether exploded . . . (*hums*) 'Again I stand before you . . .'

Arkadina Oh, I got such a shock. It reminded me of the time . . . Oh, I thought I was going to faint.

Dorn turns the pages of a magazine.

Dorn (*to Trigorin*) There was an article in here I saw – couple of months ago – from our correspondent in America, I wanted to ask you about it, just by the way . . . (*He puts his arm round Trigorin's waist and leads him to the front of the stage.*) . . . because it's something that interests me and I want to ask you to . . . (*He speaks out of the side of his mouth.*) . . . get her out of here somehow –

Trigorin looks at him sharply. Dorn, with no pause, drops his voice lower.

– the fact is, he's shot himself.